Acclaim for Michael Dobbs's

SABOTEURS

"*Saboteurs* is a riveting detective story within an engrossing war story. Meticulously researched and elegantly written, this book is that wonderfully rare thing: a first-rate work of history that is impossible to put down." —Rick Atkinson, author of *An Army at Dawn*

"Their story has been told before, but never so fascinatingly as by Dobbs." —*Chicago Sun-Times*

"Revealing. . . . Dobbs delves, incisively, into the mindset of the different participants, from the saboteurs, with their conflicting back stories, agendas and loyalties, to midlevel FBI operatives, to the legal minds summoned to work the cases. . . . Dobbs fully evokes the relentless pace familiar to readers of traditional thrillers." —*Houston Chronicle*

"Fascinating. . . . Must-reading for true crime and World War II enthusiasts. [H]ighly recommended." —*Tucson Citizen*

"Dobbs expertly deploys the wealth of detail he has unearthed to bring this crew to life. . . . [He] has a knack for historical detective work. . . . Dobbs is the first to tell the full story of a riveting episode that casts some interesting shadows on our current moment." —*Commentary Magazine*

MICHAEL DOBBS

SABOTEURS

Michael Dobbs was born in Belfast, Northern Ireland, and educated at the University of York, with fellowships at Princeton
and Harvard. He is a reporter for *The Washington Post*, where
he spent much of his career as a foreign correspondent covering the collapse of communism. His *Down with Big Brother:
The Fall of the Soviet Empire* was a runner-up for the 1997 PEN
award for nonfiction. Mr. Dobbs lives in Bethesda, Maryland.

ALSO BY MICHAEL DOBBS

Madeleine Albright: A Twentieth-Century Odyssey

Down with Big Brother: The Fall of the Soviet Empire

Saboteurs

SABOTEURS

THE NAZI RAID ON AMERICA

MICHAEL DOBBS

Vintage Books

A DIVISION OF RANDOM HOUSE, INC.

NEW YORK

FIRST VINTAGE BOOKS EDITION, FEBRUARY 2005

The Library of Congress has cataloged the Knopf edition as follows:
Dobbs, Michael
Saboteurs: the Nazi raid on America / Michael Dobbs.—1st American ed.
p. cm.
Includes bibliographical references and index.
1. Saboteurs—United States. 2. Spies. 3. Secret service—Germany.
4. World War, 1939–1945—United States. 5. World War, 1939–1945—Germany.
6. United States. Federal Bureau of Investigation. I. Title.
D753.3.D63 2004
940.54'8743'0973—dc21 2003056182

Vintage ISBN: 1-4000-3042-0

Author photograph © Claudio Vásquez
Book design by Robert C. Olsson

www.vintagebooks.com

Printed in the United States of America
10 9 8 7 6 5 4 3 2

For Alex

Contents

Contents

SABOTEURS

PROLOGUE

O<small>N THE APPROVED LIST</small> of visitors to Adolf Hitler's gloomy forest bunker for April 16, 1942, was a short, somewhat stocky German admiral with piercing blue eyes, bustling eyebrows, and a mane of carefully combed white hair.[1] He was accompanied by a very tall, almost cadaverous Austrian colonel. Together, they looked a little like Don Quixote and Sancho Panza, except the shorter man was clearly in charge. The admiral exuded a coiled-up energy; his taller colleague had a refined, aristocratic air.

They had flown that morning from Berlin, a 350-mile journey across the plains of what had been northern Poland, now part of the Third Reich. Their plane landed on a grass airstrip near a little town called Rastenburg, in a remote area of East Prussia covered by a swath of primeval forest, interspersed with lakes and gentle hills. A staff car was waiting to meet them. Soon, they found themselves driving into the woods along a winding cobblestone road, over a railway line and past several small lakes that protected the approaches to the place known as Wolfsschanze, the Wolf's Lair.

A succession of roadblocks, each more intimidating than the last, dotted the five-mile route to Hitler's headquarters. Security arrangements were in the hands of the S.S., the Führer's Praetorian guard. At each checkpoint, the black-shirted S.S. men ordered the officers to show their papers. There were telephone consultations with superiors further down the road. Once the guards were satisfied that everything was in order, they raised the barrier, giving the visitors a raised-arm, Heil Hitler salute.

After crossing a no-man's-land of minefields and pillboxes, the visitors reached the innermost sanctum of Nazi power. Here, surrounded by an electrified barbed-wire fence, lay a fortified encampment of dozens of concrete bunkers and wooden huts hidden behind thick fir trees and elaborate camouflage nets. Within this enclosure was another, even more tightly guarded, compound bristling with antiaircraft guns and constantly patrolled by S.S. men. This area contained the bunker used by Hitler as his living quarters and a single-story wooden barracks where he held his midday conferences while supervising operations against the Soviet Union.

The compound was bathed in almost perpetual gloom: sunlight rarely penetrated this deep into the woods. Apart from the barking of the Führer's Alsatian dog Blondi and the occasional shunting of trains along the nearby railway line, the sounds were those of the forest. Most of Hitler's aides detested the Wolf's Lair, finding it melancholy and oppressive. General Alfred Jodl, the army chief of staff, described the place as "a cross between a monastery and a concentration camp."[2] To Hitler's architect, Albert Speer, the Führer's bunker was like "an Egyptian tomb." But Hitler felt comfortable here, far removed from the horrors of the eastern front and the political intrigues of Berlin. The dark forest provided an ideal backdrop for his furious tirades against the outside world. He would spend a total of eight hundred days in the Wolf's Lair, more than in all his other wartime headquarters combined.

The shorter of the two visitors from Berlin was Admiral Wilhelm Canaris, chief of Hitler's military intelligence and a man of almost legendary reputation. During the First World War, he had served on a U-boat. Since taking over leadership of the Abwehr in 1934, Canaris had transformed the intelligence operation from a bureaucratic backwater to an important arm of the Third Reich. His spies had helped lay the groundwork for Hitler's stunning military successes of the last few years, including the unopposed takeover of Czechoslovakia, the blitzkrieg attack against Poland, and the invasion of the Soviet Union. The Abwehr was made up of three divisions: intelligence (Division I), sabotage (Division II), and counterintelligence (Division III).

Accompanying Canaris was the head of Abwehr II, Colonel Erwin von Lahousen-Vivremont. The scion of a noble Austrian family, Lahousen had been recruited to the Abwehr following his country's annexation by the Third Reich in 1938. He had responsibility for overseeing covert operations—from issuing German soldiers with Polish uniforms in order to stage a "provocation" on the border between Poland and Germany, to smuggling members of the Irish Republican Army back into Ireland to fight the British.

As they walked down forest paths lined with metal trees sprouting green Bakelite leaves past windowless bunkers draped with seaweed, Canaris and Lahousen could not help but get a better understanding of the dark passions driving their Führer. Named Wolfsschanze in honor of its master—"Herr Wolf" had been one of Hitler's political nicknames back in the twenties, when he was just an opposition leader—the Wolf's Lair was a monument to his paranoia and megalomania. Built by an army of racially pure workers, the fortress in the forest was a Pharaonic project that provided secure accommodation not only for the Führer, but for two thousand of his closest aides and guards. It was here that Hitler put into effect Operation Barbarossa, his plan for the invasion and destruction of the Soviet Union.

But it was not Barbarossa that Hitler had in mind when he summoned his intelligence chiefs to the Wolf's Lair on April 16, 1942. For some weeks now, his attention had been drifting away from the eastern front to the challenges posed by the emergence of a new enemy on the other side of the Atlantic, a country whose productive capabilities were so formidable that they threatened to overwhelm the military might of Nazi Germany. Hitler had a scheme that, if put into effect, would wreak havoc on America's ability to make war.

The plan was known as Operation Pastorius.

LOOKING AT a map of the territory he controlled, Hitler had every reason to feel at the peak of his power in the spring of 1942. The failed artist and retired corporal had become the unchallenged master of much of the Old World, from the Caucasus Mountains to the English Channel, from the fjords of Norway to the deserts of North Africa. He saw himself as the "greatest German ever," the more-than-worthy successor of Bismarck and Frederick the Great. He had more than avenged the humiliations heaped on Germany after World War I. Through a mixture of bullying, bluff, and blitzkrieg, his armies had sliced through supposedly impregnable defenses in Czechoslovakia, Poland, the Balkans, Belgium, Netherlands, France, and finally Russia. His plan for the annihilation of the Jewish race—a long-held dream—was well under way.

But the Führer was astute enough to understand that the propaganda accounts of an almost unbroken succession of military triumphs did not tell the whole story. Problems were surfacing that threatened the very foundations of the Third Reich and his own ability to hold on to absolute power. On the western edge of Europe, Great Britain remained a stubborn holdout, refusing to recognize the New Order Hitler had established for the rest of the continent. In the east, on the Russian front, the German juggernaut had ground to a halt in the depths of the Russian winter after a series of sweeping advances the previous summer. Ill prepared for blinding snowstorms and forty degrees of frost, tens of thousands of German soldiers had frozen to death on the windswept Russian plain, or had fallen in hand-to-hand fighting with a seemingly reinvigorated Red Army. Despite the easy capture of dozens of Soviet cities, including Kiev, Minsk, and Kharkov, Hitler's soldiers had been unable to penetrate the defenses of Moscow and Leningrad, the two grand prizes.

More troubling still, Hitler now faced a powerful new adversary following the Japanese attack on Pearl Harbor the previous December. America's entry into the war posed few immediate dangers to Germany: despite rapid mobilization, the U.S. Army was in no condition to fight a much more seasoned German army, even supposing it could somehow gain a foothold on the European continent. Over the long term, however, American involvement was likely to shift the balance of industrial, and therefore military, power in favor of the anti-Nazi coalition. It promised to provide Britain and Russia with an almost inexhaustible supply of war matériel and manpower that Germany was unable to match, even with the help of its allies, Japan and Italy.

In the end, victory was likely to go to the side that produced the largest number of airplanes, tanks, and ships. And here Germany was at a huge disadvantage. By December 1941, the third winter of the war, Hitler's armies were in the throes of a logistical crisis. Thousands of tanks and airplanes had been lost on the Russian front. Equipment that performed well in Belgium or France seized up on the frozen Russian steppes; the mighty Wehrmacht was reduced to using horses to drag its guns toward Moscow. It was not just tanks and guns that were in short supply. German soldiers fighting in Russia lacked coats, gloves, and boots, and were even showing signs of malnourishment. Their commanders made frantic appeals to civilians back home for warm clothing. In January 1942, Hitler reversed earlier statements about Germany's invincible industrial might and gave his fellow countrymen an inkling of the gravity of the situation:

The people at home know what it means to lie in snow and ice at a temperature of 35, 38, 40, and 42 degrees below zero, in order to defend Germany. And, because they know it, they are anxious to do whatever they can. It is my duty to issue the summons: Germans at home! Work, produce arms, produce munitions. More arms, and more munitions! By doing so, you will save the life of many a comrade at the front. Produce, and work at our means of transportation, so that everything will get to the front.[3]

In the meantime, on the other side of the Atlantic, America was dramatically increasing the production of iron, aluminum, and steel, the first step to churning out the tanks, airplanes, and submarines needed to win the war. At the end of 1940, President Franklin D. Roosevelt had held out a vision of America as "the great arsenal of democracy," using its "industrial genius" to "produce more ships, more guns, more planes, more of everything."[4] By 1942, the United States was well on the way to fulfilling Roosevelt's goal, producing 60,000 planes, 45,000 tanks, 20,000 antiaircraft guns, and six million tons of shipping in a single year. If these trends continued, Germany would be overwhelmed by the sheer weight of America's industrial power.

Having served in the trenches in World War I, Hitler was unimpressed by the fighting qualities of Americans, whom he regarded as hopelessly pampered and effete. "I'll never believe that an American soldier can fight like a hero," he told his associates one evening soon after America's entry into the war, as they sat around the dinner table at the Wolf's Lair.[5] American ideas of democracy and free-market capitalism filled Hitler with "hatred and repugnance." He thought of America as a "decayed country" with no future. "Everything about the behavior of American society reveals that it's half Judaised, half negrified. How can one expect a state like that to hold together—a country where everything is built on the dollar?"[6] He was even more scathing about the leadership abilities of the American ruling class, particularly Roosevelt, "a tortuous, pettifogging Jew" with a "sick brain."[7]

For all his contempt for America and Americans, Hitler had enormous respect for American industry. He admired the auto manufacturer Henry Ford, and not just because of their shared anti-Semitism. Germany had a lot to learn from the techniques of mass production pioneered by Ford, he told his subordinates. "The great success of the Americans consists essentially in the fact that they produce quantitatively as much as we do with two-thirds less labor . . . In America, everything is machine-made, so they can employ the most utter cretins in their factories. Their workers have no need of specialized training, and are therefore interchangeable."[8] And if America could produce cars in such vast numbers, at much less cost than Germany, what was there to prevent it from achieving a similar feat with tanks?

If Germany was to win the war, it would have to find a way of counteracting America's industrial power. This was not just Hitler's opinion. It was also the view of his most trusted aides, including Hermann Göring, the head of the Luftwaffe, and Heinrich Himmler, head of the Gestapo and the S.S., the shock troops of the Nazi regime.[9]

For months, both men had complained about the Abwehr's failure to establish reliable agents in the United States. Göring, in particular, was constantly warning Hitler about the threat posed by American industry. Something had to be done to sabotage the U.S. war machine.

In a series of meetings with Canaris, before and after Pearl Harbor, Hitler demanded action.[10] The Abwehr chief was skeptical of the value of sabotage operations in the United States, not for deep-seated moral qualms, but because he feared they would be counterproductive. The history of German sabotage attempts against America in World War I—such as blowing up the Black Tom ammunition depot in New York Harbor—suggested that any short-term gains were likely to be outweighed by propaganda losses and heightened anti-German sentiment. Even successful sabotage operations, Canaris felt, were unlikely to have a decisive impact on the outcome of the war.

As long as the United States remained an ostensibly neutral country, the German foreign ministry under Joachim von Ribbentrop was also opposed to acts of sabotage on American soil. Ribbentrop hoped that skillful diplomacy would keep America out of the war, but this was hardly possible if Americans found out that the Abwehr was trying to destroy American factories. Canaris was able to cite Ribbentrop's objections to sabotage as an excuse for doing nothing.[11] He told Hitler that the foreign ministry had categorically forbidden the Abwehr to build an intelligence network in the United States that could be used for sabotage operations.

The diplomatic arguments against sabotage disappeared as a result of the U.S. entry into the war. After Pearl Harbor, Hitler stepped up his demands for large-scale action against the American aircraft industry to prevent the Luftwaffe from losing control of the skies. Canaris understood that he could not procrastinate indefinitely without risking his own position. The British and American press were already talking about the Abwehr chief as a possible leader of a homegrown German opposition to Hitler. In conversations with Nazi officials, Canaris laughed off these reports as wishful thinking by the enemy and an attempt to sow high-level dissension in Berlin. All the same, he felt a need to demonstrate his loyalty to the Führer.

In the meantime, Nazi officials had produced their own scheme for infiltrating agents into the United States. The plan was the brainchild of Walter Kappe, the former propaganda chief of the German-American Bund, an American offshoot of the German Nazi Party. Kappe had lived in America for twelve years but returned to Germany in 1937 after losing a power struggle with other American Nazis. He had joined the Abwehr at the beginning of the war, with the rank of lieutenant. His real influence, however, derived from the gold button he wore in his lapel, signifying that he was one of the Nazi Party's first hundred thousand members, a Hitler loyalist dating back to the early twenties, when it was far from obvious that the Nazis would come to power.

Kappe was a loud, bombastic man—he talked like someone "trying to sell you a washing machine," in the opinion of the aristocratic Lahousen—with a grandiose vision of establishing a large network of saboteurs to cripple American industry. The core of this network would be German-Americans like himself who came back to the Fatherland prior to the outbreak of World War II full of enthusiasm for the "New Germany." Many of these returning exiles were former Bund members disillusioned with their prospects in Depression-era America who nevertheless spoke good English and had an intimate knowledge of American ways.

The problem was how to infiltrate members of Kappe's network back into America. The obvious method was by submarine—but the German navy was very reluctant to allow its precious U-boats to be used for transporting saboteurs. The head of the U-boat fleet, Admiral Karl Dönitz, was opposed to such operations as both a security risk and an unnecessary distraction. He wanted to focus his resources on a single overriding goal: cutting Britain's economic lifeline to the United States, an objective that seemed quite feasible in the spring of 1942. His U-boats were already sinking American and British ships faster than the enemy could build replacements. They were enjoying particular success along America's Atlantic seaboard, where resort cities like Miami were resisting blackout restrictions for fear they might be bad for tourism. The German U-boat captains were able to pick off targets neatly silhouetted against the brightly lit coastline.

Under pressure from Kappe's Nazi Party patrons and the Luftwaffe, Dönitz eventually backed down. But he set two conditions for his cooperation.[12] First, he insisted that "only high-class" agents be selected for the operation. Second, he demanded that any information of value gathered by the agents be shared with the German navy, and particularly the U-boat fleet. The Abwehr agreed to the conditions.

By the time Canaris saw Hitler on April 16, the navy had already agreed in principle to a sabotage operation against the United States, primarily targeting the light metal industry.[13] Eleven German-American recruits, personally selected by Kappe, had reported for training the previous week at the Abwehr sabotage school outside the Prussian town of Brandenburg. Operation Pastorius was almost ready to be launched, pending the Führer's final approval.

UNLIKE ROOSEVELT, who delegated considerable responsibility to his generals, Hitler was an inveterate micromanager. He meddled in every aspect of the war, summoning even low-ranking military officers to his hideaways around Germany for "conferences" that often lasted for hours. When they arrived, the officers were obliged to wait patiently while the Führer decided when to see them, or whether to see them at all. The experience was a little like attending an imperial court. Sometimes, Hitler would send his courtiers away without an audience; other times, he would hector them for hours, treating them to bizarre diatribes on everything ranging from vegetarianism to reminiscences of growing up in Austria to the correct way to drive a car.

In addition to the Abwehr chiefs, Hitler had sent for a large number of military and naval officers, including Grand Admiral Erich Raeder, to discuss the problems posed by America's entry into the war.[14] As usual, the intelligence chiefs did not know whether they would get to see the Führer until the last moment. When they were finally granted an audience, Lahousen submitted "a brief report" about the planned sabotage operation. In his typically sententious manner, Hitler replied that "the greatest activity will be necessary in America," a remark interpreted by Canaris and Lahousen as an order to proceed with Operation Pastorius.[15]

The British and American commentators who speculated that Canaris was the most likely leader of the opposition to Hitler were half right: although the Abwehr chief stopped well short of open rebellion, he tolerated dissident views among those around him, making him a kind of intellectual patron for German officers troubled by the dictator's excesses. The son of conservative German industrialists, Canaris had initially welcomed Hitler's rise to power, but secretly turned against him once he understood the extent of the catastrophe that had befallen Germany and Europe. Eventually, Canaris would pay for his dual loyalties with his life: he was executed along with dozens of other real and suspected opponents of the Führer after the failed assassination attempt against Hitler in July 1944 at the Wolf's Lair.

For the moment, the admiral preferred to express his opposition to Hitler through irony and ambiguity. After Lahousen said he doubted the feasibility of the sabotage operation so enthusiastically endorsed by Hitler, Canaris remarked quietly, "Well, we will lose [a few] good Nazis then."[16]

The tone of his voice suggested this would hardly be a major tragedy.

PART ONE

PASSAGE TO AMERICA

(APRIL 11–JUNE 13, 1942)

CHAPTER ONE

SCHOOL FOR SABOTAGE

(APRIL 11–30)

A CHANCE TO REHABILITATE yourself, they had told him. A chance to fulfill your obligations to the Fatherland.

He had been ordered to report in uniform to the army post in Brandenburg, a slow two-hour train ride from Berlin's Zoo station.[1] Stations with names like Wannsee and Potsdam glided past his window as the train chugged westward, packed with soldiers returning home for a few days' furlough with their families as a respite from the hell of the Russian front. From the train, the Prussian countryside seemed reassuringly permanent and serene, almost undisturbed by two and a half years of war, a collage of sparkling lakes, village churches with high steeples, children riding their bicycles down wooded lanes.

He took a streetcar from the station to the military garrison, whose old brick barracks dated back to the time of Kaiser Wilhelm. The regimental clerk took him to a storeroom, handed him a set of civilian clothes to put in his knapsack, and told him to take the Quenz Lake tramway to the end of the line. The farm was a ten-minute walk from the tram stop, along a road bordered by a drainage canal on one side and vegetable gardens on the other. The lakeside estate was impossible to miss, the clerk had insisted. There were no other farms in the vicinity.

He got off the streetcar as instructed, and walked up a country lane to a brick gatepost, beyond which he could see a two-story farmhouse at the end of a driveway lined by chestnut trees. Signs posted along the high metal fence warned intruders to "Keep out under penalty of severe punishment by the Law."[2]

As he wandered up the driveway, he caught glimpses of the lake shimmering through the woods.³ It was early spring: the chestnuts were not yet in bloom, but shoots of light green had appeared on the trees. Patches of snow still lay on the ground. To his left, he could see a converted two-story barn with a high sloping roof, along with some stables and outbuildings. The main farmhouse, fifty yards from the lake, was neat and well maintained, reflecting the Prussian virtues of thrift, hard work, and order.

Several men were lounging on the porch of the brick building as he approached. He felt a little out of place. They were all in civilian clothes, while he was still in uniform.⁴

"You must be Burger," said one of the men, a wiry fellow with a thin face and a streak of gray running through his dark hair, as he extended his hand. "My name is Davis. George John Davis."

A housekeeper showed him to a room, on the ground floor of the farmhouse, which he would share with one of the other men. After changing into the clothes the army clerk had given him in Brandenburg, he went outside to join his new companions. The man who had introduced himself as Davis suggested they take a walk around the estate.

"You will be part of my group," the man explained, as they strolled down to the lake, still half-frozen after a long, hard winter. "Eleven men have been chosen to take part in this course. Only the best will be selected to go to the United States."⁵

To outside appearances, Ernst Peter Burger had arrived at a working farm on the eastern shore of Lake Quenz.⁶ There was an apple orchard, a barnyard full of cows, pigs, and chickens, and a hothouse where vegetables were grown. Between the main building and the road, just north of the driveway, was a one-story house occupied by the people who looked after the farm. There were even a few children running around. But it did not take Burger long to discover that nothing was what it seemed at Quenz Lake.

In the first place, his new acquaintance's name was not Davis at all, but George John Dasch. Like Burger, Dasch was a German-American who had returned to the Fatherland to take part in Hitler's great experiment. Davis was merely the code name that he would use for their mission.

As Burger walked around the lakeside estate with Dasch, it became clear to him that it was not a farm at all. The barnlike building he had noticed as he came up the drive contained a classroom and a chemical laboratory above a garage. Next door was a gymnasium equipped with parallel bars and weight-lifting equipment. Beyond these buildings, on the other side of a bridge leading across a pond, was an area that looked like an abandoned movie set. It included a hundred yards of railway tracks leading nowhere, an observation tower, and a deserted house, pockmarked with bullet holes and traces of explosives. Next to the railroad tracks, bulldozers had torn a large hole in the ground. The pit was reinforced with concrete and was evidently used for setting off high explosives. At the southernmost end of the estate, beyond the explosives pit, was a shooting range.

The meaning of all this was still a puzzle for Burger. He had volunteered for intelligence work in America, for which he believed he was well suited. During the six years he had lived in the United States, he had learned good English, even though he retained a strong German accent. He felt comfortable among Americans. He had received an honorable discharge from the Michigan National Guard, and had become an American citizen. With his swarthy complexion and slightly elongated nose, he could pass himself off as a Jewish refugee. But how he would get to America—and what he would do once he got there—remained unclear.

The mystery unraveled as he talked to Dasch, who explained that Burger was the last of eleven students to arrive at the farm. Over the next three weeks, they would learn how to blow up factories. They would then be sent to America by submarine in two groups, landing somewhere along the eastern coast. Was he still interested?

Burger barely hesitated. Yes, of course, he was still interested.

They ate dinner on the ground floor of the farmhouse, in a large room overlooking the lake. They then set off through the woods for a drink at a nearby tavern. It took about half an hour to reach the place, and once again Burger found himself walking with Dasch, who began quizzing him about his past. Since Dasch was going to be his new chief, Burger thought it better to admit he had been in trouble with the Gestapo. To his relief, Dasch said he was already aware of that. He had studied the files.

"Tell me your side of the story. The other side I know."[7]

There was so much to tell that Burger scarcely knew where to begin. He was thirty-six years old, and his life had been in turmoil since his return to Germany from America nine years previously. Readmission to the Nazi Party. The elation of rejoining the storm troopers and taking part in Hitler's triumphant parades. The Night of the Long Knives. Clashes between the storm troopers and the S.S. Trips to Czechoslovakia and

Poland. Marriage. A trumped-up charge. Imprisonment. His wife's miscarriage. Release from jail.

Burger found it difficult to talk about his seventeen months in Gestapo prisons without indignation. He began to curse Heinrich Himmler, the head of the Gestapo, and "the dirty bastards who beat me up."[8] Dasch cut him short.

"That's enough. Don't say anything more. We'll talk about this later."

They changed the subject. A slip like that could have serious consequences. To Dasch, Burger seemed suddenly fearful, "a man haunted by a terrible past, happy and elated one minute and given to moody spells and silence the next."[9]

DESPITE THE secrecy that surrounded the Quenz Lake camp, little effort was made to hide the identity of the school. Burger was surprised to hear his fellow trainees chatting in English when they visited the local tavern or took walks in the countryside, even though Germany and America had been at war with each other for the past five months, ever since the Japanese attack on Pearl Harbor. They would often burst into songs like "Oh! Susannah" and even "The Star-Spangled Banner," which they remembered from their days in the States.[10]

The fact was that the people of Brandenburg—like the people of any small German town—had lost all sense of curiosity after a decade of Nazi rule. They had learned to keep their heads down, refusing to notice the most outrageous things that were being done in their name. On Sunday, April 12, the day after Burger passed through Brandenburg on his way to Quenz Lake, the remnants of the town's Jewish population were herded to the train station by half a dozen Prussian gendarmes on the first stage of a journey to the Warsaw Ghetto. As several dozen Jewish families trudged through the town in their heavy winter overcoats, hauling bags crammed with their possessions, local people simply averted their gaze.

It was not just Germans who preferred to ignore what was happening around them. Beginning in 1940, the local Opel plant, a wholly owned subsidiary of General Motors, had been using slave labor from conquered German territories to replace workers conscripted into the Wehrmacht. Every day, thousands of Poles, Belgians, and Russians were marched through the streets of Brandenburg in long columns to the Opel factory, where they worked fourteen hours a day for starvation wages. Although the American managers knew all about the use of slave labor in their

Brandenburg plant, they made no effort to divest themselves of their German holdings, and acted as if nothing were amiss.[11]

It was hardly surprising, then, that nobody would pay much attention when, as Nazi Germany geared up for war in 1939, the country estate of a wealthy Jewish shoe manufacturer on the edge of town was turned over to the Abwehr and transformed into a training camp for saboteurs.

IN ORDER to get his chance at rehabilitation, Burger had called in his Nazi Party connections, ties that dated back to his experiences as a street brawler before and after the Munich beer hall putsch of 1923. The coup had been quashed, and Hitler sent to prison, but in retrospect it marked the first big step on the Führer's road to supreme power. The putsch had become part of Nazi folklore. To have participated in the failed street rebellion was a mark of distinction that nobody could ever take away from you. None of the other men, Burger felt sure, could match his knowledge of the inner workings of the Nazi movement.

After his release from jail in July 1941, he had wangled an appointment with Alfred Rosenberg, the party ideologist, and had mentioned his interest in foreign intelligence work.[12] Rosenberg had picked up the phone and called Admiral Canaris, the head of the Abwehr. Canaris passed the message on to a Colonel Schmidt, who introduced Burger to a Lieutenant Colonel Marguerre. The lieutenant colonel called a Major Hotzel, who sent Burger to see a Captain Astor, who in turn introduced him to Lieutenant Walter Kappe.

Kappe, Burger learned, was a former editor of German-language newspapers in Chicago and New York. He had also been a high official in the German-American Bund. Some of the other men at the camp had heard Kappe speak at meetings in Chicago, railing against the Jews and urging his audience to show solidarity with the "New Germany." Fat and jovial, with an eye for the ladies, Kappe was not the kind of man you easily forgot. His flabby face was very distinctive, "a real baby face."[13] According to an unflattering portrait in the files of the American FBI, he spoke English with a strong German accent, which he tried to hide "under an atrocious and unsuccessfully affected phony Oxford accent . . . Kappe likes to play the suave, imperturbable superman but can easily be made to lose his cool."

Kappe had personally screened all the men selected for training at the sabotage school, and had arranged their transfers to Quenz Lake. In

Burger's case, Kappe had questioned him extensively about his experiences in the United States. Satisfied with his answers, Kappe made arrangements for Burger to be transferred from guarding a prison camp outside Berlin to a secret military unit known as the Lehrregiment that trained espionage and sabotage agents for the German High Command. The Brandenburg garrison, where Burger was ordered to report en route to Quenz Lake, was an outpost of the Lehrregiment.

Burger arrived at the farm on Saturday, April 11. Since classes were not scheduled to begin until Monday, he devoted the rest of the weekend to getting to know his fellow trainees. They spent much of Sunday lounging around the living room of the main farmhouse, perusing various American newspapers and magazines long banned in Germany, such as the *New York Times, Life,* and the *Saturday Evening Post.* The publications, most of which were about two months old, were stamped "Property of OKW, to be returned."[14] OKW, Burger knew, stood for *Oberkommando der Wehrmacht,* the German High Command. There were also reading materials in Hindi, Arabic, and various other languages.

The other trainees were all German-Americans who had spent varying amounts of time in the United States. Some spoke good English; others retained a thick German accent. Most had worked in menial occupations in America, such as cook, housepainter, chauffeur, odd-job man. They ranged in age from early twenties to mid-forties.

Dasch turned out to be a character, thirty-nine years old, very loquacious, and full of nervous energy. Before returning to Germany in May 1941, he had spent nearly twenty years in America, where he held a variety of jobs, including waiter, traveling salesman, and manager of a brothel. His English was a little rusty, but he had an extraordinary command of American slang, and would sprinkle his conversation with expressions that seemed to be lifted out of a *Boy's Own* magazine, such as "check and recheck," "scram," and "blow my stack." He referred to his brain as his "noodle" and people he disliked as "a bunch of nuts." Once he began to talk, it was difficult to get him to stop. Burger noticed that Dasch had the habit of waving his long, gangly arms while talking to people and holding his index finger up to his nose, as if to preempt anyone who might try to interrupt him. Dasch had been selected to lead a team of four or five saboteurs that would include Burger.

The leader of the second group was Edward Kerling, alias Eddie Kelly, a heavy-jawed man with thick wavy hair who always seemed to be smiling.

Kerling dropped hints that he was a Nazi Party member of long standing, with a membership number of around 70000, indicating that he, like Burger, was one of Hitler's early followers.[15] He had lived in America for eleven years, and had had quite an adventure getting back to Germany. In 1939, after Hitler invaded Poland, Kerling and a few friends pooled their savings to buy a small yacht, the *Lekala*, with the intention of sailing across the Atlantic and offering their services to the Fatherland. But the boat was intercepted by the U.S. Coast Guard, triggering a spate of newspaper headlines about American Nazis making illegal trips to Germany and violating the Neutrality Act. The following year Kerling managed to get his papers in order, and returned home on board a regular ship.

The "life of the party," Burger concluded early on, was Herbie Haupt, muscular, darkly handsome, nearly six feet tall, an accomplished concertina player "with classical Greek features."[16] Haupt was the youngest person selected for the school—he was twenty-two—and also the most Americanized. He had lived in Chicago from the age of five, growing up in the ethnic German neighborhoods of the North Side and becoming a naturalized American citizen. He spoke English better than he spoke German. Haupt's main interests, it soon became clear, were money and girls. He entertained the other trainees with stories of reaching Germany via Mexico and Japan, rounding Cape Horn and running the British blockade along France's Atlantic coast, a feat for which he had been awarded the Iron Cross, Second Class.

Haupt spent much of his time with a blue-eyed, blond-haired giant named Joseph Schmidt, a reserved man with a high-pitched voice and a Swedish accent. Schmidt was very strong, impressing the others with his trick of bending metal bars. His background was a little mysterious. He was an excellent shot and outdoorsman; it seemed he had worked in Canada as a hunter and trapper. Burger understood that he had become acquainted with Haupt in Mexico, and had traveled to Europe with him on the same blockade-runner. Along with a natural reticence, Schmidt had a hot temper, and was liable to fly off the handle when contradicted. Of all the trainees, Burger considered him "the most dangerous."[17]

Then there was a stocky little man whom Burger knew only as Dempsey, who amused the others with stories about his career in the United States as a professional boxer and trainer of prizefighters. Burger noticed that he spoke out of the corner of his mouth like a gangster, and that most of his front teeth were missing, suggesting that he had been bashed about a bit in his time.[18] Dempsey served as the men's first physical education instructor. Kappe wanted him to join the sabotage mission, but he pleaded a prior commitment: one of his boxers was fighting a big match against an Italian. He left Quenz Lake after a few days with a cheery good-bye and a promise to "follow you guys" to America.[19]

The remaining trainees made less of an impression on Burger. Richard Quirin and Heinrich Heinck had both worked for Volkswagen and appeared to be inseparable. Quirin had large protruding ears and walked with a forward slouch; Heinck was a "slow-moving phlegmatic type," who seemed "not quite sure of himself."[20] Hermann Neubauer, "a typical gangster type," always wore "a hat pulled down on his eyes exactly straight." Werner Thiel was a "shabby dresser" who spoke in a slow monotone. Ernst Zuber, a high-strung man with a round face, was unable to express himself clearly, in either English or German. The last member of the group was a wiry little man with large eyebrows, known to everyone as Scottie because he looked and acted like a Scotsman.

All in all, they were a mediocre lot.

AT NINE o'clock on Monday morning, after everyone had finished break-fast and calisthenics, Kappe summoned the trainees to the classroom above the garage. They sat down in front of him on rows of school benches like a bunch of eager pupils, pens and notebooks ready, watching him pace back and forth across the wooden floor. Stopping production in America, he told them, was as essential to the German war effort as the battles raging on the Russian front.[21] It would be their job to sabotage the American light metal industry and the transportation system along the East Coast. This was the first time most of them had heard the word "sabotage" mentioned in connection with their mission.

"Naturally, this work is top secret," Kappe went on, in his thickly accented version of the King's English. "You aren't allowed to leave the farm without permission, send mail, or receive mail. You must tell no one what you are doing here, not even your families."[22]

Kappe introduced the men to the two Abwehr specialists who would instruct them in the business of destroying factories and railroads: Herr Doktor Walter König and Herr Doktor Günther Schulz. The two Herr Doktors were both acknowledged masters of their trade, frequently called upon to display their tricks at Abwehr conferences. They had personally designed much of the sabotage equipment that the saboteurs would be taking with them to America. König's specialty was the theory of chemical reactions; Schulz actually built the explosives.

König was "a typical Nazi type," a tall, blond-haired man, about thirty years old, didactic and narrow-minded, with a cold stare, totally dedicated to the cause. The theme of his first lecture was how to build a simple incendiary device, using easily available materials that could be bought at a typical American drugstore without arousing suspicion. The men made detailed notes of the recipes that König scrawled on the blackboard.[23]

Two hundred parts Chile saltpeter
One hundred parts sawdust

"Dampen the sawdust and mix it with the saltpeter," König instructed. In order to light the incendiary device, they would need a rudimentary fuse. This was simple enough to create: a mixture of three parts potassium chlorate and one part powdered sugar, ignited by a drop of sulfuric acid.

König drilled the men in such basic matters as the explosive qualities of trinitrotoluene, or TNT. He showed them a block of yellow material, about the size of a brick and weighing approximately two pounds, and explained that it could be used to sever a steel rail or girder. Left by itself, the material was quite stable, he emphasized. You could fire a bullet into it, and it would disintegrate rather than explode. In order to ignite the yellow block, you needed a detonator, made up of chemicals with an explosive velocity high enough to destabilize the TNT. The detonator would in turn be linked to some kind of safety fuse and timing device, allowing a saboteur to make his getaway.

König then produced an invention that filled him with pride: a block of TNT disguised to look like a lump of coal.[24] On closer examination, the trainees could see that the explosive was covered by a plastic substance of the kind one might use to repair wood, cut into an irregular shape and painted black. König showed the class a hole that had been drilled into the plastic, permitting the introduction of a detonator.

While one group was studying theory with König in the classroom, the other went next door to the laboratory to receive practical lessons from Schulz in how to assemble fuses and explosive devices. Schulz's classes tended to be more interesting than König's because the students got to work on their own. Smaller and more agile than König, Schulz led the morning gymnastics classes after Dempsey's departure. He was less of a

Nazi than König; there were even rumors that he had been in trouble with the Gestapo.[25]

In one of his first classes, Schulz produced a test tube, some dried peas, electric wire, two screws, and two pieces of cork, and announced he would use the materials to make a simple timing device.[26] First, he filled the tube halfway to the top with the peas, along with enough water to cover them. He then sliced one of the corks to make a thin disk, with a brass screw at the center, connected to a battery by electric wire. He placed the cork disk inside the test tube, so it was floating on top of the water. One-half of the circuit was now complete. He inserted the second screw into the other piece of cork, and wired it to the battery as well. He used this piece of cork to seal the top of the test tube.

The students watched, fascinated, as the dried peas slowly expanded, pushing the brass screws together and completing the electric circuit, setting off a small explosion. They spent the next lesson experimenting with test tubes of different sizes, and different quantities of water and dried peas. They discovered it was possible to delay or hasten the detonation of a bomb by playing with the different variables.

In all, the men learned to make at least ten such contraptions. Another device, for use in sabotaging railroads, consisted of a rubber ring separating two metal plates connected to a battery. Schulz showed them how to place a metal thumbtack inside the rubber ring, which could then be attached to a railroad track. When a heavy object such as a railway locomotive ran over the plates, contact would be established through the thumbtack, igniting the bomb.

During noon recess, Schulz and König took the students out to the explosives pit and mini-railroad at the end of the estate for practice in blowing things up. They explained that two pounds of the "yellow stuff" or the "black stuff" was sufficient to blow up a rail. They showed the students how to place the TNT by the side of the rail, drill a hole in it, place a detonator in the hole, and light a fuse. The first time they did this, everybody dived for cover as the device went off. When they returned to the site, they found a section of rail missing.[27] As the trainees got more proficient in handling explosives and timing devices, they practiced their skills on objects scattered around the estate, such as a wooden post buried in sand or an iron bar in a cellar. They learned that it was usually unnecessary to totally destroy a target: the same result could be achieved by applying a small quantity of explosive to a critical point, causing the entire structure to collapse.

The instructors did their best to simulate the conditions that the saboteurs were likely to encounter in America by organizing mock exercises. For these exercises, the students were required to wear an outfit of black pants, black shirt, and a black cap.[28] They were then divided into pairs, and given detailed instructions on what to blow up. Obstacles were placed around each target, in the form of harmless explosive devices that went off when someone approached them. Schulz and König posed as guards, leaping out from behind trees and doorways and throwing firecrackers at the nervous trainees.

BY THE end of the first week, the students had slipped into a routine.[29] Reveille at seven a.m., followed by calisthenics, making of beds, and cleaning of rooms. Breakfast was at eight, classes from nine to noon. Back to the farmhouse for lunch, and an hour reading English-language newspapers and magazines. Afternoon classes ran from two to four. Then sports, consisting of soccer games, boxing instruction, discus throwing, wrestling, and occasional pistol shooting. Dinner was at six, followed by a rest period, during which the men got together with group leaders to go over what they had learned.

The classes with Schulz and König were from Monday to Thursday. On Friday, Kappe arrived from Berlin to help the men with the cover stories that they would use in America, and see how well they stood up to interrogation. The stories had to sound plausible, not only to chance acquaintances but also to the U.S. authorities: if necessary, they would be provided with false documents to back up their claims.[30] As the trainee with the most extensive knowledge of America, Dasch helped Kappe drill the men in their new identities.

The trick was not to change too many personal details. That way, there would be less chance of the men becoming forgetful and giving themselves away. As far as outsiders were concerned, Dasch was now Davis. His birth date was shifted from 1903 to 1900, and his place of birth from Speyer-on-the-Rhine, Germany, to San Francisco, California. Kerling, alias Edward J. Kelly, an Irish-American bartender, also had his birthplace shifted to San Francisco. On Kappe's instructions, Kerling added five years to his age, so that his birth date was now the spring of 1906, shortly before the Great

Fire, which would conveniently explain why it was impossible to find records relating to his origins. Kappe told Dasch to look up the precise date of the fire in order to make sure the story held up.

Kappe decided that Burger and Haupt could keep their own names as they were naturalized American citizens and would therefore arouse less suspicion than German immigrants. Burger would pretend to be a Jewish refugee who had spent time in a Nazi concentration camp. His name sounded vaguely Jewish anyway. During his time in the hands of the Gestapo, he had met many German Jews, so it would not be difficult to come up with supporting details for this story. Burger wanted to know whether he should pose as an Orthodox or Reform Jew. Since he knew nothing about Jewish religious ceremonies, Kappe and Dasch decided he would be better off as a Reform Jew.

Haupt would simply keep his old identity as a German-American boy brought up in Chicago who had run off to Mexico on a lark, to avoid getting married to a pregnant girlfriend. If questioned, he would say he had spent the last year in Mexico, and deny that he had been anywhere near Germany. The only problem was that he had failed to register for the draft before he left home, even though he was of draft age. His superiors decided that when he got back to Chicago he would go to the local draft board and clear the matter up. In the meantime, he would be issued a false draft card in the name of Lawrence Jordan, a young man he had once known in Chicago.

The other men would variously claim to be Polish, Lithuanian, and even Portuguese. They would have jobs requiring very little documentation, such as painter, dishwasher, or farmhand, which were not too far from their actual occupations. Because Schmidt spoke English with a Swedish accent and had a vaguely Scandinavian appearance, he would pose as a Swede, Jerry Swensen.

Kappe cross-examined the men on their new identities, firing off questions like "Where was your father born?" "What schools did you attend?" and "Where were you last week?"[31]

Often, the stories would then begin to fall apart. That is what happened with the slow-witted and unimaginative Heinck. Because Heinck's English was not that good, Dasch had suggested he pose as Henry Kaynor, the son of a Polish coal miner from Wilkes-Barre, Pennsylvania. His cover story was that he left Wilkes-Barre at the age of fifteen after his mother died, working in a series of Polish restaurants.

"How do you spell Wilkes-Barre?" Kappe asked Heinck one evening in the classroom.

Heinck—who had never left New York during his thirteen years in the United States—was stumped. Although he made a valiant attempt to spell the name of the town where he supposedly grew up, it was clear he either was lying or was illiterate.

"You've done a poor job," Kappe scolded Dasch. "You must get the boys together and go over their stories so there are no more holes."

Dasch promised to create better stories for the men as soon as they got to America.

As the most committed Nazi among the saboteurs, Edward Kerling prided himself on his optimism and positive outlook. "This war is won for us already," he liked to boast to anybody who would listen.[32] "With these soldiers, we can't lose." He felt America had been tricked into going to war with Germany by "a small group of Jews," and did not really have the will to fight.[33] But now, perhaps for the first time since returning to Germany, Kerling began to have doubts about German invincibility. Halfway through the course, he went to Kappe with a series of complaints about his fellow trainees.

"These fellows you've got to do this job, they're useless. Some of them haven't been in America for years. Some of them are mentally unfit."

"Who do you think is unfit?"

Take Dasch, for example, Kerling replied. You only had to be around Dasch a little while to have doubts about him.[34] Dasch was the kind of person who seemed to take pleasure in doing the opposite of what was expected. His greatest passion was playing cards: whenever they got any time off, Dasch could be relied upon to organize a game of pinochle. He seemed uninterested in the sabotage lessons.[35] He would arrive at classes late and affect a superior air. In conversation, he talked like a true Nazi. But there were times when everybody else snapped to attention and shouted "Heil Hitler" and Dasch would just smirk and keep his hands in his pockets.

Or Burger. Kerling conceded that Burger was an excellent student. Unlike Dasch, he paid great attention in class, memorizing the different formulas and taking elaborate care with the experiments. On the other hand, there were rumors that Burger had spent time in a concentration camp, which raised questions about his political reliability.

Kerling went on down his list. Neubauer had "splinters on top of his brain" as a result of the injuries he had suffered in Russia.[36] If the pieces of metal moved around, he would have to go to the hospital, and his cover would be blown immediately, endangering everybody. Zuber had also served on the Russian front and was now "a mental case." He knew little about America, having been away for five or six years, and had expressed a marked antipathy to sabotage work. Then there was Thiel, whose knowledge of English was very limited, and Haupt, who could barely look at a pretty girl without chasing after her. Finally, there was the man known as Scottie, who drank so heavily that he was a danger to the mission.

Kappe had heard enough. He told Kerling that he had checked Dasch and Burger out carefully, and had confidence in both men. In fact, Dasch had been Kappe's first recruit, plucked out of the foreign broadcast monitoring section of the German foreign ministry the previous year. The previous December, he had written a long memorandum outlining various kinds of sabotage work and suggesting possible targets in America.[37] The memorandum had greatly impressed Kappe, who asked Dasch to help him go through the Nazi Party files of German-American returnees to find suitable candidates for a sabotage mission. Dasch's intimate knowledge of American ways was also a major plus, in Kappe's view. For example, he was thoroughly familiar with baseball, in contrast to Kerling, who had never been to a ball game during his eleven years in America.[38]

Kappe knew that Dasch had difficulty applying himself to the lessons on sabotage techniques.[39] One of the instructors had complained about this as well. When Kappe asked Dasch what was the matter, his protégé had replied that he was preoccupied with his responsibilities as group leader. He did not have to know all the technical details. It would be sufficient if his subordinates learned their lessons perfectly. Kappe accepted the explanation.

As for Burger, Kappe conceded that he had been in trouble with the Gestapo, but that did not mean that he was disloyal. In order to understand Burger, you had to understand the history of the fratricidal split between the storm troopers—also known as *Sturmabteilung*, or S.A.—and the S.S., which had come to a head soon after his return to America in 1933. Burger had been a follower of Ernst Röhm, the S.A. leader and one of Hitler's closest associates in the early days of the Nazi movement. The Führer had concluded that Röhm had become too powerful, and was threatening to undermine the new regime with his bullying storm trooper ways and wild rhetoric about the betrayal of the "German revolution." Tactics that were appropriate for the period when the Nazis were struggling to gain power were counterproductive now that Hitler was master of Germany. So he ordered the S.S. to crush the storm troopers, murdering Röhm and hundreds of his top aides during the Night of the Long Knives in 1934.

Burger had been fortunate to escape with his life. He had ended up in a concentration camp after making a trip to Poland on behalf of a Nazi Party political science institute, during which he had submitted an incautiously worded report about conditions there. But now he wanted a chance for political rehabilitation, and Kappe was willing to give it to him. Burger, Kappe thought, was a good soldier.

As a concession to Kerling, Kappe agreed to get rid of Zuber and Scottie. But he insisted the others were "all right."[40] So it was decided. Two of the men would be dismissed. Nine would stay.

THE NAVY had agreed to transport the saboteurs to America by U-boat, but the question remained: how would they get from the submarine to shore? Kappe's first idea was to equip them with collapsible rubber canoes, each of which had room for two men. The trainees practiced assembling and disassembling the boats, and took them out on the lake for practice landings. They quickly concluded it would be foolhardy to use the canoes on the ocean, particularly if the surf was high.

Kappe brushed aside their concerns. "They will be easier to navigate once they are fully loaded and are deeper in the water." He pointed out that the canoes would also be transporting several boxes of sabotage equipment.[41] The men were skeptical, but continued to practice with the canoes.

One day, while Dasch's group was in the laboratory experimenting with explosives, screams were heard from the direction of the lake. An instructor rushed in with the news that one of the canoes had overturned. Everybody rushed down to the lake, where they saw Kerling and Haupt flailing about in the icy water. The lake had only begun to thaw a few weeks before, and the men were wearing heavy blue uniforms and boots that had been seized from the Polish army. Kerling had the presence of mind to pull his boots and pants off in the water; Haupt was practically drowning.

The instructors and some of the other men pushed a large rubber boat into the lake and mounted a rescue mission. Both men were dragged aboard, teeth chattering, faces blue-white. Back in the farmhouse, the hapless canoeists were rubbed down with alcohol, given some schnapps to drink, and sent to bed.

The next day, Kappe went to Berlin to report. That evening, he called Dasch by phone to announce that the navy had agreed to land the saboteurs in America in large rubber dinghies, to be manned by professional sailors.

THE LAST lesson at Quenz Lake was a two-hour course in secret writing. An instructor from Berlin taught the men some simple techniques, using a variety of everyday tools, such as laxative tablets, aspirin, and toothpicks. He began by demonstrating a method that relied on water, paper, and pencil.[42]

First he soaked a piece of paper in a bowl of water. To prevent the paper from becoming wrinkled when he removed it from the bowl, he held it up by the top two corners, allowing the excess water to drain off. He laid the paper on a glass surface, and placed a dry sheet of paper on top of it. Using a black pencil, he then wrote a secret message on the top sheet of paper, pushing down hard enough so that an imprint was left on the wet sheet below. He removed the dry sheet, leaving the wet sheet on the glass until it had thoroughly dried. By this time, the writing had become invisible, and a camouflage letter could be written over it. The instructor showed the class how to get the secret message to magically reappear: simply immerse the now-dry paper in water again.

Other methods of secret writing left a jumbled impression with the men, particularly Dasch, who was confused by the whole business. "You buy a laxative," he recalled later.[43] "You use so many grains, add something, and you have the works. You use a toothpick and cotton and start writing, but you could never see it."

The idea behind the training in secret writing was to give the men a secure way of communicating with one another in America, particularly if they were living in different cities. But when one of them asked the instructor whether the secret inks they had studied would withstand chemical analysis by the enemy, he replied bluntly, "No." This set off a round of low muttering.[44]

Most of the men concluded they were unlikely to have much use for secret writing.

FINAL EXAMS got under way at noon, on Wednesday, April 29. The instructors divided the men into pairs and handed out secret instructions on what to blow up. The targets—symbolizing a factory, an oil refinery, a railroad—were scattered around the estate. The Abwehr sent an additional fifteen observers from Berlin to assist the instructors and act as guards. The goal was to carry out the mission by noon the next day without being caught.

Dasch teamed up with Quirin, one of the men in his group.[45] Unlike Dasch, Quirin was good with his hands, having worked as a machinist in the new Volkswagen plant in the town of Braunschweig in central Germany and, before that, as an odd-job man for rich Americans in Westchester County, New York. Together they were ordered to disable a make-believe manufacturing plant. They had twenty-four hours to prepare their materials, sneak into the factory, plant the bomb, and return safely to base. Since this was a trial run, they would use incendiaries rather than explosives such as TNT.

Dasch and Quirin returned to the laboratory to get everything ready. Together, they mixed the chemicals, just like Schulz had shown them. Then they prepared a detonator, fuse, and timing device. For the timer, Quirin chose a cheap pocket watch with a celluloid face. He opened up the watch and drilled a tiny hole in the side. He also removed the minute hand. He threaded some electrical wire through the hole, and attached one end to the hour hand and the other to a battery. He replaced the face of the watch, drilling another hole in the celluloid opposite the position for six o'clock. He inserted a small metal screw in the hole, also linked to the battery by electrical wire. When the hour hand came into contact with the screw, the circuit would be complete. By adjusting the hour hand, the saboteurs could now explode their bomb with a delay of up to eleven hours.

That night, when they thought the coast was clear, Dasch and Quirin crept up to the imaginary factory, an abandoned building at the edge of the estate. They reached the designated spot, and placed their bomb, hooking up the fuse and timer. But as they were leaving, instructors jumped out of the shadows, throwing firecrackers at them.

At least they had completed most of the assignment. Some of the others did not get that far. Heinck set off a loud explosion when he stepped on a booby trap as he approached his target.[46] Another man was overcome by tear gas as he pried open the door of a small stone house, representing some kind of industrial plant. Throughout the night, the farm reverberated with the sound of firecrackers, explosives, and Molotov cocktails.

The most successful pair was Burger and Schmidt, alias Swensen.[47] Their assignment was the destruction of a fictitious oil tank, located in a cellar of one of the buildings on the estate. First, they had to get into the cellar without being seen and find out the exact dimensions of the oil tank, which had been marked on the floor with chalk. After completing this part of the test, they returned to the laboratory to prepare the timing devices and explosives. Even though the cellar was guarded, they managed to sneak back inside a second time and set off their miniature bomb without being detected.

Kappe pronounced the exercise a success. Not everybody had done as well as Burger and Schmidt, but they had all been exposed to something approaching real-life conditions. Their nerves had been tested, and they had approached their tasks with enthusiasm. A lieutenant colonel who came from Berlin to observe the final exam was generous in his congratulations, remarking, "Never since the school started have I seen a bunch of men so eager."[48]

ON THE final day of class, Thursday, April 30, everyone gathered in the classroom to hear Kappe reveal their assignments in America. He produced a series of maps of the United States, with a detailed list of targets, along with graphs of American industrial production and photographs of bridges and railroads.[49]

The first map showed the locations of aluminum and magnesium plants along the eastern seaboard, marked with blue and red crosses. Several of the crosses were clustered around the town of Alcoa, Tennessee, center of the American aluminum industry and site of the largest aluminum plant in the world. Kappe explained that aluminum was the basic material in the construction of modern aircraft: its outstanding property was its light weight, roughly one-third that of steel. He pointed to a graph that showed that American aluminum production had increased from under 300,000 pounds in 1937 to more than 600,000 by 1941. The 1942 target was 1.2 million pounds. If the saboteurs could cripple or severely disrupt aluminum production, they might be able to prevent the United States from ever developing an effective air force to fight the Luftwaffe.[50]

Disrupting aluminum production was simpler than it sounded. The process for manufacturing aluminum—invented by a young American chemist named Charles M. Hall in 1886—was heavily dependent on the supply of huge amounts of electricity. In fact, aluminum was formed through a process known as electrolysis, a kind of electric bath in which aluminum oxide was dissolved in melted cryolite ore. If the power supply was interrupted for long enough during this procedure, the molten metals would congeal, wrecking the stoves and baths in which the aluminum was manufactured. By downing critical power lines for a period of eight hours, saboteurs could permanently disable an aluminum plant.

An American pamphlet produced at the beginning of World War II summarized what was at stake in a neat formula:

Electric power → aluminum → bombers → victory.[51]

It was the task of the Nazi saboteurs to reverse this formula:

Sabotage of power lines → less aluminum → fewer American planes → defeat.

Kappe assigned the job of attacking aluminum plants to group number one, which would consist of Dasch, Burger, Schmidt, Quirin, and Heinck. Dasch, at least, already understood the importance of aluminum to the war effort, and America's ability to vastly increase its production of war matériel. Back in January, while still working at the foreign broadcast monitoring center, he had jotted down U.S. war production plans announced by Franklin Roosevelt in his State of the Union address to Congress. According to Roosevelt, America would increase its production of planes from 60,000 a year in 1942 to 125,000 in 1943.

"Kids, this war has not even begun," Dasch warned his friends.[52]

If there was any time left over from these activities, Kappe suggested several targets of opportunity, such as planting small explosive devices in Jewish-owned department stores or in the baggage-claim rooms of large railroad stations. The idea was not to kill and maim, he emphasized, merely to spread panic.

Group two, Kappe announced, would be made up of Kerling, Haupt, Thiel, and Neubauer. Their primary objective would be the transportation system. He turned the floor over to his assistant, Reinhold Barth, a former employee of the Long Island Rail Road, who produced maps of the American railroad and canal systems and photographs of critical bottlenecks such as the Hell Gate Bridge, connecting Long Island to the Bronx, and the great Horseshoe Curve of the Pennsylvania Railroad. Putting the Hell Gate Bridge out of action should not prove too difficult, Barth insisted. It was constructed out of metal plate rather than cast iron.

Kappe and Barth had done their homework. Among the targets they selected were two cryolite processing plants in Pennsylvania, which produced the aluminum oxide used to produce aluminum. The U.S. War Department had given the cryolite plants a P-3 classification, indicating a relatively minor importance for national defense. A subsequent investigation by American military intelligence showed that destruction of the two plants would practically halt aluminum production throughout the United States. The director of the Federal Bureau of Investigation, J. Edgar Hoover, would later comment that the German High Command was "better informed as to the importance of these two plants to our war production than was the United States Army."[53]

Because of difficulties in arranging U-boat transportation, Kappe had decided to grant the men two weeks' furlough, to allow them to say goodbye to their families. Before they left Quenz Lake, however, there were a couple of personnel matters to be addressed.

The rumors about Burger's problems with the Gestapo were true, Kappe said. But he repeated what he had already told Kerling: Burger was working toward his political rehabilitation and deserved their support. Besides, Kappe had special plans for the former concentration camp inmate.[54] He wanted Burger to establish himself in Chicago either as a draftsman or as a violin teacher: he had talents in both directions. After renting a studio, he would signal to the spymasters back in Germany that all was well by taking out an advertisement in the *Chicago Tribune*. Burger's studio would serve as a point of contact for subsequent sabotage groups arriving in America.

Kappe also confirmed the appointment of Dasch and Kerling as group leaders. Schmidt and Quirin were aghast at the choice of Dasch, and could not understand why Kappe had so much confidence in the garrulous former waiter. Privately, they talked about killing Dasch if he didn't change his attitude by the time they reached America. When speaking to Kappe, they were more diplomatic: how should they deal with someone who proved untrustworthy?

This time, Kappe told the saboteurs what they wanted to hear. If there were grounds to suspect anyone of betraying Operation Pastorius, he replied, that person must be removed, if necessary by force.[55]

CHAPTER TWO

FAREWELLS

(MAY 1–21)

M OST OF THE MEN spent the furlough with their relatives. Peter Burger helped his wife move out of their small apartment in Berlin to his parents' home in Bavaria. Dasch visited his parents in Speyer, in southern Germany; Quirin and Heinck returned to the Volkswagen plant in Braunschweig, where their wives and children were living in factory-supplied housing; Kerling went back to his family home in Wiesbaden.

Herbie Haupt took a train to the Baltic port of Stettin to visit his grandmother, who had given him a place to live after his around-the-world adventures. Having been in the United States as recently as June 1941, he was taken aback by the austerity and paranoia of life in Nazi Germany. From the land of plenty, he had arrived in a country where everything was rationed, and people had to make do with two cigarettes a day. He learned how to smoke the cigarettes down to a butt of a quarter of an inch and extract the remaining tobacco to put in a pipe. Fuel was in such short supply that his grandparents only heated one room of their house, and spent most of their waking hours there. Haupt resented the frequent visits from Gestapo officials checking up on the suspicious German-American. He "counted the days and hours" until he got back home to his family in Chicago.[1]

The food shortages seemed to get more severe as the war progressed. At the sabotage school on Quenz Lake, Haupt and his fellow trainees had been relatively well fed, eating meat or some kind of stew four or five times a week. Much greater sacrifices were required of ordinary civilians. The official weekly ration per person was ten ounces of meat, four and a half ounces of butter and margarine, three ounces of cheese, three pounds of

potatoes, and three-quarters of a pound of sugar. Eggs were only distributed at Easter, Christmas, and other special holidays. Frequently, food supplies were so tight that shops were unable to sell customers even their
official rations.

Most of the men did not tell their families where they were going. Some
invented cover stories, saying they were being drafted into the army.
Others said they were being sent on a mysterious top-secret mission. The
most candid was Burger, who told his wife he was going to America, but
not what he would be doing there. As a communication system, he
instructed her in one of the methods of secret writing he had learned at
sabotage school. He also gave her a password to authenticate a message
sent through a trusted intermediary.[2] If someone introduced himself to
her with the password, she was to immediately follow that person's
instructions.

Dasch told his parents he was being transferred to Chile to do propaganda work for the foreign ministry. It must have been difficult for him to
display such restraint. His mother—a "battleaxe," in Dasch's word—had
always insisted that her children tell her everything.[3]

GEORGE JOHN DASCH was the fifth of thirteen children, known in the
family as Knöppel, German slang for "short, wiry boy."[4] His mother,
Frances, was a social worker elected to the Speyer city council on the Social
Democratic ticket following Germany's defeat in World War I. At her insistence, he entered a Catholic seminary to study for the priesthood, but was
expelled for "utterances and acts which were in conflict with teachings of
the Church." She later encouraged him to fight for the rights of his fellow
workers. Throughout his life, he venerated his mother as the person who
had influenced him most, describing her as the "teacher" who had given
him his "basic socialist ideas."[5]

Dasch retained his socialist ideals after moving to America in 1922,
working his way up the ladder from soda fountain clerk to busboy to
waiter. Although he made several attempts to get out of the restaurant
business—he dreamed of becoming a pilot, and worked for a few months
as a traveling salesman selling Catholic missionary supplies—he kept
coming back to waiting on tables. During the Depression, Dasch spent
much of his free time trying to unionize his fellow waiters. He became
obsessed by union politics, and got into frequent battles with both the far

right and the far left. The bosses viewed him as a Communist trouble-maker; the Communists in Local 17 of the Bartenders' and Waiters' International Union detected Nazi sympathies.

As he watched the rise of Nazism across the Atlantic, Dasch initially had little sympathy for Hitler. But his views began to change in the late thirties as friends and relatives arrived from Germany with stories of how life was getting better under the Führer. After the turmoil and hyperinflation of the Weimar years, the country was moving forward once again. Everybody had a job and a sense of direction. The humiliations heaped on Germany after World War I by the Treaty of Versailles were being overcome and the Fatherland was regaining international respect. The dictatorship imposed by Hitler seemed a small price to pay for the return of prosperity and national self-esteem.

To Dasch's great surprise, even his mother "praised the work of Hitler" when she arrived in the United States in early 1939 on a brief visit.[6] The former Social Democrat political activist described how workers and farmers were protected by new labor laws, how living conditions had improved, and how "people in general were very happy." She supported Hitler's quest for "Lebensraum" in eastern Europe. When Nazi Germany and Soviet Russia signed their non-aggression pact in the summer of 1939, thereby sealing the fate of Poland, Frances Dasch hurried back enthusiastically to Germany, telling her son that "this means war."

Confronted with these arguments, Dasch began to rethink his opposition to Nazism. "I said to myself that perhaps I had been wrong all along about Hitler; perhaps I had a prejudiced mind that had been closed to the truth." His political views now underwent a 180-degree turn. From viewing Nazism with hostility and suspicion, he decided he should follow his mother to Germany, even though this meant abandoning an application for U.S. citizenship, then in its final stages. To stay in America at a time when his own country was threatened by so many enemies would be like a rat deserting a sinking ship, he reasoned.

There was an additional and perhaps determining reason for Dasch's decision to leave America: his own fortunes had recently taken a sharp turn for the worse. His clashes with the group that controlled the Waiters' Union, and his attempts to set up a new union, had led to an expensive lawsuit.[7] He was forced to sell his wife's beauty parlor and move out of his Bronx home for nonpayment of rent. After eighteen years in America, he was almost back to where he started, forced to take whatever menial job he could find. The experience left him "disgusted" and "nearly a nervous wreck."[8]

Since it was very difficult to book passage back to Germany, and he could not afford to pay for his own ticket in any case, he pestered the German consulate in New York for assistance to return home and perform his duty "as a German citizen." He also needed a passport, because his previous one had expired. At first, the officials just laughed at him, saying there was no way to get back to Germany in the middle of a war. Dasch was sure he could find a way, even if it meant smuggling himself aboard an Italian steamer as a stowaway. After months of pleading, he finally discovered the real reason for the consulate's refusal to help him get back to Germany: he was not Nazi enough.

Dasch would later recall that the doubts about his political soundness "got my fighting Dutch up."[9] He went to the German embassy in Washington, and stated his case to a higher official. After questioning him at length about his political beliefs, the official finally agreed to issue him a new German passport and sponsor his return home. The passport came through in January 1941. Now it was just a question of waiting for a ship to take him from America to Japan, on the first stage of a very roundabout trip back to Germany via California, Japan, China, and Russia. (Most Atlantic ports were closed to German ships.)

The only remaining snag was his wife, Rose Marie, known to Dasch as Snooks. She was an American citizen. She was also gravely ill with an infected uterus and was admitted to a hospital in the middle of February, her life threatened by dangerous blood clots. By the time Dasch got word of the imminent departure of a Japanese ship from San Francisco, his wife was getting better but was still in no condition to travel.

The consulate gave him ten hours to make up his mind. Having overcome so many obstacles to get this far, he decided it was now or never. "I thought of my wife in the hospital and at the same time I also remembered the hell I had raised with the consulate for the chance of going home . . . I reached a quick decision to sail."[10] His wife would have to follow later. He did not even have time to say goodbye, instead asking his brother and sister "to go to Snooks at the hospital the next day and explain the circumstances of my sudden departure."

He took a bath and packed two suitcases, the maximum permitted for the journey across Russia on the trans-Siberian railroad. His brother drove him down to the New York bus terminal for a five-day trip across the country to San Francisco. He arrived just in time to catch a Japanese steamer, the *Tatuta Maru,* bound for Yokohama, giving a California acquaintance the impression that he was "overjoyed" to return to Germany and enthusiastic about assisting the Nazi war effort. "If I don't succeed in Germany, I will kill myself," Dasch insisted.[11]

Most of his fellow passengers were German-American Bund members returning home to fight for Hitler. They greeted him with a chorus of Sieg Heils. As he boarded the steamer on March 27, and sailed through the Golden Gate Bridge, Dasch had few regrets about leaving America. His failure to advance beyond waiting on tables was a recurring source of annoyance and grievance. While some Americans had been kind and hospitable, others had been "cold and rude."

DASCH'S INITIAL attempts to find fulfillment in Germany were as unsuccessful as they had been in America. He told Nazi officials he wanted "to do my duty for my country," by which he meant something more elevated and patriotic than the mundane jobs he had held in America.[12] But when he approached the army for a job that would draw on his experiences traveling around the world, he received a sharp rebuff. "What do you think?" a colonel asked sarcastically. "You want us to fry an extra fish for you?"[13] He got a similar response from Dr. Goebbels' propaganda ministry when he suggested that he could help improve Nazi propaganda efforts in the United States, which were "not correct." It was more or less the same story everywhere: Nazi bureaucracy, he concluded, was even more obtuse than the American variety.

Dasch turned for help to someone he had known in America: his wife's cousin, Reinhold Barth, who gave him an introduction to Walter Kappe of the Abwehr. After questioning Dasch in detail about his experiences in America, Kappe told him he was "crazy" to want to join the army and unlikely to last two weeks there.[14] Instead he proposed helping Dasch find a job in the Nazi Party office that monitored foreign broadcasts. For his radio monitoring work, he would receive a salary of 525 marks a month, a respectable sum by wartime standards. When Dasch said he felt he should be doing "something bigger and better for my country," Kappe told him to be patient. "In due time, I will call on you."[15]

The monitoring work consisted of listening to foreign radio broadcasts, and transcribing and translating anything that might interest senior

Nazi officials. Dasch spent up to eight hours every day, six days a week, with his ears glued to headphones, listening to crackly American news broadcasts coming in over shortwave frequencies from places like New York, Ankara, and Cairo. He paid particular attention to commentators like Cyrus Sulzberger and Martin Agronsky who were believed to reflect the views of the American establishment. A teletype machine connected the monitoring station to the offices of Nazi leaders, allowing them to receive Dasch's translations virtually simultaneously.

Toward the end of November, after he had been working at the monitoring station for six months, Dasch received another summons from Kappe. The Abwehr lieutenant made him sign an oath of secrecy, and then asked if he would like to "go back to America."[16] He proceeded to give Dasch a sketchy outline of a plan to carry out sabotage attacks against American industry. It was a few days before Pearl Harbor, and the United States was still officially neutral, but Kappe explained that America was helping Germany's enemies and had thus become an "indirect enemy" of the Third Reich.

"It is time for us to attack them."

Dasch told Kappe he was ready for anything.

His mother had always urged him to do something "bigger and better" with his life—and now that dream seemed closer than ever to fulfillment. He was going back to America as leader of a special wartime mission for the Fatherland. His boyish delight at his new role was reflected in the password he gave his parents to authenticate any message he succeeded in sending back to them while he was away. For this latest adventure, he would be known to his family by his old childhood nickname: Knöppel.

THE FURLOUGH had a particularly bittersweet quality for Hermann Neubauer, the young soldier wounded on the Russian front. Neubauer had an American wife whom he had met while working at the Chicago World's Fair in the summer of 1933. When Neubauer decided it was his duty to return to Germany in 1940 to fight for the Fatherland, Alma had been strongly opposed, even though her family was also of German origin. She remained behind in Chicago. He eventually persuaded her to join him, and she arrived in Berlin around Easter, 1941.

Alma spoke scarcely any German and had a hard time adapting to life in Hitler's Berlin. The living conditions were terrible, at least from an

American perspective, and everyone seemed suspicious of the pretty young girl from Chicago. Soon after her arrival, Neubauer was ordered to report to his unit. By midsummer, he was in Russia. The only tangible reminders of their married life were some snapshots of Hermann in uniform in some miserable Russian village and hastily scribbled notes saying he expected to be sent into action soon. A few weeks later, he was back in Germany, in a military hospital in Stuttgart.

And now Neubauer was going back to the United States as a saboteur while his wife, the pampered daughter of a Republican precinct captain who had never wanted to come to Germany in the first place, was staying behind in the Third Reich. What made the situation even worse was that he was not allowed to say where he was going. He told her simply that he expected to be sent back to Russia.

They had spent most of his furlough on a farm outside the former "free town" of Danzig, the Baltic port city that had served as the pretext for Hitler's blitzkrieg attack on Poland. The farm belonged to one of Hermann's aunts. It was easier to get food in the countryside than in the cities, and Neubauer said he wanted some peace and quiet before returning to the front. To Alma, her husband seemed depressed and unhappy. He spent much of the holiday complaining about severe headaches and talked with foreboding about the hardships he would have to endure in Russia.

On their last day on the farm, Hermann told Alma to get ready to go to Berlin, where he was to meet some friends before reporting back to his company. He mentioned one of his officers by name, saying, "I must see Herr Kappe in Berlin concerning arrangements for our journey to Russia."[17]

The evening after their arrival in Berlin, Hermann took his wife to a tavern "to meet some friends and fellow soldiers." The dimly lit dining room was practically deserted, except for a long table in the middle, at which sat a dozen men and three women. The orchestra was playing English and American music, and Alma concluded that the entire tavern had been specially reserved for the group. As soon as she and Hermann approached the table, all the men rose to their feet with a collective clicking sound, and the conversation died down.

The only person she recognized was Eddie Kerling, an old friend of Hermann's from the States. Eddie and Hermann had shared many adventures, including the failed attempt to cross the Atlantic on the yacht *Lekala*.

When Alma and Hermann were married in January 1940, Eddie had served as best man. Six months later, Hermann and Eddie had returned to Germany together.

Whenever Alma had met him before, Kerling had been smiling and upbeat. But on this occasion, he too seemed downcast. He mentioned how much he wanted to see his wife, Marie, whom he had left behind in America.

Hermann made no attempt to introduce Alma to anyone at the table, other than a mumbled "This is my wife." The conversation was dominated by a fat, middle-aged man who sat at the middle of the table. This man was evidently the "Herr Kappe" Hermann had mentioned as his reason for coming to Berlin. Kappe in turn lavished most of his attention on a young, well-dressed woman with dyed red hair sitting next to him. Since smart clothes were practically unavailable in wartime Berlin, Alma guessed that the woman was probably a prostitute.

After ordering a couple of rounds of drinks for the rest of the group, Hermann and Alma got up and left. They were accompanied to the door by Kerling, who told Alma that he and Hermann would be leaving very soon for the Russian front.

Back in the hotel, Alma poured out all her frustrations and disappointments, telling Hermann that he should have stayed with her in America.[18] She felt as if she was being constantly watched. The police had kept on asking why she didn't go to work, why she didn't have a baby, what her family did back in the United States. She was being treated like a criminal.

They said goodbye the following morning. As they hugged and kissed, Hermann seemed more than usually emotional, telling Alma this might be the last time they would ever see each other.

AN ENTHUSIASTIC conspirator, Walter Kappe maintained two different offices in Berlin. His official office was in room 1025 of the headquarters of the German High Command, at Tirpitzüfer 76/78, on the Landwehr canal near the Tiergarten in the heart of the imperial city. Abwehr II, the sabotage division of military intelligence, occupied one wing of the handsome four-story classical building, which had been built on the eve of World War I. Sixty years later, the same building would house the ministry of defense of a reunited Germany.

In addition to his Abwehr office, Kappe also had a conspiratorial hideaway known as "the bunker" in the commercial district of the city at

Rankestrasse 6, a tree-lined street leading down from the Kaiser Wilhelm Church on the Kurfürstendamm. Here he held court in a fourth-floor safe house behind a smoked-glass door with a sign that read *Schriftleitung Der Kaukasus,* the Editors of The Caucasus.[19] The name over the bell was Röhrich. Both Herr Röhrich and the *Kaukasus* magazine were figments of Kappe's fertile imagination.

Visitors to the bunker were ushered into a reception room decorated with Baroque furniture. A concealed microphone and spy hole permitted Kappe to keep an eye on whatever was going on in the reception room from his secretary's office next door. The rest of the apartment consisted of a bedroom, dining room, kitchen, and bathroom, each opening into an L-shaped corridor.

Over the previous five months, Kappe had invited several dozen German-American returnees to the bunker for screening as potential saboteurs. Some, like Dasch, had approached the Abwehr by themselves, looking for a job with foreign intelligence. Most had been the targets of an aggressive recruiting campaign by Kappe. The former Bund rabble-rouser had spent hours poring over the files of the Ausland Institut, the Nazi Party office that coordinated relations with foreign countries. By sifting through questionnaires submitted by returnees, Kappe was able to identify candidates for a future sabotage mission. He also addressed reunions of former Bund members around Germany, during which he insinuated that there were ways to "help the Fatherland" back in America. This was how he came across Heinck and Quirin, two returnees who had found work with Volkswagen.

Kappe had ordered Dasch and Kerling, the two group leaders, to report to Abwehr headquarters on May 11, the day before the rest of the men, for further instructions in secret writing. They spent that Monday morning in the laboratory, dabbling with handkerchiefs and matches impregnated with an invisible ink. Abwehr officials also gave them the address of a mail drop in Lisbon, through which they could communicate with Berlin with some delay. As a neutral country, Portugal still had mail service with both the United States and Germany.

They had lunch at Kappe's favorite restaurant on the Nollendorfplatz, a fifteen-minute stroll from Abwehr headquarters on the other side of the canal. As they walked to the restaurant, Kappe raised the question of finances.[20] He proposed giving each group leader $50,000 "for operational purposes," and $5,000 for each agent. In addition, every man on the mission would carry a specially designed money belt containing $4,000, plus $450 in ready cash for immediate use. In all, the two groups would take over $180,000 with them to the United States, the equivalent of two million dollars today. Dasch suggested sewing his cash into the lining of an old Gladstone bag that he had picked up in America.

After lunch, the discussion turned to the best landing places on America's two-thousand-mile eastern coastline. Dasch knew Long Island well, particularly the Hamptons.[21] He had worked as a waiter at various inns in East Hampton and Southampton, and thought that the broad expanse of sand on the southeastern tip of Long Island would be the perfect place to bring in a dinghy. For his group, Kerling proposed the beaches of northern Florida around Jacksonville. He was familiar with this stretch of coastline as a result of his adventures on the *Lekala* two years earlier. After intercepting the boat off Atlantic City and impounding it for three weeks, the U.S. authorities had permitted Kerling and his friends to sail it down to Florida so they could sell it. But there was a stringent condition designed to prevent the Bundists from making a dash across the Atlantic: they were obliged to report to every Coast Guard station between New York and Miami.

When the rest of the men reported to the bunker the following day, Kappe announced that submarines were not immediately available for their voyage across the Atlantic.[22] Instead, they would take part in a field trip intended to familiarize them with the targets of their sabotage mission.

First stop on the tour was the canal system around Berlin. Their guide was Dasch's relative Barth, a mousy, nearsighted man who had worked for six years on the Long Island Rail Road cleaning coaches and repairing railway cars.[23] While in America, Barth had also served as the Bund's logistics expert, organizing special trains to transport large groups of American Nazis to parades and training camps around Long Island. This was how Barth had first come into contact with Kappe.

Rain was pouring down as the saboteurs clambered aboard a boat, making Berlin seem even grayer and bleaker than usual.[24] The first lock they inspected had wooden doors on large metal hinges, which opened to permit water levels to rise and fall. The best way to destroy such a lock, Barth instructed, was to apply a couple of sticks of dynamite to the hinge, the weakest point in the lock. Once one or two locks had been destroyed, the force of tumbling water would usually be sufficient to rip out all the locks lower down in the system.

Next, they inspected a more modern type of lock that rose up and down with a pulley-and-cable mechanism. Barth recommended putting this kind of lock out of action by disabling the machinery that pulled the doors up and down. Another method of putting a canal out of action was to sink a concrete-laden barge in the middle of the stream.

The next day, Barth took the saboteurs to see a railroad repair shop. They were introduced as counterintelligence agents, studying how to combat sabotage by Russian partisans.[25] The chief engineer seemed satisfied with this explanation. He took them through the shop, pointing out the kind of targets that might interest a saboteur and describing the workings of a steam engine.

After lunch, they walked to a nearby railroad yard. At Quenz Lake, Barth had already given the men a detailed explanation of American rolling stock, identifying the weak points on different types of equipment. Climbing on top of a locomotive, he pointed out a simple way of disabling the engine by putting sand in the cylinders or in the oil boxes, a method favored by Russian saboteurs.

A more sophisticated way of achieving the same result, Barth explained back in the *Kaukasus* office, was to use the exploding coal designed by Abwehr specialists, which was armed by a detonating cap. Several lumps of such coal thrown into the tender of a locomotive would eventually make their way into the furnace, causing the train to "go high up in the air."[26]

THE HIGHLIGHT of the inspection tour was a two-day trip to the aluminum and magnesium plants of the IG Farben group. In addition to the nine saboteurs, half a dozen officials went along for the trip, including Kappe, a representative of the Army High Command, a man from Farben headquarters, and the two Herr Doktors from the sabotage school. They left Berlin by train at six o'clock on Thursday morning, arriving in Bitterfeld three hours later. From the rail station, a bus took them to the aluminum plant, the biggest in Germany.

The group listened to a lecture on the aluminum manufacturing process, with frequent reminders on the importance of destroying the power supply. Then they inspected the plant, whose layout was very similar to facilities run by the Aluminum Company of America, the company that dominated aluminum production throughout the United States. Some of the Farben engineers were able to talk very knowledgeably about the challenges facing the saboteurs as they had been to the Alcoa factories before the war.

First stop on the tour were the electric baths where molten ores were turned into aluminum. They moved on to the main powerhouse to inspect the transformers that reduced the incoming power voltage from a hundred thousand volts to the much lower level necessary to feed the electrolysis machines. Farben officials showed them how to destroy the transformers by placing explosives next to the air-cooling system, which would cause the oil to drain out of the cooler. An alternative method was to shoot a high-velocity bullet between the metal ribs of the cooling system.

Nearby, the engineers pointed out some tall porcelain insulators; a hammer blow to one of these insulators would destroy the vacuum and knock out the power supply. In order to gain access to the porcelain jars, they would probably need to "immobilize" the man in the control room.

Security at the sprawling aluminum plant was hardly perfect, the saboteurs observed with satisfaction.[27] Burger and Dasch noted numerous ways of gaining access. The director told them that as an experiment he had instructed his guards to try to smuggle dummy packages of explosives into the plant. Out of twenty-seven men selected for the exercise, twenty-six managed to complete their mission without being caught. In order to strengthen security, the director had appointed guards with shotguns to patrol the exterior and interior of the plant. With his military training, Burger quickly spotted at least one of the guards walking around with an unloaded shotgun over his shoulder, a detail he delighted in pointing out to the director.

Their work completed, the saboteurs and their hosts retired to the company dining room for a feast complete with cigars and bottles of wine. It impressed Dasch as "the swellest dinner I ever had in Germany... We were treated like kings!"[28] They spent Thursday night in Bitterfeld, traveling on to Dessau the following morning.

From Dessau, a bus took the party to the brand-new aluminum and magnesium plants at Aachen, which were still being completed. They made the usual inspection tour, but what most struck Dasch and some of the other saboteurs was the system of forced labor recently introduced by Hitler. Ninety percent of the workers at the two plants had been shipped in from conquered areas of the Soviet Union. Many appeared to be starving. Over another lavish lunch, the director explained that these "free" workers—as opposed to prisoners of war—earned around thirty-five marks a week. Out of this amount, they had to pay around thirty marks for food and lodging. In order to buy luxuries, such as beer and cigarettes, they needed special coupons, which were only handed out to the most deserving.

The Russians, Dasch noted, were escorted to and from the camp by armed guard. Even though the weather had turned fairly warm, they came to work dressed in winter clothes, including scraps of old furs. "They wear everything they possess," one of the German managers explained. "They go to bed with those clothes on and they come to work with them on."[29] He seemed unconcerned that the workers had a tendency to "drop down, just like flies."

The men returned to Berlin by train that night, arriving at two in the morning. Kappe gave them the rest of the weekend off, telling them to report back on Monday. It had been an exhausting but instructive week.

BEGINNING ON May 18, Kappe called in the men individually to the Rankestrasse bunker to go over final arrangements for their trip. He wanted to make sure that their service papers were all in order before they left for America. Nobody knew what would happen to Kappe and the other Abwehr officers who had ordered the sabotage mission—any of them might be sent to the Russian front at any moment—so it was best to put everything in writing.

Kappe handed each saboteur three documents.[30] The first was a financial contract, stipulating the man's salary and how much his family would receive in the event of his death. It stipulated that the saboteurs would report to the Vertrauensmänner Abteilung, the Trusted Agents' section of the Abwehr. The second document committed the Abwehr to find an appropriate civilian job for the V-man—as agents were known—once the war was over. The third was a pledge of secrecy, obliging the V-man never to talk about his work to outsiders on penalty of death.

The salary scale depended on the individual saboteur. As group leaders, Dasch and Kerling would receive 600 marks a month. Most of the others would earn from 250 to 500 marks, similar to what they had been making as civilians. The two soldiers, Neubauer and Burger, would continue to receive their regular army pay. Neubauer objected to this arrangement and, after some argument, persuaded Kappe to increase his salary. Burger merely asked for the inclusion of a clause promising him complete reha- bilitation in the eyes of the Nazi Party if he carried out his mission suc- cessfully.[31] The papers had been countersigned in advance by senior Abwehr officers. As Kappe produced each document for signature, he carefully covered up the names of the Abwehr officials. One by one, each V-man signed his name on the dotted line.

From now on, the saboteurs were not permitted to communicate with their families. In order to reassure family members, Kappe made a list of their birthdays. He planned to send each relative birthday greetings from the saboteur announcing that he was alive and well and serving the Fatherland in an undisclosed location.[32] If the relatives wanted to reach the saboteur, they could write to Kappe c/o *Der Kaukasus.*

Next, Kappe made sure his agents were properly clothed for their jour- ney to America. He had been able to scrounge some civilian clothing from a tightly guarded, two-story warehouse on the outskirts of Berlin that con- tained an array of used clothes, all neatly sorted. Suits and overcoats were on the first floor; hats, underwear, and luggage on the second; shoes down in the cellar. Many of the clothes had foreign labels, from places like Sweden, Czechoslovakia, France, and even America. When Dasch visited the building to help Schmidt pick out a faded blue double-breasted suit and bright yellow shoes, he guessed that the clothes had previously belonged to Jews sent to concentration camps.[33]

Some of the men, including Dasch, still had American outfits they had brought back with them to Germany. Kappe told them to make a list of all their belongings so they could wear each other's clothes.[34] Dasch ended up giving away a pair of black shoes, some shirts, and underwear to the other men.

Kappe did not want his agents to wear their civilian clothes when they landed in America. If they were captured, they might be executed as spies. So he took them to a navy warehouse to fit them out in military fatigues, consisting of khaki pants and jacket, wool socks, black boots, and a cap decorated with the swastika. Although none of the uniforms carried any sign of rank or other insignia, Kappe assumed they would be sufficient to identify the men as German soldiers, to be treated as prisoners of war if captured.

Abwehr experts made sure that the V-men had sufficient documenta- tion to support their cover stories in America. They provided them with false ID papers, Social Security cards, and draft registration cards. In Burger's case, they cleaned up his U.S. naturalization certificate, which showed he had been issued a passport in 1933 to return to Germany. Kappe took the certificate away, returning it a few days later with the incriminating rubber stamp removed.[35]

In the meantime, eight wooden crates containing explosives, detonators, and fuses were delivered to the *Kaukasus* office.[36] The boxes—eleven inches wide, eight and a half inches tall, and twenty-one inches long—were all expertly packed. An inner container of galvanized steel made the contents completely waterproof. Six of the boxes, identified with a large X, held yellow blocks of TNT and pieces of exploding coal of the kind the saboteurs had used for training sessions at Quenz Lake. The two other boxes contained various types of detonator, fourteen-day timers, and several dozen "American fountain pen" sets in small leather cases. Each pen concealed an ingenious delay mechanism for setting off explosives: a capsule of sulfuric acid that, once released, would slowly eat its way through a piece of celluloid and ignite a charge of potassium chlorate.

The two group leaders, Dasch and Kerling, needed to settle on a rendezvous point and a system for getting in touch with each other if all else failed. For the meeting place, Kappe suggested Cincinnati. Both group leaders knew the city well, and it was conveniently located between Dasch's area of operations in the Midwest and Kerling's in New York State and Pennsylvania. Kappe wanted to give both groups enough time to get across the Atlantic and find their way around America. For the date of their reunion, he proposed July 4, which was both easy to remember and had a patriotic ring to it, appealing to Kappe's none-too-subtle sense of humor.

Dasch and Kerling agreed to meet at the grill of the Hotel Gibson in Cincinnati at lunchtime or, as a backup, dinner.[37] If the first rendezvous failed, they would return to the hotel on subsequent Sundays until they either met up or decided their partner was in trouble. The instructions were to sit in different parts of the restaurant, giving no sign that they recognized each other. Once they were sure nobody was watching them, one of them would leave, and the other would follow.

During their last two days in Berlin, Dasch and Kerling returned to the Abwehr laboratory for a final round of instructions in secret writing. A female technician presented the two men with a packet of three matches impregnated with invisible ink, and watched them practice writing. "You pressed too hard," she scolded Dasch. "Do it again."[38]

After showing the two men how to apply just a light amount of pressure with the matchstick, she took them next door to a dark room, and placed the paper under a machine that produced ultraviolet light. Within about ten seconds, the secret writing appeared.

The two group leaders also used secret ink to exchange addresses of friends and trusted family members to contact in an emergency. Dipping a toothpick in a solution made out of pyrimidine—the basic ingredient for laxatives—Dasch copied names and addresses provided by Kerling and Kappe onto a white handkerchief:[39]

> Maria Da Conceicao Lopez, Lisboa, Rua Ecorias 52.
> Father Krepper, c/o Gene Frey, R.F.D. 2, Box 40, Rahway.
> *Bingo:* Walter Froehling, 3643 Whipple, Chi.
> Helmut Leiner, 2158 39th Street, Astoria.
> FRANZ DANIEL PASTORIUS.

Lopez was the cutout in Portugal, to be used for communications with Kappe. Father Krepper was a pro-Nazi Lutheran priest in New Jersey, who could help out with false birth certificates and identification papers. Bingo was Haupt's Abwehr code name; Froehling, the name of his uncle in Chicago, who might be able to help Dasch's group find a farm to use as a hideout for their sabotage materials. Leiner was Kerling's best friend in New York, a thoroughly reliable Nazi. Pastorius was the name of the mission, and also the code word by which the saboteurs would announce themselves to other V-men. In order to make a connection, both parts of the name had to click.

They had practiced the drill many times, both at Quenz Lake and in Berlin:

"Greetings from Franz Daniel."

"Pastorius."[40]

BERLIN IN the spring of 1942 was a depressing city, relieved only by a grim determination to enjoy life's few remaining pleasures. Hopes of a quick victory over the Red Army had faded and rumors were beginning to circulate of huge numbers of casualties on the eastern front. The Wehrmacht no longer seemed invincible, despite Hitler's pledge on the nation's Memorial Day to destroy "the Bolshevist hordes" by the end of the summer.[41] The city itself was now almost completely "Aryanized," most of the Jews having been deported to the East. The few that remained had to wear a yellow star on the outside of their clothes to distinguish them from Aryans. Their ration cards were stamped with purple Js, a sign for shopkeepers to serve them last.

On the surface, life seemed normal enough. Despite some bombing by the Royal Air Force the previous year, the city was reasonably intact, with little obvious damage. Some monuments, including the Victory Column in the Tiergarten, were disguised by camouflage netting. Newspaper kiosks trumpeted the latest successes of German U-boats in the Atlantic and "enormous losses" inflicted on the Soviets in Russia. There were fewer people in the streets, and not nearly as much traffic as before the war, but the zoo was crowded with families and off-duty soldiers. As in prewar years, Berliners indulged their love for asparagus, a springtime delicacy, with daily newspaper reports on the market price.

It was, however, a distinctly threadbare normality. The shop windows along the Kurfürstendamm were still full of shoes, dresses, and suits, suggesting at least a hint of prewar plenty, but when a customer tried to buy what was advertised in the window, the items were usually unavailable.[42] When goods did appear, long lines formed immediately.

The one exception to this economy of scarcity was the entertainment business. In the absence of any other outlet for spending their reichsmarks, off-duty soldiers and Nazi officials alike flocked to the city's concert halls, nightclubs, beer halls, movie houses, and prostitution dens, most of which had remained open. In mid-May, Berlin newspapers listed twenty-six functioning theaters, four cabarets, and sixty-eight movie houses, most of them showing escapist romances like *Dance with the Kaiser,* starring Marika Rokk, the sweetheart of the Third Reich.

There seemed little point in saving money. Even if one stayed alive, the marks would probably soon be worthless. During their last week in Berlin, the saboteurs became avid connoisseurs of the city's nightlife, quickly using up the spending money distributed by Kappe. To Dasch, who had worked half his life in American restaurants, the food he ate in Berlin "filled you up for a moment but in an hour or so you were hungry like a dog."[43] The beer had "lost all its strength" and tasted as if there were "hardly any malts or hops in it." But the restaurants and clip joints were still "jammed to the gills."

The nightclubs offered a window into the political structure of the Third Reich. Rivalry between the army and the S.S. was so intense that soldiers and S.S. men usually patronized different clubs. When they mixed, there was often trouble. One evening, Burger wandered into a club frequented by Luftwaffe officers, several of whom wore the Knights Cross around their collars, indicating that they had shot down at least forty enemy planes. One of the officers asked the bandleader to play an American tango.[44] As the band struck up the music, a man in civilian clothes jumped up from his seat near the back of the club, walked over to the conductor, and flashed a Gestapo badge. American songs were *verboten*. The conductor pointed in the direction of the war hero, who got up to talk to the Gestapo man. Within a few seconds, the Gestapo man was escorted to the door by the Luftwaffe officers, who announced they had evicted "a Gestapo rat." The officers received a standing ovation, and the band played on.

On their next-to-last night in Berlin, the V-men were invited to a farewell dinner at the city's celebrated Zoo restaurant. Kappe told them that "the big chief" himself would be present, leading to some speculation that the Führer might put in an appearance. The banquet took place in a private dining room. The "big chief" turned out to be a tall man in a well-cut civilian suit who was greeted with a flurry of Heil Hitler salutes when he walked into the room. He was introduced only as "Dr. Schmidt," but some of the Abwehr officers addressed him as *"Herr Oberst,"* Herr Colonel.[45] The V-men eventually figured out that "Dr. Schmidt" was in reality Colonel Erwin von Lahousen.

Hitler failed to show up, but everyone had a good time nevertheless. Most of the guests—including "Dr. Schmidt" and Lieutenant Kappe—got quite drunk from repeated toasts to the success of Operation Pastorius. The speeches went on until well after midnight. If they were successful, the colonel told the men in his soft Viennese accent, they could do more damage to the enemy than several divisions of fighting men. They might even decide the outcome of the war.

As leader of the V-men, Dasch thanked the Abwehr officers for their confidence and promised that he and his men would prove themselves worthy of the Fatherland. In between speeches, he asked Lahousen to settle an argument he had been having with Kappe, who had encouraged the saboteurs to try to recruit former German-American Bund members in the United States to assist in their mission. "Promise them heaven on earth if you like," Kappe had urged.[46] "Work on their nationalistic sentiments, their homesickness."

To Dasch's relief, Lahousen was much less adventurous. He told Dasch not to trust anyone, and to bear in mind that Bund members were closely watched by the American authorities and could have changed their political views since the outbreak of war. Dasch should exercise great caution.

When it was Kappe's turn to address the saboteurs, he revealed the meaning of the code name "Operation Pastorius."[47] Franz Daniel Pastorius, he explained, had been the leader of the very first group of Germans to arrive in the New World, back in 1683. The immigrants, thirteen families of Mennonites and Quakers, had settled in a place that soon became known as Germantown, now a suburb of Philadelphia.

If all went well, the nine Nazi saboteurs would be spearheading a new—and much more deadly—wave of German migration to America.

CHAPTER THREE

"THE MEN ARE RUNNING WILD"

(MAY 22–28)

A S WALTER KAPPE looked around the breakfast table at the men he had selected for Operation Pastorius, he was in a relaxed, jovial mood. It was May 22, a Friday, and soon they would be leaving Berlin for Paris on the first stage of their journey to America. He had invited the men to the Rankestrasse safe house for breakfast before setting off for the train station. He would accompany them as far as Lorient, a German submarine base on the southern coast of Brittany. If all went well, he planned to join the V-men in the United States in a few months and create an extensive sabotage network to wreak havoc on American industrial production.

Kappe was pleased by the way the men had responded to five weeks of intensive training. All seemed ready for the adventure. Only Neubauer, the soldier shipped back from the Russian front with pieces of shrapnel in his head, appeared nervous and apprehensive.

He tried to make a joke out of Neubauer's sour face. "Everyone else seems to have the right spirit. It's only Hermann here who doesn't seem to be enjoying himself."[1]

Kappe was thirty-seven years old. His girth was widening, his hairline receding, his face fuller and more florid than ever, but he finally felt he had found his true calling. It had not been easy. His life had been full of ups and downs. He had been born to a moderately well-off family from Hanover that lost all its possessions in the Great War. Like many alienated and restless young Germans, he joined one of the paramilitary organizations banned by the Versailles treaty that later became the basis for Hitler's storm troopers. He and his friends spent much of their time traveling around the country, fighting with Communists and breaking up strikes. He belonged to a movement known as the Wandervoegel, the Wandering Birds, a name intended to invoke the medieval tradition of groups of young craftsmen wandering around Germany in search of work. In modern times, the Wandervoegel had become a breeding ground for political fanatics, who had little in common with their predecessors.

After the failure of the Munich beer hall putsch, thousands of Wandervoegel immigrated to the United States. Kappe arrived in New York in March 1925, and was granted permanent resident status. He found work in a farm implement factory in Bradley, Illinois, where, according to his FBI file, he was "considered a jovial sort of fellow who liked to entertain folks with stories, songs, and piano playing."[2] He considered factory work beneath him: he boasted that he knew six languages and was meant to be "a journalist, not a mechanic."

By the following year, Kappe had realized his dream, and was working for *Abendpost,* a German-language newspaper in Chicago. Colleagues described him as very capable and energetic, but totally without scruples. He joined the Teutonia Club, a forerunner to the German-American Bund, whose members paraded through the streets of Chicago with swastikas and German flags. Instead of translating news agency reports into German, as his superiors wished, he rewrote them with a strong pro-Nazi slant. The editors of *Abendpost,* which was dubbed "a Jew-sheet" in American Nazi circles, disapproved of Kappe's political activities and open admiration for Hitler, and found an excuse to fire him.

Kappe then got a job on a Nazi broadsheet in Cincinnati, where he devoted much of his time to Bund politics. He also attracted the attention of U.S. military counterintelligence, which opened a file on him. One government informant reported that Kappe was a "heavy drinker" who talked loudly about his exploits. "He is oversexed," the informant went on, "consistently seeking the comradeship of prostitutes or women hanging around taverns. With such women, [he] invariably plays the part of a dashing Prussian officer, obviously trying to impress everyone within reach. He has a definite Prussian military bearing, clicking heels when meeting strangers and coming to attention during the introduction."[3] But beneath the "bluff and braggadocio," the report concluded, Kappe was in reality a coward. Another informant reported that no matter how busy

Kappe was with Bund affairs, "he always found time for one or two girls on the side, in addition to his wife."[4]

Soon Kappe had become a full-time propaganda worker for the Bund, and was appointed the organization's "press and propaganda chief" in early 1933, the year after Hitler attained supreme power in Germany. He corresponded with Joseph Goebbels, persuading the Nazi propaganda minister to donate $50,000 for the establishment of a weekly Nazi newspaper in the United States, to be known as *Deutsche Zeitung*, or German News. He also spoke at mass meetings in Chicago, Cincinnati, New York, and other cities with a large population of ethnic Germans, drawing crowds of up to ten thousand. Interrupted with repeated chants of "Heil Hitler" and the singing of the Horst Wessel Song, the meetings frequently degenerated into open fighting between Nazis and anti-Nazis; on several occasions, Kappe was beaten up by enraged Communists.

In an article for an American Nazi newspaper in August 1933, Kappe poured vitriol on those German-Americans who refused to accept the swastika. He described them as "neither German nor American."[5]

You are nothing. You are too narrow to conceive what it means to be German; too cowardly to take advantage of your rights as Americans. You have become slaves and vassals of those who spread hatred against the country of your birth. Here in America, the German people will change some day. They must change, if they want to keep in spiritual contact with the Fatherland, for the roots of our strength lie in the homeland. And when change comes, your game will be up, Gentlemen!

As a member of the Nazi inner circle in America, Kappe soon got caught up in the squabbles over who would become the American Führer. An article in the *Washington Post* in September 1934 referred to Kappe as one of the "Big Three" led by Bund leader Fritz Gissibl.[6] Unfortunately for Kappe, Gissibl lost a power struggle with Fritz Kuhn, who wanted to "Americanize" the Bund, replacing German nationals with American citizens. Unlike Kuhn, Kappe had never taken out U.S. citizenship. According to one newspaper account, Kappe was frog-marched out of the New York City offices of the Bund newspaper by Kuhn's storm troopers in February 1937.[7] Kuhn accused Kappe of spying for the German consulate in New York, and fomenting a revolt against him, in addition to financial irregularities. Four months later, the disgraced Bund leader boarded the SS *St.*

Louis, together with his wife Hilde and their two young children, and set sail for Hamburg.

With Germany gearing up for war and America still sitting on the fence, Kappe felt he had returned to the center of the action. He joined the Ausland Institut under Gauleiter Ernst Bohle, churning out anti-American propaganda. After war broke out, he transferred to military intelligence. Abwehr networks in the United States had been virtually wiped out in early 1941 when a renegade German agent named William Sebold went to the FBI and told them all he knew, leading to the roundup of dozens of German spies. In conversations with colleagues, Kappe railed against "that son of a bitch" Sebold, adding darkly, "There is no stone big enough for him to hide under."[8]

One of Kappe's goals in launching Operation Pastorius was to repair the damage caused by the traitor.

TWO COMPARTMENTS had been reserved for the saboteurs on the noon express from Berlin to Paris with a sign RESERVED FOR OKW, the German High Command. They were an incongruous sight: nine young men in an assortment of ill-fitting American clothes, led by a rotund, heavyset Wehrmacht lieutenant, accompanied by a pile of wooden boxes and seabags. Had a fellow passenger been able to look into their luggage, he would have discovered an array of sophisticated sabotage equipment, naval uniforms and shovels, and a small fortune in American dollars.

When the train pulled into the Gare de l'Est at eight o'clock the next morning, a representative of the Paris branch of German military intelligence was on the platform to meet them. He took the V-men to the Hotel des Deux Mondes, a fin de siècle establishment near the opera house,[9] one of several hotels in Paris that had been commandeered by the German occupation authorities. After the men were assigned their rooms, Kappe handed them wads of francs and told them "to go out and have a good time."[10]

Compared to drab, oppressive Berlin, Paris was magical. Even under wartime occupation, the half-deserted city had a melancholy charm. The chestnut trees were in bloom along the Champs-Elysées and the banks of the Seine. There was still plenty of food around. The famous landmarks—the Eiffel Tower, the Louvre, Montmartre—were as beautiful as ever. Even the girls seemed prettier and better dressed than in Germany.

Armed with Kappe's money, they raced around the city, seeing the sights and visiting nightclubs. Several of them got into trouble. Heinrich Heinck, the dour-looking Volkswagen worker assigned to Dasch's group, got drunk at the Deux Mondes bar, and announced that he was "a secret agent."[11] There was a disturbance at the hotel late one night when Herbie Haupt, who never had any difficulty picking up girls, refused to pay a prostitute who had accompanied him back to his room. Either he had run out of money or he imagined she had fallen for his charms, like the girls back home in Chicago, and had no right asking for payment. After she began screaming at him in French, a language he did not understand, one of the other V-men settled his debt.

Some of the saboteurs found time to have serious conversations about their mission. Kerling and Burger were strolling past the navy ministry on the Place de la Concorde, watching the German guards march up and down, when Kerling suddenly blurted out, "What do you think of your group?"[12]

"Not very much," Burger replied cautiously. "Heinck is not what you would call a hundred percent saboteur, and Dasch is not the ideal leader for this kind of mission."

Kerling, the most committed Nazi of them all, nodded his head, and said vaguely, "Well, perhaps there will be a way to get out of this."

Burger did not ask what he had in mind.

Normally tolerant of loose behavior, Kappe tired of his subordinates' antics after a weekend in Paris. When a naval intelligence officer came to his hotel and told him the U-boats were ready, Kappe breathed a sigh of relief. "Thank God! The men are running wild with booze and girls."[13]

KAPITÄNLEUTNANT Wilhelm Ahlrichs, of the Security and Intelligence Office of the German High Command, had top-secret orders from Berlin to put the saboteurs on board the U-boats that would take them across the Atlantic. He joined the V-men in Paris, and escorted them on the overnight train to Lorient. Prior to transferring to intelligence work after the outbreak of war, Ahlrichs had been a captain in the German merchant navy, and knew both America and England well. A pessimist by nature, he was unimpressed by the overall quality of the saboteurs.

There were some exceptions. Kerling was obviously an idealistic Nazi. Haupt—who was dressed in an open-neck silk shirt and flashy, light-green checkered coat—looked like a decent kid, a real American boy, Ahlrichs thought. Burger seemed depressed. The other men struck Ahlrichs as incompetent. The worst impression of all was made by their leader. When Ahlrichs asked Dasch what his men would be doing in America, he boasted, "Just look inside our boxes. We're going to blow up factories."[14]

After their three-day break in Paris, the V-men were getting more tense. On the train to Lorient, the normally reticent Schmidt taunted Dasch and Burger, saying Dasch did not deserve to be in charge and Burger could not be trusted because he had been in a concentration camp. As he talked, Schmidt became flushed and angry, thrusting out his jaw. It seemed to Burger that he was attempting to foment an insurrection against Dasch and replace him as leader.[15]

In Lorient, the men were taken to the Jour de Rêve hotel, which was reserved for U-boat crews. The leaders—Kappe, Ahlrichs, Dasch, and Kerling—met to go over final details of where the two groups would land in the United States. The plan was for Kerling's group to leave for America that very evening; the others would follow two days later.

In the afternoon, Kappe assembled Kerling's men to distribute the money they would take with them to America. As previously arranged, each received a wad of $50 bills in a specially designed money pouch to go around his waist, as well as $450 in smaller denominations. As Haupt was going through his pile of $50 bills, he noticed that some were not green-backs at all, but so-called yellowbacks, gold certificates withdrawn from circulation in 1934, after the United States went off the gold standard.

The men were furious with their Abwehr superiors, but particularly with Kappe. Such carelessness could cost them their lives. They imagined trying to use the yellowbacks in America to make purchases and immediately being turned over to the FBI as German spies. They clawed through the money belts, removing the incriminating bills. Kerling took Kappe into the next room and told him bluntly he did not feel like going ahead with the operation: it was too dangerous.

It was too late to back out now, Kappe insisted. "You have enough money anyway, even without the gold certificates. Just throw those bills out."[16] Kappe argued that it was a trivial matter, nothing to worry about. Ahlrichs wanted to phone Berlin for instructions. The men eventually calmed down, but their confidence in Kappe had been severely shaken.

Dasch, meanwhile, had gone missing. He had disappeared, without saying a word, on the way to a lunch hosted by Ahlrichs after suddenly remembering that he had left his identification papers on the train. His American Social Security card was in a notebook that also contained jottings from lessons at Quenz Lake, along with some snapshots of his mother and wife. He had taken the notebook out of his pocket during the night as he lay in his bunk on the train trying to get to sleep. In the rush to unload the boxes at Lorient, he had forgotten all about it.

As soon as Dasch could get away from his colleagues, he rushed back to the railroad station and asked to see the German official in charge. In his excitable fashion, he explained he had left some "hot papers" on the train, which must on no account fall into the hands of the enemy.[17] The official told him to come back later that afternoon: the train was now at a depot further down the line. When Dasch returned, he found another official on duty who demanded his papers. Unimpressed with Dasch's attempt at a Heil Hitler salute and his explanation that he was traveling incognito, the official reported him to the Gestapo.

Dasch realized that the only way out of the mess was to call Kappe at the hotel. Kappe arrived at the station at about the same time as a major from the Gestapo. After insisting that everybody else leave the room, Kappe gave the officer a rough outline of Operation Pastorius and let him inspect the orders issued by the High Command. The Gestapo major berated everybody for being so careless, but permitted Dasch to leave with Kappe. Dasch's documents were never found.

Up until this point, Dasch felt he had the trust of Kappe, who had always defended him against the complaints of others. In some ways, the two men were rather alike: loud-mouthed, ingratiating, quick-witted, always coming up with grandiose ideas, but also careless, even clueless about certain things. But now Kappe's confidence seemed to be waning rapidly.

As they drove back to the hotel, Kappe said it would be very dangerous for Dasch to travel around America as George John Davis, the name on his mislaid Social Security card. Not to worry, Dasch replied cheerfully, he would use the name of George John Day.

Kappe was exasperated, but too exhausted to argue.

THE *U-584*—with Kerling, Haupt, Neubauer, and Thiel aboard—left Lorient harbor late that evening in the pouring rain. Ahlrichs made sure that the crew was confined to barracks while the V-men boarded the boat with their equipment. Once Kerling's men were safely below deck, the crew returned to the U-boat. From that point onward, nobody was allowed to leave the submarine until it sailed.

That left Dasch, Burger, Quirin, Heinck, and Schmidt. The next day, Schmidt complained to Ahlrichs that he had caught some kind of sexual disease, probably from a prostitute in Paris. The intelligence officer had Schmidt lie down on a bed and pull out his penis, which was covered with a nasty brown foam. Ahlrichs took one look at the foam, decided that Schmidt was suffering from gonorrhea, and ordered him to report to Berlin immediately for treatment.

When Ahlrichs told Kappe of his diagnosis, the Abwehr officer was beside himself. Schmidt was the toughest member of the group and, with the possible exception of Burger, the most resourceful. A burly outdoorsman with years of experience farming and trapping in Canada, he was the obvious choice to run the farm that they planned to use as the hiding place for their explosives. Without him, the whole mission might be at risk.

Ahlrichs refused to back down. As the representative of the German navy, he would not permit a man with a venereal disease to board the U-boat. If Schmidt was so essential to the mission, it would be necessary to cancel the departure of the second party altogether. "I take full responsibility for my decision," Ahlrichs said firmly.[18]

Kappe relented. They would leave Schmidt behind.

THE DAY scheduled for the departure of Dasch's group was Thursday, May 28. That morning, Dasch had another heated argument with Kappe over how the group should operate in America. Kappe wanted the men to begin sabotage work almost immediately, even if in a small way. Dasch insisted they lie low for three or four months to develop good cover stories. He referred to his conversation with Colonel Lahousen at the farewell banquet in the Zoo restaurant: the "big chief" had counseled caution.

They then quarreled over whether the saboteurs should contact former comrades from the German-American Bund. Heinck, who had been an active member of the Bund when he lived in the United States, wanted to look up a friend in Long Island whom he thought he could recruit. Dasch said that any such meeting would "take place over my dead body."[19] He accused Kappe of failing to follow instructions, reminding him that

Lahousen had been opposed to contacting former Bundists on the grounds it was impossible to be sure whether they were still loyal to the Fatherland.

The conversation quickly degenerated into an argument over political loyalties. With the departure of Schmidt, Dasch was the only member of the group who had never been active in Nazi politics. Kappe complained that Dasch had "no confidence in our people in America who have been in the Bund."

"You dirty bastard, we Bund members had to fight people like you in America," Heinck chimed in.

Now it was Dasch's turn to get angry. Privately, he felt only contempt for the swarthy Heinck, whom he considered a "typical German spy, dumb and big mouthed when he is safe, yellow as a coward when in danger."[20] But he kept these thoughts to himself, and instead yelled, "I'll kill you if you call me a bad German again."[21]

They then began arguing over who would team up with whom in America. Kappe wanted Dasch to pair with Quirin, and Burger with Heinck. Burger would be leader of the second team, ready to replace Dasch if anything happened to him. Dasch said he did not fully trust Burger because of his old troubles with the Gestapo. He preferred to keep an eye on Burger, and let Quirin be responsible for Heinck. Quirin and Heinck knew each other well, having worked together at Volkswagen. Kappe eventually let Dasch have his way.[22]

There was one final dispute that afternoon, as they were preparing to board the submarine. Dasch, who had not been too worried about the gold certificates, now discovered that some of his dollar bills had small Japanese characters scrawled on them. This suggested that they had been acquired through Japan, which was allied with Nazi Germany. "This money I don't want," Dasch told Kappe, throwing the bills out. "You should be ashamed, supplying us with money like that."[23]

By the time Kappe escorted the men to the submarine that evening in a navy car, he was glad to be rid of them. The U-boat could not be seen from the shore as it was anchored behind a freighter. Dressed in navy fatigues and hauling their bags, the V-men boarded the freighter by a gangplank, crossed over to the other side, and then climbed down a ladder onto the deck of the submarine. The captain invited them all for a drink in his cramped quarters, but Kappe only stayed long enough to wish everybody "good luck."[24]

ALTHOUGH DASCH and his men had never been on a U-boat before, they felt at home. German newspapers carried frequent reports about life on board submarines, hailing the achievements of the U-boat fleet, particularly in the North Atlantic.[25] "Our submarines are endangering U.S. oil supplies," boasted the *Berliner Lokal-Anzeiger* as the saboteurs were preparing to leave Berlin. "Liquid gold is flowing into the ocean." A cartoon depicted Churchill telling Roosevelt, "You can find our ships all over the ocean," as the two leaders used telescopes to spot a graveyard of Allied ships at the bottom of the sea.

At a time when German armies were beginning to falter on other fronts, Dönitz's U-boats provided a steady stream of propaganda triumphs. The Nazi press painted a picture of gallant U-boat captains stalking their prey, and American seamen quaking in fear at the thought of running into a German submarine. "Deadly eye on the Atlantic," said the *Berliner Illustrierte Zeitung* above a picture of a periscope peeking through the waves.[26] "Meeting it means certain destruction. Millions of tons of enemy ships have fallen victim to this magic eye that can observe the sea and the sky at the same time."

The same newspapers gave the saboteurs a skewed picture of life in America. To the extent that the Nazi press covered daily life in America at all, it was to mock American popular culture, and the country's lack of preparedness for war. There were many jokes about the profits made by Wrigley's chewing gum now that it was being issued to U.S. soldiers along with their rations. Another favorite technique was to run pictures of big-breasted American girls in uniform, under headlines like "Roosevelt's Freedom Fighters." It was the Nazi equivalent of soft pornography, making fun of the enemy and selling newspapers at the same time.

"Into battle with girls in shorts" ran the headline in the *Berliner Illustrierte Zeitung,* beneath a picture of drum majorettes. "Hundreds of actresses trained in seducing screen heroes have become soldiers and are now supposed to seduce American men into going to war."

SOON AFTER *U-202* departed from Lorient harbor, Kapitänleutnant Ahlrichs was surprised to run into Schmidt in the dining car of the Paris–Berlin train. Both men were on their way back to Germany, Ahlrichs to report to naval intelligence, Schmidt to get medical treatment. Far from being despondent about being left behind, the ninth saboteur seemed exceptionally cheerful. He told Ahlrichs that the V-men, particularly those belonging to Dasch's group, had quarreled with one another constantly. Dasch was very mistrustful of Burger, threatening to kill him or betray him to the FBI.

When Ahlrichs asked Schmidt whether he had been to see a doctor, the Canadian trapper smiled sheepishly. He didn't have gonorrhea. He had injected his penis with a soda solution in order to get out of going to America.[27]

CHAPTER FOUR

ACROSS THE ATLANTIC

(MAY 28–JUNE 13)

WHEN HE WELCOMED the four saboteurs on board his submarine on the evening of May 28, Kapitänleutnant Hans-Heinz Linder had been in charge of *U-202* for just over a year. It was his first command, and he was proud of what he and his men had accomplished during their previous five patrols: several trips across the Atlantic, half a dozen enemy ships sunk, and many hair-raising escapes.

A stout man with blue eyes and a ruddy complexion, Linder made no claim to being one of the aces of the German submarine fleet. Unlike the U-boat captains whose feats in sinking dozens of Allied ships and threatening Britain's lifeline to North America were celebrated by the Nazi propaganda machine, Linder had the reputation of being a solid, reliable officer who was calm during a crisis and did not take too many risks. At twenty-nine, he was already a veteran of the U-boat service, older than many of his fellow skippers. His crew members, most of them boys just out of school, looked up to him as an ancient.

On board his ship, a U-boat captain had almost godlike status. He was required to exude confidence at all times, even in the face of disaster. If a U-boat was "a community bound together by fate," in the phrase of the fleet commander, Admiral Karl Dönitz, the captain was at once its savior and its scourge.[1] His exploits could bring glory to the ship and the crew, but a single mistake could send them all to their deaths.

Of the various branches of the German armed forces, the U-boat fleet was perhaps the most glamorous but also the most deadly. Before the end of the war, the Third Reich would lose 785 out of 1,162 submarines, and 28,000 out of 41,000 crewmen. Even during the early part of the war, when the U-boats achieved their greatest successes, the life expectancy of a German submariner could often be measured in weeks or months. In these circumstances, it was an achievement for a captain to bring his men back alive. The survivors felt they belonged to an elite.

Linder and his men had had a very narrow escape on their fourth patrol back in December, when they were ordered to break through to the Mediterranean via the Strait of Gibraltar, which was controlled by the British.[2] A Royal Air Force plane had dropped four bombs on the U-boat, destroying its diesel engines. For thirty-six hours, the ship lay on the seabed at a depth of six hundred feet, waiting for the enemy to disappear, then limped back to the French port of Brest on its electric motors. When asked about the incident, Linder would shrug his shoulders and say simply, "I was lucky to get home."[3]

After major repairs, *U-202* set out again in March to join the submarine "wolf packs" that were causing havoc along America's Atlantic coast in Operation Drumbeat, one of the most successful Nazi naval operations of the war. According to Dönitz's figures, U-boats managed to sink 303 Allied ships, a total of two million tons, in a period of just four months. This rate of destruction would soon outpace America's ability to build new ships. Linder's luck held once again. This time, he and his men survived a depth charge attack by a U.S. destroyer.

Linder only found out about the mission for his sixth patrol a few hours before his submarine was due to sail from Brest, when he received a sealed package labeled "MOST SECRET" direct from Dönitz. The orders specified that he was to take a group of saboteurs across the Atlantic and land them on the southern coast of Long Island. The landing should be timed to coincide with a "new moon night" in the middle of June.[4] Since darkness was vital to the success of the "special operation," it would take priority over the sinking of enemy ships. Nevertheless, Linder was authorized to seize "opportunities of attack" if they presented themselves.

The U-boat High Command war diary listed the following objectives of Operation Pastorius:

1. To carry out sabotage attacks against vital economic targets.
2. To stir up discontent and lower fighting resistance.
3. To recruit fresh forces for these duties.
4. To reestablish disconnected communications.
5. To obtain information.

THE CREW of *U-202* were in a good mood as they took their ship out of the harbor at Brest, the headquarters of the German submarine fleet, on the evening of May 27. There were cheers of "Hurrah" and "Good luck" from their comrades and friends gathered on the pier.[5] All the crew members knew was that they were setting off on another mission across the Atlantic. Before heading out, they had been instructed to put in at Lorient to receive supplies. There were rumors that a war correspondent would join them: the navy sometimes allowed reporters to accompany the U-boats and write up their exploits for a public eager for nautical victories.

The next day, they took on board not just one civilian but four, along with four wooden crates and a large seabag. The civilians were all dressed in navy fatigues. Except for Linder, none of the crew knew who they were, or what they were meant to be doing. They did not look like war correspondents: for one thing, they seemed far too reticent for reporters. New rumors began to circulate: could they be secret agents?

Linder showed the men their bunks in the petty officers' quarters, on either side of his own minuscule cabin. In order to make room for the saboteurs, he had had to leave several less essential crew members behind, including the ship's doctor. Every square inch of available space in the U-boat seemed to be occupied by bodies, torpedoes, crates of food, or some kind of dial or gauge.[6] For the next two months, forty-five men would be living, working, eating, sleeping, and fighting for their survival in a cigar-shaped space just 211 feet long on the outside and 142 feet on the inside, about the length of two subway cars. Linder, who was six feet tall, could barely stand erect in his own control room. Most parts of the ship were no wider than ten feet; much of that space was crammed with equipment, leaving just enough room for one person to squeeze by at a time.

As his ship sailed out of Lorient harbor on Thursday evening, Linder made a note of the time in his neatly kept ship's log: 1957. He invited his guests up to the bridge to see *U-202* leave the concrete submarine pens constructed by the Germans as protection against Allied air raids. The sub was accompanied by a small flotilla of ships: patrol boats on either side and a minesweeper in front, trailing a long wire with various electronic antimine devices. Leading this procession was a large tramp steamer weighed down with concrete. Linder explained that this ship was a "punch absorber," to shield U-boats from floating mines dropped by British warplanes.[7] If a mine went off, it would do little more than damage one of the steamer's many airtight compartments.

As *U-202* left the harbor, the crew tested out the antiaircraft gun mounted to the rear of the bridge, firing some tracer bullets into the night sky. An officer was able to steer the boat from a panel on the conning tower underneath the bridge, which duplicated the instruments in the control room below.

The escort ships pulled away once the U-boat had cleared the most dangerous waters in the immediate vicinity of the port. For the rest of the night, the ship remained on the surface, tossed around on the ocean like a cork on a rushing stream. Four seamen stood watch on the bridge, scanning the horizon with binoculars for any sign of an enemy plane or warship. Each man faced in a different direction, and was responsible for a ninety-degree segment of sea and sky. A few seconds' delay in spotting a plane and ordering an emergency dive could mean the difference between life and death. In order to make any headway at all, they had to travel on the surface as much as possible. On the surface, the boat could use its diesel engines and travel between ten and twelve knots, about the speed of a bicycle. Submerged, it was restricted to its electric motors, and could go no faster than two and a half knots, the pace of a leisurely walk.

As they lay in their bunks that first night, Dasch and the other saboteurs tried to adapt to the strange sensations of life aboard a U-boat. Sleep was practically impossible. They already felt seasick from the violent rocking of the boat back and forth on the waves. And then there was the constant din from the two 1,160-horsepower diesel engines, known affectionately to the crew as Max and Moritz, in the stern of the ship. The diesels made a gurgling sound as they sucked in air from a pipe mounted in the bridge.

At dawn, the U-boat dived to avoid being spotted by the Allied planes constantly patrolling the Bay of Biscay in a circular loop from their bases in Cornwall, on the southwest tip of England. When the ship was below the surface, everything seemed much more peaceful to the saboteurs huddled in their bunks. The roar of the diesels was replaced by the hum of the battery-powered motors. The violent rocking and shaking subsided, and it was as if the submarine were floating gently through space.

For the first two days, the crewmen were told nothing about their new passengers. On the third day out of Brest, Linder finally made an announcement over the loudspeakers, his voice echoing from the forward torpedo room to the engine room in the stern. He informed the crew that their four guests were undertaking a "special assignment" to America.[8] The crew members were to treat the visitors well, refrain from asking questions, and observe strict secrecy on pain of death.

As *U-202* was leaving Lorient harbor, a battle of wits was under way on the grounds of a rambling English manor house that would eventually determine the outcome of the Battle of the Atlantic. Hundreds of cryptanalysts were attempting to unscramble the latest batch of top-secret telegrams from the German High Command to military and naval units all over Europe and North Africa. Bulky machines known as "bombes" spun their rotors to discover the precise match of letters and numbers that would break the German code.

Crude precursors of the computer, the bombes were meant to simulate the operation of the Enigma machine, the supposedly unbreakable cipher system used by the German army and navy for their daily communications. Breaking the German code was somewhat like solving a vast jigsaw puzzle while blindfolded: a combination of inspired guesswork and trying every single logical possibility. What made the process even more mind-numbing was that the Germans kept rescrambling the puzzle.

By late 1941, the code breakers of Bletchley Park had developed a system that allowed them to read secret German messages within a few hours of receiving them. By dint of analytical brilliance, a captured German codebook, and mechanical force, they gained priceless insights into Hitler's plans and intentions, which they passed on to British Prime Minister Winston Churchill and other wartime commanders. The code-breaking operation opened up intelligence on a vast range of subjects, from Hitler's decision to invade the Soviet Union in the summer of 1941 to Luftwaffe raids on Britain to the mass murder of Jews in Nazi-occupied territories. British commanders were also able to use the decrypted messages to plot the movements of German U-boats around the Atlantic, and order Allied convoys to make adjustments in course to steer clear of the submarine menace.

At the beginning of February 1942, disaster struck. Suspicious of Allied successes in evading his U-boats, Admiral Dönitz ordered the installation of a new, and even more complicated, cipher system on board the submarines. By adding a fourth rotor to the three-rotor Enigma machines, he increased by a factor of twenty-six the number of possible letter combinations available to German cipher clerks.[9] What had become a manageable deciphering operation was now beyond the capabilities of even the cryptological geniuses of Bletchley Park, at least until they succeeded in building faster and more powerful code-breaking machines. Almost overnight, the task of tracking down Dönitz's U-boats became far more difficult.

There were still some small windows into the movements of U-boats, however. One was a network of radio direction finders built by the Americans and the British, which detected the emission of radio signals from submarines. By triangulating the data from several direction finders, Allied intelligence officers were able to plot the location of a U-boat with considerable accuracy, particularly along the coast. The system was not much help in predicting where the U-boats would move next, or where they were when they maintained radio silence, but at least it gave the Allies a sense of the maritime battlefield. A second window was provided by messages from support ships, not all of which had made the transition from three-rotor to four-rotor Enigma machines.

By decrypting messages from the commander of the seventh German naval flotilla to U-boat escort ships, Bletchley Park was able to track the departure of *U-584* and *U-202* from Lorient at the end of May.[10] The information was immediately transmitted to the Submarine Tracking Room in the British Admiralty in London, where it was plotted on a giant wall map. Messages were sent to the Royal Air Force to watch out for German U-boats in the Bay of Biscay.

But the mission of the two U-boats remained a closely guarded secret from Allied intelligence, as did the presence on board of eight Nazi saboteurs.

A DAY after *U-584* left Lorient with Kerling's party, a lookout spotted a dot on the horizon, soon after the submarine came to the surface. "Alarm!" he yelled into the intercom connecting the bridge to the control room below. "Enemy plane!"

From down below came the command "Flood!" There was a loud gurgling sound, as water rushed into the buoyancy tanks, expelling the air that kept the boat afloat. Within seconds, the watch officer and three lookouts had scrambled down the ladder that connected the bridge to the control room through the conning tower.

The plane had seen them as well, and was heading in their direction. "All hands forward!" yelled the captain, sending crew members slipping and sliding toward the forward torpedo room. As the bow of the boat tipped forward, dirty pots and plates scattered around the galley, and crates of vegetables slithered into the gangway. The U-boat was already several hundred feet down by the time depth charges began to explode in the water above.[11]

With the exception of the V-men, everybody on board had a specific job. One crew member turned a valve to flood the ballast tanks, and send the boat plummeting downward. A second was responsible for closing the hatches. A third ensured that the ship was properly balanced. And all the time, the captain and chief engineer were relaying information and barking out commands over the loudspeakers.

"Eighty meters."

"Sounding."

"Twenty-two hundred in compartment one."

"One hundred meters."

"Eighteen hundred in two."

The saboteurs sat huddled in their bunks, seasick and frightened, wondering how much longer they had to live. They counted the depth charges exploding around them, battering the boat as if it were a tin can.

Three.

Four.

Another huge explosion.

Six.

Seven.

Eight.

The last explosion was followed by a prolonged silence. Some of the crewmen broke out in grins: the worst was evidently over. They were out of range of the depth charges. The plane had given them a fright but had failed to score a direct hit, and their ship was undamaged.

The saboteurs on *U-202* were spared such drama, but they quickly understood that the sea around them was alive with danger. Linder instituted daily diving drills, practicing every conceivable kind of dive: fast, slow, deep, shallow. At the end of each practice session, the captain would announce, "Alert over, dive for exercise only."[12] Until the dive was over, Dasch and the others never knew whether an alert was for real or for practice.

At the end of a dive, the whole submarine was "as quiet as a church," Dasch noted.[13] Nobody said a word. The slightest sound might give them away.

. . .

By the fourth day out of Lorient, the saboteurs had settled into the routine of life aboard *U-202*. Even as it traveled westward, through several time zones, the ship stuck religiously to Berlin time, as did the entire U-boat fleet.[14] Wake-up time was at 6 a.m., followed by breakfast at 6:30 and ship cleaning at 7. The main meal was at 12 noon, and there was a light supper at 5:15 p.m. The day was divided into six four-hour watches; the watch officers and lookouts were each responsible for two watches over a twenty-four-hour period.

Once the ship was out in the ocean and the risk of being spotted by enemy planes had receded, it traveled mainly on the surface. "Submersible" might be a better term than "submarine" for a Type VII-C German U-boat such as *U-202*, which was only capable of traveling relatively short distances underwater. It needed to come to the surface frequently in order to recharge its electric batteries and make more rapid progress. At the average underwater speed of two knots, it would have taken nearly two months to cross the Atlantic.

Although surface travel was faster, it was also much more uncomfortable. The ship was tossed about on the ocean, and battered by the winds and the waves. The crew was accustomed to these conditions, and reported calm weather throughout the trip. But the four saboteurs felt wretched and spent most of their time in their bunks, trapped in a seemingly endless roller-coaster ride. With the exception of Heinck, who had worked as a seaman as a young man, the saboteurs got violently seasick.[15]

The most seasick of all was Dasch, a poor seaman, whose most fervent wish was "to get this thing over." He kept asking Linder and the other officers if they could make the ship go a "little faster," only to be told that ten knots was the optimum speed for fuel consumption. In theory, the 750-ton ship could make up to eighteen knots, but that was reserved for an emergency.

Type VII-C boats like *U-202* were considered the "workhorses" of the German submarine fleet.[16] Dönitz favored them because they were extremely maneuverable and had quick diving times and a low silhouette, meaning they were difficult for the enemy to spot. They could be refueled at sea from larger submarines, enabling them to make return trips across the Atlantic, and were small enough to be mass-produced. Of the U-boats commissioned during the war, nearly half were VII-Cs, a slightly more sophisticated variant of the original Type VII.

Although Linder gave the V-men freedom to move around his ship, with the exception of the radio room and its top-secret Enigma machine, Burger found it "impossible to walk around very much because of the fact that the boat was fully manned."[17] The gangways were crammed with food supplies, including hard-crusted black bread, cheese, potatoes, various kinds of sausage, noodles, and large cans of coffee. On long voyages, the crewmen would first eat their way through the fresh food and then open the cans. When someone needed to move about the ship, he would have to alert the rest of the crew to maintain a proper trim, particularly underwater. Phrases like "man going aft" or "man going forward" were constantly echoing through the ship.[18]

By the third or fourth day out, the entire boat, plus the ship's company, had started to stink. The smell was a mixture of burning diesel oil, human sweat, cooked food, and the cheap perfume that the men used to disguise the other unpleasant odors. There was barely enough fresh water to drink, let alone to wash. The entire company shared two toilets: one for officers and senior petty officers, and another for other members of the crew. As guests, the saboteurs were permitted to use the officers' toilet.

Soon, Linder and his crewmen were sporting mustaches and full beards. They wore the same clothes every day, in Linder's case a slate-blue leather coat and pants that became ever more grimy and stained as the trip progressed. As captain, Linder wore a white cap, to distinguish himself from the rest of the crew, who wore blue caps.

Despite the difficulties of moving around, Dasch eventually explored the entire ship, beginning in the forward torpedo room, where a total of ten torpedoes were stored: four in the tubes, ready to fire, and another six among the bunks and hammocks and in the bilges. This area was so jampacked with men and gear that some submariners called it "the cave."[19] The missiles aboard *U-202* were a mixture of air-propelled torpedoes and electric torpedoes powered by battery, the latest in German marine technology. The crew used an ingenious pulley system to lift the torpedoes from the bilges and ram them into place. "Just take a look at how wonderfully the torpedoes are stored away," the torpedo officer boasted to Dasch. "Our enemies often wonder how a little submarine can carry this many torpedoes."[20]

The next compartment aft was the chief petty officers' quarters, where Dasch and Burger had two upper bunks. This compartment also contained the captain's quarters, screened by a curtain to give him some privacy, and the radio room, where the Enigma codebooks were kept under lock and key in steel drawers. The control room occupied the center of the ship, underneath the conning tower, and was packed with "a million gadgets" that indicated speed, depth, balance, and revolutions per minute of the engine. There were numerous other dials and valves, most of which were meaningless to the V-men but had a vital role to play in the operation of the ship. When the boat was a few feet below the surface, the captain could also use the periscope in the control room to scan the horizon for the enemy and order torpedo attacks.

The petty officers' quarters, where Quirin and Heinck were bunked, was the next compartment aft. This compartment was alongside the galley, where a young round-faced Swabian boy from southern Germany named Otto Wagner prepared meals for the entire crew on three small electric plates and a tiny oven, in a space that measured 59 inches by 27.5 inches. As cook, Wagner was known as Smutje, a special nickname that reflected his vital contribution to shipboard morale. He served up meals on collapsible wooden tables in the aisle, which had to be dismantled whenever someone was moving through. Despite the lack of culinary resources, the saboteurs agreed that the food on board *U-202* was "exceptionally good," much better than regular army meals.[21]

The last two compartments aft were the domain of the chief engineer, the second-most-important man on the ship after the captain, and housed the diesel and electric engines, as well as most of the electrical equipment. The chief engineer was responsible for the smooth technical functioning of the submarine, leaving the captain free to concentrate on waging war. There was always something that needed fixing; during the first few days of the voyage, the ship was plagued by rudder problems.[22] While the main rudder was out of operation, the chief engineer rigged up a hand rudder. The stern of the ship also contained another torpedo tube, plus a spare torpedo, but these were rarely used.

The saboteurs were occasionally allowed to join the officer of the watch on the bridge for fresh air and a cigarette. During one of these smoking breaks, Dasch noticed a three-foot-long metal plate shaped like a porcupine hanging from the conning tower, alongside the ship's official name, the *Innsbruck*. He was told that the porcupine was the ship's unofficial emblem, tolerated by the navy as a way of promoting a fighting spirit among the crew.

Dasch was so taken by the emblem that he asked the chief engineer to stamp out eight miniature porcupines, similar to those worn by crew members on their caps as good luck charms.[23] The other saboteurs had been showing signs of frustration with his leadership, and he wanted to make things up to them. He distributed two of the little porcupines to each saboteur, saying they would come in handy as a secret communication system in America. If one member of the team wanted to send a message to a comrade, he would give the intermediary a porcupine to identify himself, and the recipient would know that "the man is all right."

FOR THE V-men on board *U-202*, this was easily the most uncomfortable of several trips across the Atlantic. All four had arrived in America for the first time in the twenties as refugees from the street violence, mass unemployment, and hyperinflation afflicting the Weimar Republic. For these new arrivals, America represented a beacon of peace and prosperity, a chance to make a new life far away from European conflicts.

Dasch's story was typical. After dropping out of the Catholic convent of the Sacred Heart in Düsseldorf in 1920 at the age of seventeen, he was desperate to find a means to support himself. He earned some money as a housepainter and working in the mines, but was unable to get a regular job and was constantly broke. In 1922, he went to the north German port of Hamburg hoping to stow himself away on a ship bound for America. The harbor was guarded, but he got into the docks by mingling with a large group of workers.

He looked for a ship with an American flag and attracted the attention of a cook, who was throwing scraps overboard. "I'm hungry and need work," Dasch shouted, gesturing to his stomach and hands.[24] The cook took pity on him and helped him board the ship by acting drunk. Once on board, he washed dishes for the cook in return for his first American-style meal of corned beef and cabbage.

One of the crew members on the Kerr Line's SS *Schohary* was a German-American from Philadelphia who entertained Dasch with tales of life in America, strengthening his determination to get there. During his free time, he looked for a place to hide when the boat sailed. He settled on a storeroom on the second deck, amidships, where he could come and go as he pleased. Just before the ship sailed, he bid farewell to his new friends but, instead of going ashore, went to his hiding place. The only document in his possession was his birth certificate.

He slept during the day and came out of his hiding place at night to scrounge for leftover food from the mess hall. The Atlantic crossing took seventeen days, and the ship reached Philadelphia on Columbus Day, 1922. At Government Pier, he walked down the gangplank with a group of workers and sailors, evading immigration officials, and went into the city looking for work. A German baker offered him a job as a dishwasher, paying him five dollars for a week's work and allowing him to sleep in his cellar. That was enough to bum his way to New York.

A succession of restaurant jobs followed, such as caterer's assistant, fry cook, and soda fountain clerk. By the end of his first year in America, Dasch had saved eight hundred dollars and was anxious to rectify his status as an illegal immigrant. At that time, immigration authorities took a relatively benign view of hungry European seamen jumping ship in American ports. After determining that he had saved up some money and had "the makings of a good American citizen," they instructed him to pay $8.16 in head tax and issued him an alien seaman identification card bearing the stamp "Legally admitted to the United States."[25]

Heinrich Heinck and Richard Quirin left Germany for similar reasons, because they were penniless and needed work. Heinck got a job as a seaman on the Hamburg-American Line and jumped ship on his third trip to New York. Quirin received a quota immigrant visa in Germany with the help of an affidavit from an uncle living in Schenectady, New York, who promised to support him once he got to America.

Peter Burger's motives for fleeing Germany for America were slightly different. As an early supporter of Hitler, he felt threatened by the political backlash that followed the failure of the Munich beer hall putsch in 1923. There seemed "very little future for remaining in Germany," and he was constantly in "fear of terrorist acts" by Communists and other left-wingers hunting down the remnants of the Nazi Party.[26] An aunt living in Milwaukee sent him an affidavit for a quota immigrant visa, and Burger sailed to New York aboard a German steamer in February 1927. At the time he left Germany, the prospect of Hitler coming to power appeared remote.

Of the second group of saboteurs, on U-584, only Kerling was an early Nazi Party member. Like Burger, he was discouraged by the political setbacks experienced by the Nazis in the twenties, and immigrated legally to the United States as a quota immigrant in March 1929. His first job was smoking hams in Brooklyn. Both Werner Thiel and Hermann Neubauer left Germany for economic reasons, Thiel arriving in America in 1927 as a quota immigrant and Neubauer jumping ship in 1931 after working his way across the Atlantic as a cook. Herbie Haupt arrived in the United States at the age of five in 1925 with his mother, following in the footsteps of his father, an unemployed World War I veteran.

By the late thirties, the political and economic dynamic that had caused this wave of German immigration to the United States was at least partially reversed. The effects of the Depression were still lingering and it was difficult for new immigrants to find good jobs. America had lost some of its allure: all of a sudden, it was Hitler's Germany that seemed to represent the wave of the future. The tired and huddled masses yearned for a sense of direction, and the Fatherland beckoned them home.

LINDER PLOTTED the course of *U-202* every day on charts attached to the table in the control room, marking out the distance traveled the previous day. He followed the route established by the German government as a safe zone for neutral shipping, from Lorient southwest to a point just north of the Azores, and then a sharp turn to the northeast toward Labrador.[27] Here, in the warm waters of the Gulf Stream, they enjoyed a few days of the "most marvelous weather."[28] Linder took advantage of the calm weather to send the crew out on deck to grease the ship's 88 mm and 20 mm guns and practice inflating the rubber dinghy to be used for landing the saboteurs on Long Island. The weather turned much colder when they reached the vicinity of Newfoundland.

Even though their primary mission was to transport the V-men across the Atlantic, the crew of *U-202* were hunters by profession. They greeted each other in the morning with talk like "I hope we are going to shoot something today" and boasted about becoming the first to spot a steamer when they went on watch duty.[29] Near the Azores, they spotted a steamship and a three-masted Portuguese schooner sailing close to the wind. Linder let the schooner pass as a neutral, and decided he did not have enough time to chase the steamer, which was headed in the wrong direction. "I have no time for a long hunt, as I have only ten more days to take care of my special assignment," he noted in his log for June 2.[30]

A few days later, as *U-202* traveled down the Newfoundland coast, it received a radio message from another U-boat, alerting them to a 20,000-ton Allied steamer traveling from Halifax to Boston. His hunting instincts aroused, Linder at once ordered an increase in speed to twelve knots, but confided to Dasch that there was only "one chance in a hundred" of sinking it.[31] Catching up with the steamer was impossible: it could make twenty knots, four knots more than the U-boat. The only hope of intercepting it was by chance. After a day or so, Linder abandoned the chase, and resumed course for Long Island.

As they approached their destination, Linder permitted Dasch into the radio room to let him listen to broadcasts from American stations and hear the news. A lot had been happening since the beginning of their trip. The Germans had destroyed Russian forces near the city of Kharkov. Resistance fighters had assassinated the Nazi gauleiter of Czechoslovakia, Reinhard Heydrich; the Germans retaliated by destroying the town of Lidice and murdering several hundred inhabitants. America had achieved a measure of revenge for Pearl Harbor by inflicting heavy losses on the Japanese fleet at the Battle of Midway.

From America itself, the radio reported preparations for a huge military parade through the streets of New York on June 13, the very day the saboteurs were likely to arrive in the city. But the big news was the institution of gasoline rationing along the eastern seaboard, a move that could seriously complicate the logistics of Operation Pastorius.[32] The V-men had been ordered to hide their bomb-making equipment as soon as they came ashore. Once established in America, they were to buy a car or van, return to the landing spot, dig up their sabotage gear, and take it to a safe place. If it was difficult to get gasoline, this plan would have to be reconsidered.

The principal reason for gasoline rationing was a shortage not of oil but of rubber. On June 12, President Roosevelt explained in one of his fireside chats that 92 percent of America's normal rubber supply was now under the control of the Japanese.[33] Since modern wars could not be won without rubber, every ounce of the nation's precious rubber stockpile would have to go to the military. By using their cars less, Americans would buy fewer tires, which would reduce civilian consumption of rubber. The government authorized gas stations to pay a penny a pound for old rubber products. Within days, Americans had responded to Roosevelt's appeal by flooding government collection centers with old tires, rubber shoes, and garden hose.

During one of his trips to the control room, Dasch observed the operations of the top-secret Enigma machine.[34] To his untrained eye, it looked like a cash register attached to a typewriter. The radioman received coded messages in Morse, wrote them down, and then typed them into the machine. Whenever he typed a coded letter, a different letter would appear in a panel on the top of the machine, spelling out the secret message. When the operator wanted to send a coded message to another U-boat or back to headquarters, the process was reversed.

In a neighboring cubbyhole, another crew member was glued to headphones, listening obsessively to the sounds of the sea, which were magnified as they traveled underwater. An experienced operator could tell a fishing boat from a destroyer by listening to the sound of its engine and counting the number of revolutions. He was also able to tell precisely where the sound was coming from with the help of a locator device shaped like a round disk.

One day near the end of their trip a coded distress signal arrived from another U-boat in American waters. The crew reported they had been "shot to hell" and were unable to pump any more water out of the leaking vessel.[35] There was a silence on board *U-202*: they all felt for their fellow submariners but were too far away to be of any assistance.

"Another gang gone," murmured the radio operator.[36]

"We die like rats and have to fight like snakes," said the torpedo mate. "I wouldn't mind dying with a gun in my hand if it meant I could at least come face to face with the enemy."

As THEY sailed around Newfoundland, a medical crisis erupted that typified the challenges facing a U-boat captain. A technician named Zimmermann developed violent abdominal pains and a high fever combined with chills and nausea. Soon he was unable even to walk and could only lie down. In the absence of a doctor, one of the radiomen was serving as a medic. He diagnosed acute appendicitis.[37]

Eventually, it might be possible to transfer the stricken crew member to one of the large supply submarines that cruised around the Atlantic with full medical facilities and refueling capabilities for smaller U-boats. But none of the supply boats was in the vicinity, so Linder had to improvise and treat the patient with opium and ice compresses, which did little to reduce his agony. If Zimmermann came close to death, Linder was prepared to remove the appendix himself using crude kitchen utensils—there was no scalpel on board—but he wanted to postpone that decision for as long as possible.

As *U-202* worked its way down the coast, the fine weather gave way to heavy fog, and Linder was forced to order lengthy dives for fear of running into American patrol boats. As he explained to Dasch, American destroyers and subchasers had better sonic monitoring equipment than German U-boats: above water, they would hear a submarine sooner than a submarine could hear them.[38] Traveling underwater threatened to delay their arrival in Long Island beyond June 11, the first night of the new moon, the best time for landing the saboteurs on the beach.[39] The U-boat High Command expressed irritation with Linder, criticizing him in a coded message for failing to adopt "the most efficient course."

Linder may have been making slower progress than his superiors would have wished, but he was doing better than the commander of the second U-boat, Kapitänleutnant Joachim Deecke. Submarine *U-584* had been following a more southerly route than *U-202*. Linder received a message from Deecke informing him that he would not be able to land his saboteurs in Florida until around June 17, four or five days after the *U-202* group.

Aboard *U-202*, the saboteurs' nerves were getting frayed. Burger noticed that Quirin and Heinck kept to themselves, talked in a low voice, and shut up whenever he or Dasch approached. Heinck, in particular, seemed more and more apprehensive the closer they came to America.[40]

Burger was also nervous, and worried about his wife back in Germany. During the trip, he had made friends with a crew member who had previously served with the storm troopers, like Burger himself. He bribed the former storm trooper to ignore the strict instructions of the captain and deliver a letter to his wife, assuring her he was fine.[41]

Burger also made friends with the ship's cook, Otto Wagner, a fellow Swabian. Before he left the boat, he wanted to eat something that reminded him of home, so he asked Wagner to prepare a meal of Swabian noodles, or spaetzle, with sauce. Decades later, Wagner would still remember Burger's explanation for his special request:

"I have a feeling that our expedition is going to go wrong."[42]

THE AMERICAN system for tracking U-boats was still very primitive in June 1942, when *U-202* appeared off the Long Island shore. The commander of the U.S. Navy, Admiral Ernest King, was a notorious Anglophobe, unwilling to accept advice, much less direction, from the British, despite their long experience in combating the U-boat menace. A sailor of the old school, King believed that it was very difficult, if not impossible, to predict U-boat movements, and that the gains were not commensurate with the effort.

American attitudes began to change in the spring as a result of the carnage inflicted by the German shooting spree along the East Coast. Allied losses in this sector alone in March, April, and May totaled 142 ships, or 818,000 tons. In May, King finally agreed to set up a U-boat tracking room in Washington, modeled on the British submarine tracking room in the Admiralty in London.[43] Even though Allied code breakers were still unable to break the four-rotor Enigma system used by the U-boats, other intelligence flowed into the room from the British, the U.S. Coast Guard, and a network of wireless direction finders along the eastern seaboard.

The Allies had lost track of *U-202* after it left Lorient on the first stage of its trip across the Atlantic. As it surfaced off Long Island, on the afternoon of Friday, June 12, the boat emitted a burst of radio signals clearly audible to American monitors. By plotting the source of the signals from several points along the coast, the monitors were able to fix the location of the U-boat: roughly twenty-eight miles south of the fishing village of Amagansett in the Hamptons.

ABOARD *U-202*, Linder was trying to chart a course through the fog, much like a blind man tapping his way along a street.[44] The only way to determine his exact position was the traditional one—by using a sextant to fix the position of the boat relative to the sun and the planets—but the heavens had been invisible for the past two days because of the fog. He believed he was off East Hampton, the agreed-upon landing point for the saboteurs, a few miles down the coast from Amagansett. But it was impossible to be sure.

Meanwhile, final preparations were under way for the landing of the V-men. Dasch gave each member of his group a money belt and pocket money. Linder ordered the men to go through their belongings and remove potentially incriminating German items such as cigarettes. The saboteurs also tried as best they could to straighten out the civilian clothes they would wear in America: after three weeks in a seabag, they were very wrinkled.[45]

As the submarine nosed its way toward the shore, Linder summoned his officers and the saboteurs to decide how to carry out the landing operation.[46] He planned to sail toward the coast at very slow speed using just his electric motors, rather than the noisy diesel engines, to avoid alerting the Coast Guard. He would keep the deck a few inches above the surface of the waves until the boat scraped the sandy sea bottom, indicating that it was close to the shore. He would then land Dasch and his men, blow his water tanks to lift the U-boat off the bottom, and make off.

For the landing operation itself, Linder selected two of his strongest sailors to row the saboteurs ashore in a rubber dinghy he had brought along for this purpose. A line would be attached to the dinghy to guide the boat back to the submarine once the V-men were ashore. If the landing party encountered anyone patrolling the beach, Linder ordered, they were to overpower him and send him back to the submarine for interrogation. In addition to removing a potential threat to the mission, the capture of a coastguardsman would provide the German navy with intelligence on American coastal defenses.[47] The sailors would also bring back the navy fatigues worn by the saboteurs during the landing operation.

When the U-boat surfaced, it was still extremely foggy. As planned, they had arrived on an almost moonless night, with visibility less than a hundred yards. From his post in the control room, Linder could not make out the shoreline, but he could hear the pounding of the surf against the beach, suggesting they must be very close to land.

The U-boat touched the sea bottom with a shudder and then swung around with the tide so it was parallel to the shore, with the heavier starboard side facing land.[48] By now, it was nearly midnight, U.S. Eastern War Time, six o'clock in the morning in Berlin, the time kept by the U-boat fleet. Linder ordered the landing party up on deck, along with their crates of bomb-making equipment and the seabag full of civilian clothes. "Christ, this is perfect," murmured Dasch, as he emerged onto the fog-shrouded deck.[49]

The saboteurs were dressed in the navy clothes they had picked up in Berlin. Quirin and Heinck wore German marine caps with swastika insignias, Dasch a dark brown fedora hat. They scrambled into the dinghy, Dasch squatting in the stern, Burger next to him clutching both the seabag and a briefcase crammed with bundles of fifty-dollar bills.

Linder told the sailors to pull away from the submarine at a ninety-degree angle so they would be heading toward the shore. But after a few minutes' rowing, they lost their sense of direction. The fog was so thick it was impossible to make out either the shoreline or the submarine. At times the roar of the surf seemed to be coming from the right, at other times from the left. They must have been going around in circles.

"Come on boys, let's go to it," yelled Dasch, straining to listen to the crash of the waves against the beach.[50] Somehow, they managed to sort out the correct direction of shore, but then a succession of three huge waves hit the dinghy with full force, drenching everybody and filling the little boat with water. The crates with explosives had been carefully water-proofed, but the seabag was dripping wet. Two of the men lost their paddles, another his cap. As the waves propelled them across the surf, Dasch used a long oar to reach out for the ocean bottom. When he felt the sand, he jumped out of the boat together with the two sailors, landing in waist-high water.

"We made it, boys."[51]

They dragged the boat onto the beach, along with the boxes. As their eyes became accustomed to the different shades of black—dark black sea, gray-black sky, silvery black sand—the men from the U-boat could just make out a broad expanse of beach stretching up a gentle incline to brush-covered dunes. They hauled the boxes to a rickety fence by the dunes, hurriedly covering them with sand in case they ran into a coastguardsman. Burger pulled a raincoat out of the seabag and spread it on the sand.[52] He then removed bundles of sodden clothing from the bag, one for each man, and placed them on the raincoat.

As his colleagues were attending to the baggage, Dasch took a quick walk around the beach. After a few steps, he cursed quietly to himself. He could see a beacon flashing in the distance: they must have landed near a Coast Guard station. There was no time to lose. He ordered his men to hurry changing out of their naval fatigues into civilian clothes. He then ran back to the seashore to the sailors, who were searching for the lost paddles. He was helping them get the boat out of the water and drain it when he realized to his horror that there was someone else on the beach.

A tall figure was walking toward them through the fog, swinging a flashlight.[53]

PART TWO

FREEDOM

(JUNE 13–27, 1942)

CHAPTER FIVE

THE BEACH

S IX MONTHS after Pearl Harbor, foreign-inspired terrorism was low on the list of the concerns of ordinary Americans. Even though German U-boats were known to be off the East Coast, the idea of Nazi saboteurs coming ashore to wreak havoc behind American lines seemed far-fetched, even ludicrous. Enemy sabotage missions were the stuff of Hollywood movies rather than daily newspaper headlines.

For most Americans, the war in Europe and Asia was still a long way away. American boys might be dying in places like Corregidor and Bataan, but there was still a quality of innocence about domestic life. People had grown accustomed to the protection afforded by two great oceans: the American homeland seemed an oasis of peace and relative prosperity, somehow insulated from the murderous passions afflicting the rest of the world. Saks Fifth Avenue was still advertising its semiannual clearance sale; Irving Berlin was still performing on Broadway; Joe DiMaggio was still hitting home runs in Yankee Stadium.

The sense of American invulnerability was reflected in the low priority placed on homeland security. The defenses set up along the eastern seaboard in the immediate aftermath of America's entry into the war were "scanty and improvised," in the words of the army's official history.[1] They were strengthened somewhat in April as a result of the growing U-boat menace and intelligence reports that the Germans might be trying to land saboteurs along the coast. But there were many glaring holes, caused in large part by bureaucratic turf fights between the agencies responsible for homeland defense.

In theory, the navy was responsible for combating the enemy at sea; the

Coast Guard patrolled the beaches; the army defended the coastline. In practice, all these responsibilities overlapped. Both the army and the navy ran radio interceptor stations along the coast, listening to U-boat communications. The army's Eastern Defense Command included mobile infantry units charged with responding to enemy incursions; as a result, army commanders were perpetually feuding with the Coast Guard over who was responsible for beach defense. The navy had primary responsibility for the anti-U-boat campaign, but ordering and enforcing a blackout to prevent submarines from attacking ships silhouetted by lights on shore was the job of the army.

To make matters even more complicated, the Federal Bureau of Investigation was charged with combating attempted subversion or sabotage, assisted by the Office of Naval Intelligence and the Military Intelligence Division of the army. The head of the FBI, J. Edgar Hoover, had a reputation as a skilled, sometimes ruthless, bureaucratic infighter constantly seeking to advance the interests of his agency, even if it meant running roughshod over everyone else.

Each of the agencies responsible for homeland defense had its own chain of command and jealously guarded its rights and prerogatives, some of which dated back to the War of Independence. Although War Department officials had tried to cut through the red tape and come up with a workable system of interagency cooperation, the people who actually patrolled the beaches, manned the coastal defense guns, and listened to enemy communications were barely on speaking terms with one another.

If there was one person in Washington who took the threat of internal subversion very seriously, it was President Franklin Delano Roosevelt. As assistant secretary of the navy during World War I, Roosevelt had been responsible for naval intelligence, and he constantly suspected the Germans of plotting attacks against American military installations. Some of these suspected plots were the figment of his own hyperactive imagination and lifelong fascination with the cloak-and-dagger, but others were real enough. In July 1916, saboteurs blew up a huge ammunition depot on Black Tom Island in New York Harbor opposite the Statue of Liberty, killing seven people and destroying two million pounds of munitions intended for Allied forces in Europe.[2] It was the greatest explosion in the history of New York City, and could be heard in Philadelphia, nearly a hundred miles away. Thousands of heavy plate-glass windows fell out of skyscrapers and office buildings in Manhattan and Brooklyn, and pieces of shrapnel landed as far away as Governors Island. Six months later, in January 1917, the roar of exploding munitions again shook New York City, this time from a fire in a shell assembly plant near Kingsland, New Jersey.

Responsibility for the Black Tom and Kingsland explosions—which took place at a time when the United States was still officially neutral—was eventually traced to the German secret service. Among those implicated in the plot was Franz von Papen, a former German military attaché in Washington and future mentor to Adolf Hitler. It seemed reasonable to conclude that the Germans would try something similar in World War II.

Roosevelt's suspicions were piqued by an intelligence report dated March 15, 1942, from the U.S. embassy in Switzerland warning that German submarines were transporting groups of "two or three agents at a time" to the coasts of north and central America.[3] The report cited a trusted source who had just returned from the German port of Kiel, where he met with the relatives of U-boat men.

Agents carry communications and very valuable explosives . . . They are very familiar with area where they will work and very amply supplied with dollar bills obtained in Sweden and Switzerland. During darkness submarines proceed very near inshore (some commanders related having seen glare New York skyline), whence member submarine crew takes them ashore in hard rubber boats with outboard motors. Well developed plan prescribes that, at moment ordered, agents and accomplices in America will commence simultaneously everywhere on continent a wave of sabotage and terror, chief purpose of which is to cause United States military authorities to keep greatest possible number of troops on home front, reducing thereby to minimum number sent abroad.

The report was discussed by the Joint Chiefs of Staff on March 30, and passed on to the intelligence agencies "for appropriate action." A week later, the president had his naval aide send a memorandum to the navy and the Coast Guard alerting them to the possibility of saboteurs coming ashore. An effective way of dealing with the threat, Roosevelt suggested, would be a "reasonable expansion" of the Coast Guard's beach patrol service.[4] In particular, he proposed equipping the one-man beach patrols with portable radio sets that would allow them instantly to alert their superiors to an enemy incursion. Two-way radio sets were a relatively novel innovation: Roosevelt had seen them used by the Secret Service at his country retreat at Hyde Park in upstate New York, and was much impressed.

As often happened with such missives, FDR's suggestion about two-way radio sets was filed away and forgotten as one more passing presidential enthusiasm.

AGED TWENTY-ONE, with keen blue eyes, a ruddy complexion, and a deep wave in his hair, John Cullen had been working at Macy's department store for just over a year when war broke out. As was the custom at Macy's, he had started out delivering small packages and worked his way up to delivering furniture. His main interests outside work were bowling, dancing, and dates with his girlfriend.

The day after the Japanese attack on Pearl Harbor, Cullen and his best friend decided to enlist in the marines. They reported to a recruiting station in the Bronx, where a gruff sergeant told them, "If you fellas are ready to ship out tonight, we will take you. If not, leave now."[5] Their patriotic enthusiasm did not extend to missing Christmas with their families, so they joined the Coast Guard instead.

The Coast Guard was expanding rapidly to deal with the threat posed by German U-boats, and new recruits were sent to a receiving station on Ellis Island, where they were stacked in three-tier bunks. After several weeks' training, they were dispatched to lifeboat stations along the East Coast for the unglamorous duty of "sand pounding"—walking up and down the beaches to look for ships in distress, drowning swimmers, and German submarines. The lifeboat stations were strung out some six miles apart from each other in a two-thousand-mile chain from Maine to Florida.

Cullen ended up in the little resort town of Amagansett, near the eastern tip of Long Island, on a stretch of coast known as the site of a large number of wrecks and groundings. A false sandbar a few hundred yards offshore had tricked numerous mariners over the years, stranding their boats as the tide washed out. A powerful hurricane had blown through Amagansett in 1938, flattening many beach houses and turning the area behind the seashore into half-empty scrubland.

The lifeboat station was a two-story wood-and-shingle building topped by a lookout tower, with a large boat room downstairs and sleeping quarters upstairs for sixteen men. When on beach duty, Cullen was required to walk or run three miles to a navigation beacon, punch a clock he carried with him to prove that he had reached his destination, and return to the station. At night, he had to make sure that every house facing the sea was completely blacked out. The six-mile circuit took about two hours to complete.

Coast Guard headquarters had responded to the alert for German saboteurs coming ashore by ordering simultaneous patrols on either side of the lifeboat station whenever practical.[6] At the Amagansett station, however, the men only had one clock to share between them, so it was necessary to wait for a patrol to return before sending another out. This meant that each stretch of beach was patrolled twice in four hours, once on the way out and once on the way back.

The chance of a coastguardsman running into anyone coming ashore—assuming that the intruder spent roughly twenty minutes on the beach before moving inland—were approximately one in six.

ON THE night of Saturday, June 13, Cullen was assigned the midnight patrol east from Amagansett Lifeboat Station. The west patrol was late getting back, so Cullen did not leave until ten minutes past twelve. He made his way down from the lifeboat station through the sand dunes and past an observation tower and a naval radio station to the beach.

He was alone and unarmed, wearing the standard Coast Guard uniform of dark blue pullover, pants, and black dress shoes. He was unable to see more than a few yards in front of him because of the fog. There were rumors of German U-boats offshore but, even if he were to run into a Nazi sailor or saboteur, Cullen had no idea what to do or how to get help. Apart from a flare gun, he had no means of communicating with his lifeboat station.

Since the tide was out, the beach was particularly wide, almost a hundred yards from the water's edge to the dunes. Cullen did not want to get lost in the fog, so he stuck close to the ocean where the sand was firmest. He amused himself by singing the latest hit songs, such as "I've Got a Girl in Kalamazoo" by Glenn Miller. There was one tune, in particular, that he could not get out of his head. Played by the Jimmy Dorsey Orchestra, it had been the number one song in America for the past five weeks:

Tangerine,
She is all they claim
With her eyes of night and lips as bright as flame
Tangerine.
When she dances by
Señoritas stare and caballeros sigh
And I've seen
Toasts to Tangerine
Raised in every bar across the Argentine.[7]

He had been walking for about fifteen minutes, and had covered just under half a mile, when he spotted a group of three men holding a dark object in the surf, silhouetted against the misty sea. It was rare to run into anyone at this time of night: under the blackout regulations, everybody not in uniform was meant to be off the beach.

"Who are you?" Cullen yelled.[8] He shined his flashlight in the direction of the strangers, but it was of little use in the fog, so he turned it off.

One of the men came toward him, shouting out a question.

"Coast Guard?"

"Yes. Who are you?"

"Fishermen. From East Hampton. We were trying to get to Montauk Point, but our boat ran aground. We're waiting for the sunrise."

"What do you mean, East Hampton and Montauk Point?" said Cullen, surprised that the fishermen would run aground less than five miles from their starting point and fifteen miles from their destination. Logically, they should be further out to sea. "Do you know where you are?"

The stranger acted cagey. "I don't believe I know where we landed. You should know."

"You're in Amagansett. That's my station over there," the coastguardsman replied, gesturing back over his head through the mist. "Why don't you come up to the station, and stay there for the night?"

The other man hesitated a little, before murmuring, "All right." They walked together a few steps in the direction of the lifeboat station. Then the stranger changed his mind.

"I'm not going with you."

"Why not?"

Another hesitation.

"I have no identification card, and no permit to fish."

"That's all right. You better come along."

"No, I won't go."

Cullen made a motion to grab the stranger's arm. "You have to come."

Although the stranger spoke fluent English, he seemed strangely out of place. He didn't look much like a fisherman. He was wearing a red woolen sweater with a zipper up the front, a gray mechanic's coat, gray-green dungarees, white socks, tennis shoes, and a dark brown fedora hat.[9] His pants, Cullen noticed, were dripping wet. The stranger seemed anxious to distract Cullen's attention from his two companions. Rather than submit to the coastguardsman's authority, he abruptly changed the subject.

"Now listen, how old are you, son?"

"Twenty-one."

"You have a mother?"

"Yes."

"A father?"

"Yes."

"Look, I wouldn't want to kill you. You don't know what this is all about."

The stranger reached into the left pocket of his pants and pulled out a tobacco pouch with a thick wad of bills.

"Forget about this and I will give you some money and you can have a good time."

"I don't want your money."

Another man appeared out of the fog, from somewhere higher up the beach, wearing only a dripping bathing suit and a chain with some medallions around his neck. He was dragging a canvas bag, which was also wet, through the sand. "Clamshells," said the man in the fedora hat by way of explanation. "We've been clamming."

The newcomer began saying something in a language that Cullen could not understand but that sounded vaguely like the German he had heard in war movies. The use of the foreign language seemed to upset the man in the fedora. He immediately put his hand over the other man's mouth, ordering him, in English, to shut up and "get back to the other guys." He then took Cullen's arm, saying, "Come over here."

After a few steps, the stranger produced more money from the tobacco pouch, shoving what he said was three hundred dollars into Cullen's hands. By now, Cullen was very worried. His life had been threatened, and he was outnumbered, at least four to one.

"Take a good look at my face," said the stranger, removing his hat and coming closer. "Look in my eyes."

The stranger's eyes were dark brown, almost black. He was thin, and seemed to be about five feet six inches tall. He had unusually long arms, a large hooked nose, and prominent ears. His most noteworthy feature, apart from a thin, elongated face, was a streak of silvery gray that went through the middle of his combed-back black hair.

"Look in my eyes," the stranger repeated. "Would you recognize me if you saw me again?"

"No sir, I never saw you before."

"You might see me in East Hampton some time. Would you know me?"

"No, I never saw you before in my life."

"You might hear from me again. My name is George John Davis. What's your name, boy?"

It had been a bizarre conversation, and Cullen was not about to reveal his real name.

"Frank Collins, sir," he mumbled.

With that, he backed away from the strangers, clutching the bills in his hand. The man in the fedora seemed willing to let him go, even though he and his companions could easily have overpowered him. Once Cullen reached the safety of the fog, he ran for his life.

It took Cullen no more than five minutes to run back to the lifeboat station. Most of his fellow coastguardsmen had gone to sleep; he woke them with shouts of "There are Germans on the beach" and "Let's go." Nervous and out of breath, he spilled out his story to his immediate boss, Boatswain's Mate Second Class Carl Jennett, an old salt who thought he had seen everything. Jennett had spent too much time responding to false alarms to believe his subordinate's story immediately: it was not until Cullen produced the crumpled bills from his pocket that Jennett began to take him seriously.[10]

Jennett opened up the storeroom, and handed out .30 caliber Springfield rifles and ammunition to his men, none of whom had handled firearms before. He loaded the rifles for Cullen and six others, put the safety catches on, and gave them a two-minute lesson in how to fire the guns. Before heading out the door, Jennett called the neighboring lifeboat station, six miles up the coast at Napeague, to alert them to what was going on.

Outside the station, the men saw a car coming down the road, its headlights dimmed to a narrow slit in accordance with the blackout regulations. Not knowing who was in the car, and thinking it might be headed toward the beach to pick up the Germans, Jennett and his men hid on the side of the road. But the car turned toward the lifeboat station. The passengers turned out to be two coastguardsmen returning from a party.

By the time they got back down to the place where Cullen had run into the man with the streak in his hair, it was close to 1 a.m., half an hour after the incident.[11] They fanned out across the beach, combing the area carefully, but there was no sign of the strangers.

"Stay here while we search the dunes," Jennett ordered, leaving Cullen at the spot where he had last seen the Germans.[12] Two other coastguardsmen kept him company.

As they waited on the beach for the return of the others, Cullen and his companions caught whiffs of what smelled like burning diesel fumes wafting in from the sea. The fog was still very thick. But somewhere beyond the breaking waves, they could make out the silhouette of a long, low-lying boat that tapered down at each end, with a kind of deckhouse in the middle. A light blinked through the mist. Every few minutes, the boat would turn on its engines, as if attempting some kind of maneuver.

Thinking that the Germans might be coming back, or that the boat might fire on them, Cullen and the others ducked behind a fence. They felt scared and vulnerable: a war that a few hours ago had seemed far away was suddenly right there, on the beach.

ABOARD *U-202*, the mood had turned from elation at a relatively successful operation to panic. At first, everything appeared to go smoothly. The thick fog had provided perfect cover for the landing of the V-men. The sailors who rowed the saboteurs ashore in the rubber dinghy had kept a line attached to the U-boat. They tugged on the line when they wanted to return, and were hauled back in.

When Linder heard about the encounter with the coastguardsman, he was angry with Dasch for failing to send him back a prisoner, in accordance with his orders.[13] But his anger was soon overshadowed by a more immediate crisis: his ship was stuck on the sandbar.

The U-boat had swung around parallel to the beach during the disembarkation of the saboteurs. Preoccupied with the dinghy, Linder did not pay enough attention to his own boat, which was being pushed further onto the sandbar with every swell of the waves. By the time he realized what was happening, the tide was running out and the U-boat was stranded.

From the bridge of *U-202*, Linder could just make out a man with a flashlight moving about on the beach. He assumed it was one of the V-men signaling that everything was all right. He tried to free the submarine from the sand by running the diesel engines and the electric motor at full power, but nothing happened. He then ordered the torpedoes to be removed from their tubes to raise the bow. To make the boat as light as possible, he blew the water tanks and dumped diesel fuel overboard. By switching one of his propellers to forward and the other to reverse, and pushing the rudder in the direction of the backward-running propeller, he was able to rock the boat, a maneuver known to English-speaking sailors as "sally ship." But although *U-202* "hopped around like a frog on the beach," it failed to come free.[14]

"No luck," Linder recorded in his log. "Boat stuck too fast. I flooded down further so I wouldn't wash further up on the beach. I tried the same maneuver (blowing with air and full speed astern) in spite of the danger of being heard on the land. This attempt also failed."[15]

By 1 a.m., the mist was getting lighter and land was becoming visible. By comparing his position to the charts, Linder could see that his ship was lying about two hundred yards from the beach, almost perpendicular to the Amagansett Naval Radio Station. Despite navigating in the fog, he was within a couple of miles of his intended landing place. He could see a "house and some sort of tower" on the beach, as well as two tall masts of the radio station, off slightly to his left. "Automobiles are going by all the time in both directions, but do not stop at our landing place. A dog barks long and loudly. Periodically a single machine gun is fired, but at some distance away."

Linder was amazed that his ship was not discovered and fired upon immediately. Searchlights were scanning the sea from a point near the lifeboat station, but were ineffective because of the low visibility and the fact that they seemed to be directed upward. He concluded that the Americans on shore had mistaken his diesel engines for the drone of aircraft.

By now, the ship was "fairly high and dry, with a cant of 40°." Low tide was due at 2:14. In contrast to his chief engineer, who was a nervous wreck, and the rest of the crew, who were worried about spending the rest of the war in a prisoner of war camp, Linder was calm and controlled. He prepared to scuttle the boat and destroy the top-secret Enigma codebooks. His engineers placed explosive capsules around the ship.

A further nightmare was the crewman with appendicitis, Zimmermann, now in the sixth day of his agony.[16] Linder had used up the ship's entire supply of opium on the stricken mechanic, to little apparent effect: he was in greater pain than ever. The only solution now was to send Zimmermann ashore with one of his officers and to prepare the rest of the ship's crew for surrender.

Sadly, Linder addressed his men over the ship loudspeakers, ordering them to pack a few items of clothing in diver-rescue bags, and prepare to abandon ship. He wrote out a coded message to the U-boat command announcing that he had been forced to surrender after completing his mission of landing the saboteurs. *U-202* was "ready for demolition," he noted in his log. "Radio ready for the last message. There is very little hope left. Worst of all is the helpless waiting for the return of the tide."

As SOON as he had finished speaking to the coastguardsman, Dasch ordered the two sailors to get back to the submarine immediately without waiting for the navy fatigues worn by the V-men. He then rejoined the other saboteurs further up the beach. Quirin and Heinck had heard about his encounter with Cullen from Burger, who had blundered into the middle of the conversation. They were angry at him for failing to carry out the captain's orders to overpower anyone they met on the beach and send him back to the U-boat.

A flare exploded somewhere in the distance, straining everyone's nerves to breaking point. "They are looking for us and it's all your fault, George," complained Quirin. "You should have killed that guy on the beach, or we should have done it."[17]

"Now, boys, this is the time to be quiet and keep your nerves," said Dasch, boasting that he had managed to "buffalo" the coastguardsman into thinking he was someone important.[18]

The men were still changing out of the sodden navy fatigues into civilian clothes. Dasch hurried them up, saying undiplomatically, "It takes years to dress bums, let's get going." They followed him along the beach, carrying and dragging the heavy wooden crates, until they reached a little gully where a sandy path opened out onto the beach. "Dig," he ordered, pointing to the ground. "Let's get that evidence right down here."

At this point, Dasch discovered he had left his own clothes and a notebook near the original landing spot, up on the dunes. Burger and Quirin had also lost papers and items of clothing. Cursing to each other and shivering in the cool night air, they crept back along the dunes through the fog, until they stumbled on Dasch's clothes. Dasch ripped off his drenched socks and navy fatigues, and put on a pair of Scotch tweeds that he had bought at Macy's a few years earlier for playing golf. He then ordered the others to collect all the navy clothes in the seabag, and bury it at the top of the dunes, together with the shovels.

Terrified of being discovered, they began crawling inland through the scrub until they reached a row of bungalows. A few hundred yards away, they could see cars and trucks loaded with sailors passing along a road. Searchlights appeared from the direction of the beach, and signal flares exploded in the sky. Sometimes the fog would clear slightly, and they could make out activity along the beach, where coastguardsmen were patrolling.

"We're surrounded, boys," Heinck kept repeating, rattling his companions' nerves even more.[19] As they lay in the scrub grass, wondering what to do next, they could hear the roar of diesel engines from out at sea. The noise could mean only one of two things, Dasch told the others: a U.S. patrol boat moving along the shore or *U-202* going full speed ahead.

A light came on in one of the bungalows near where they were sitting and a door creaked open.[20] A telephone rang. They could hear the sound of muffled conversation.

It was time to move further inland, in the direction of the main road.

WHEN CULLEN got back to the lifeboat station, he reported his sighting of a stranded boat offshore to his superiors, who were beginning to arrive on the scene. Chief Boatswain's Mate Warren Barnes, the man in charge of the Amagansett station, put a call through to Coast Guard intelligence in New York at 1:45 a.m. Lieutenant (j.g.) Fred Nirschel, a thirty-nine-year-old former football player who had spent the Prohibition years chasing bootleggers across Lake Erie, picked up the phone in his office on Broadway.[21]

Anxious to maintain control of the investigation, Nirschel instructed Barnes to keep his information "entirely secret" and admit nobody to the lifeboat station.[22] He then jumped into a station wagon with another Coast Guard lieutenant, Sydney K. Franken, telling the driver to keep his foot pressed down on the accelerator until they reached Amagansett.

Before leaving Manhattan, Nirschel had alerted Navy Intelligence and the Eastern Sea Frontier—the navy command with responsibility for the entire eastern seaboard—to the incident in Amagansett. Nobody treated the matter as very urgent. According to the war diary of the Eastern Sea Frontier, "the frequent reports of mysterious flares, lights, strangers and other phenomena had become so familiar as false alarms that the customary procedure . . . was to turn the information over to the Intelligence Officer" without further action. The people at headquarters had become thoroughly skeptical of U-boat sightings: the war diary dismissed Cullen's claim of spotting a U-boat as of "dubious foundation."[23]

A special submarine tracking room had been installed at Eastern Sea Frontier headquarters on the fifteenth floor of the Federal Building at 90 Church Street, Manhattan. It was staffed by just one officer, a Princeton University geology professor named Harry Hess, who held the rank of lieutenant in the U.S. Navy Reserve. Hess was a brilliant scientist who fully understood that locating German U-boats was key to winning the Battle of the Atlantic. He was constantly looking for new ways to predict their movements from various scraps of evidence, including radio direction finding. But even though Hess had pleaded with the navy to give him enough men for a round-the-clock operation, and had asked for secure telephone communications to be installed between Washington and New York to permit a "direct and immediate" assessment of German U-boat movements, nothing had been done.

There was still little sense of urgency in Washington about transmitting direction fixes on enemy submarines to the field. There were many in the U.S. Navy, including the commander in chief, Admiral King, who dismissed the efforts of Hess and other submarine-tracking enthusiasts as little better than "the mysterious use of a crystal ball, tea leaves, and a Ouija Board."[24]

On this particular occasion, reports of a German U-boat off Long Island had reached Washington the previous evening on the basis of intercepted radio traffic. By plotting the source of the radio signals, submarine tracking stations had placed the U-boat at a location roughly twenty-eight miles south of Amagansett at 8:53 p.m. But this information was not transmitted to Eastern Sea Frontier headquarters on Church Street until 11:30 that night. By this time, Hess had gone off duty. In his absence, the report was handled by the surface controller, who alerted the operations officer of the Third Naval District. The operations officer promised that a Coast Guard cutter would be sent to investigate.

ON AMAGANSETT Beach, several people had spotted the U-boat in addition to Cullen, but they also had difficulty getting anyone to take them seriously. Chief Radioman Harry McDonald was in charge of the Amagansett Naval Radio Station, part of the top-secret network that tracked the movements of enemy submarines all over the Atlantic. By an extraordinary coincidence, a U-boat was now washed up on a sandbar right next to his own radio station. McDonald no longer needed his sophisticated tracking equipment to find a submarine in the middle of the ocean: he could both hear and smell the roar of *U-202*'s diesel engines.

His first thought was that the ship might be landing a raiding party to destroy the radio station. Afraid that the Germans were coming, he decided to evacuate the station, sending his family to stay with friends. He then called the Coast Guard for further information but was given a curt bureaucratic brush-off.

"I am not permitted to discuss details of possible enemy activity," said the man who answered the phone.[25]

Next McDonald called the army post five miles down the beach, to say he believed a mini-invasion was under way and to ask for extra protection. The duty officer of the army's 113th Mobile Infantry Unit was unconvinced. "I'm sorry, we can't leave the premises without orders from the captain." When the coastguardsmen got through to the army post, they received a similar response: "What are you doing, trying to start something?"[26]

Cullen's direct superior, Jennett, was more concerned about a light in a cottage along the beach than the threat of a Nazi invasion. Such lights were prohibited under blackout regulations, and Jennett believed that someone might be trying to send a signal to the U-boat out at sea. He had already complained about the light to the people who lived in the cottage, but they had paid no attention. He saw a man switch on the light of his front porch and whistle loudly, as if whistling for a dog, return inside, switch the light off, come back outside, and repeat the whole process all over again. It seemed very suspicious. He assembled a group of coastguardsmen and went to investigate.

In the meantime, evidence was turning up to corroborate Cullen's story. Cullen found a pack of German cigarettes near the spot where he had had his bizarre encounter with the man in the fedora. As dawn was breaking, Barnes and two other coastguardsmen followed some tracks along the beach to the top of the dunes, where they discovered a freshly turned mound of sand. Poking around with a stick, they felt something hard. In a few minutes they came across four wooden crates bound with marlin that could be used as a handle.[27] Barnes pried open the crate with a bayonet and discovered a hermetically sealed tin container.

A short distance away, in another newly dug hole, the coastguardsmen found a canvas seabag and two trench shovels. A pair of light blue bathing trunks was lying on the sand, along with a belt and a shirt.

Barnes sent one of his men back to the station to bring up a truck.

AT 3 A.M.—nearly three hours after *U-202* first ran aground—Linder noted that the tide was coming in, lifting his boat slightly off the sand. The time had come for one last attempt to escape. In another hour, it would be light, and they would certainly be spotted from land. He must either get off the sandbar now or blow up the boat.

"We will make one last try to free the boat," he told the crew, his voice echoing through the ship's loudspeakers. "If it fails, we will go together to captivity. Remember the first commandment: silence is golden."

He ordered all the men aft so the bow would lift clear from the sand. The torpedoes had already been removed from the tubes. He blew the water tanks again, turning the diesels to full speed ahead, and running the electric motors as well. With each swell of the waves, the boat moved slightly, rocking back and forth like a cradle. "After about four tries she came free," Linder noted at 3:10. "Hurrah!"

There were "cries of joy" from the men crowded in the stern of the ship as they felt water rushing in under the keel. The cook, Otto Wagner, would later recall that the crew "could hardly believe" the seemingly miraculous twist of fate. "We hugged each other out of sheer happiness."[28] The thirteenth was obviously their lucky day.

There was still one problem to overcome. Believing that the ship was doomed, Linder had ordered one of his officers to take the crewman with appendicitis to the shore. After *U-202* had managed to free itself, the officer abandoned the plan and rowed back to the submarine. Both men were hauled back on board.

"This was the only chance for us to get away, otherwise we could have marched in the military parade in New York," Linder noted in his log, referring to the big "New York at War" procession announced for later that day in Manhattan. "Now we are off, while it is still dark. Evidently no one noticed us from land. All activity was not on the coast, but further inland."

In fact, they had been seen from the shore. Standing by the water's edge, several coastguardsmen could see the outlines of a long, narrow boat lying very low in the water. They watched, fascinated, as the U-boat revved up its diesel engines, turning slowly in the direction of the sea. "It was so close it looked as if it was ashore," one of the men later recalled.[29]

Barnes, the petty officer in charge of the Amagansett Lifeboat Station, was also on the beach when the diesel engines started up for the final time. The engines were so loud he immediately concluded that a boat must be trying to pull itself off the sandbar. He noted "a heavy odor of oil in the air." As he returned to the station, he saw the boat proceeding west, in the direction of Manhattan. When he phoned his superior to report what was happening, the noise of the engines was clearly audible at the other end of the line.

By the time Barnes emerged from the station, the submarine had turned around, and was heading toward the ocean. "Which way is it going now?" he yelled to a coastguardsman on top of the observation tower.

"Eastwards," the lookout replied.

Barnes was not quite sure that the boy knew his east from his west, so he asked if he was facing the ocean.

"Yes."

"Which hand is it moving towards?"

"My left hand."[30]

The boat was indeed moving east, toward the Atlantic. According to the Eastern Sea Frontier war diary, Coast Guard headquarters failed to respond to the original report of a German submarine in the vicinity of Amagansett the previous evening. "No ships were dispatched to the area until after the reported landing," the war diary concluded, and "no action was taken" as a result of the radio direction finding.[31]

Despite ample opportunities to capture it, *U-202* was permitted to escape.

DAWN BROKE over Amagansett Beach to reveal an expanse of golden sand at the edge of a prairie. The Hamptons in 1942 bore little resemblance to their appearance today: there were no sprawling beach communities, no smart boutiques, no immaculately manicured lawns and glistening swimming pools, hardly any paved roads. There were not even many trees. Instead there were miles of rough scrubland and a few sandy paths leading down from the East Hampton–Montauk highway to a wide, windswept beach.

Since it was June, vacationers were already coming out from New York to occupy the dozen or so modest bungalows strung along the beach. Amagansett had recently been discovered by a circle of avant-garde painters around the heiress Peggy Guggenheim and her lover, Max Ernst, but it was still a quiet, secluded spot. The lifeboat station stood out from the other buildings because of its size and location next to the beach; it has since been sold and moved inland, and is today dwarfed by multimillion-dollar mansions.

It was now four hours since the landing of the saboteurs and an hour since *U-202* had pried itself loose from the sandbar. America's military machine was belatedly mobilizing itself. Several dozen soldiers from the 113th infantry unit arrived on the beach, followed by an army lieutenant, alone and somewhat bewildered. He had been roused from his bed by repeated phone calls and was "looking for his men."[32] Barnes suggested diplomatically that the army keep behind the sand dunes, well clear of the beach itself. His own men were patrolling the beach, and they were armed and jittery, not a good combination. He himself had almost shot one of the soldiers as a suspected Nazi.[33]

Around 4:15 a.m. the men on the beach again heard the sound of a boat revving up offshore.[34] This was either *U-202* making its final escape after picking up the seaman with appendicitis or, more likely, a Coast Guard cutter investigating the reports of a U-boat washed up on the sandbar. The sound died away after a few minutes, as the boat went out to sea.

The Coast Guard intelligence officers, Nirschel and Franken, arrived at the lifeboat station at 4:30, having made the three-hour trip from Manhattan in just over two hours. Barnes returned from the beach at the same time, together with his haul of four wooden crates and a very wet seabag. The two lieutenants used a can opener to slice open the sealed container inside the crate already opened by Barnes. A variety of sabotage devices—including time bomb mechanisms, detonator caps with lead wires attached, and vials containing inflammable liquids—spilled onto the floor of the boat room.

"Timing devices," murmured one of the lieutenants, as he examined the fake pen and pencil set. His colleague discovered a German inscription on the pack of cigarettes found on the beach—"D. Mosel, Hamburg-München"—and the French words "Allumettes de Sûreté" on a box of matches.[35] Soon the floor of the boat room was littered with German naval uniforms, explosives, and other instruments of sabotage.

Excited by their findings, the officers imagined a starring role for themselves in uncovering a Nazi sabotage plot. They ordered Barnes to return to the beach and fill in the holes he and his men had dug "in such a manner it would not be noticeable that the material had been removed."[36] They also insisted that their own visit to Amagansett be kept secret. Their idea at this point was to return the following night in civilian clothes and keep watch over the beach near the arms cache, on the assumption that the Germans would return to pick up their equipment. In the meantime, they instructed the coastguardsmen to load the sabotage gear into their station wagon.

Before leaving for New York, Franken questioned Cullen about his strange encounter on the beach, and signed a receipt for the money offered him as a bribe. It turned out not to come to $300—as the stranger had claimed—but $260, consisting of two fifty-dollar bills, five twenties, and six tens.

In the excitement, nobody thought to ask the obvious questions: If the invaders were not on the beach, where were they? And where were they likely to be headed?

DASCH'S MAIN concern was to get away from the beach as soon as possible. This meant heading in the opposite direction from the sound of the surf. As dawn was breaking and he could see a little better, he led his men away across the scrub to the East Hampton–Montauk highway. He knew from the coastguardsman he had met on the beach that they were somewhere near Amagansett. He had a vague sense of the local geography, having worked in the area a few years previously, but had no idea whether the village lay to the left or to the right.

The saboteurs decided to explore along the main road, without knowing where it would lead. To avoid being seen, they kept behind a hedgerow. They were wet and exhausted, and suspicious of one another. Quirin insisted they all go through their pockets, looking for anything that might give them away. They were alarmed to discover that Burger had two draft registration cards, one in his real name, another waiting to be filled up.[37] Dasch demanded that he tear up the empty registration card.

Soon they came to a house with lights on in the front, and a parking space out back for several cars. It turned out to be a campground. "Jesus Christ, I'm falling into a trap," thought Dasch, as he steered his men around the campground. Nobody noticed them. Behind the campground, they found some railroad tracks.

Looking at the tracks, Dasch was struck by "one outstanding fact":[38] he could see a single track to his right, but a double track and then a triple track to his left. He concluded that the village of Amagansett must lie to the left. They took that direction and, after a mile or so, reached the railroad station. It was around five o'clock in the morning, and the ticket office was closed.

"Filthy and wet and as stained as anyone could have been going through water and wet grass," they cleaned themselves up as best they could. Dasch got rid of his wet clothes—swimming trunks, tennis shoes, tattered shirt, and a pair of socks—by throwing them into a hedge opposite the station.

At six, Dasch noticed smoke coming out of the station chimney, suggesting that the stationmaster was up and about. He examined the timetable. The first train of the morning—an express from Montauk all the way through to Jamaica, in Queens—was due at 6:59.[39] Dasch went up to the ticket office, feigning nonchalance as he asked for four one-way tickets to Jamaica.

"We were going fishing, but it's a nasty foggy morning, and I guess we will go back home," he told the stationmaster, Ira Baker.[40]

They were the only passengers to board the train at Amagansett. Soon afterward, Baker discovered some wet clothes in the station hedge. Thinking nothing of it, he threw the items into the incinerator.

CHAPTER SIX

New York, New York

(JUNE 13, AFTERNOON)

IT WAS AN ENORMOUS relief to be on the train. They felt exposed and out of place—four young men just off a submarine, wearing filthy, tattered clothes, embarking on a crazy adventure—but, to their relief, none of the other travelers seemed at all interested in them. Soon, they were soaking up half-forgotten glimpses of Americana through the train window: outsize American cars running alongside the track, single-family homes, loud clothes, big-boned meat-and-corn-fed people.[1] They began to sense that they had already accomplished something unique just by making a seemingly impossible journey across the ocean between two warring nations.

After suspecting Dasch of double-crossing them on the beach by allowing the coastguardsman to go free, the other saboteurs were now more trusting of their unpredictable chief. The most dangerous part of their trip seemed to be over. "I accept you as our leader," murmured Heinck, shaking Dasch's hand.[2]

Dasch sat behind Heinck and Quirin so that he could help them out if they were questioned by the conductor: their English was not as good as his or Burger's. While boarding the train, he had picked up a stack of newspapers which he handed out to his companions so that they could blend in with all the other early morning travelers. He used his own paper to conceal an embarrassing gash in his golf pants, which he had ripped on a nail in the Amagansett station.[3] The headlines offered a picture of a war still hanging in the balance and a nation gearing up for greater trials:

JAPANESE MAKE LANDINGS IN ALEUTIAN ISLANDS

ENEMY LOST 15 WARSHIPS IN CORAL SEA BATTLE

RUSSIANS REPORTED HURLED BACK
AT VITAL POINT

MARRIED MEN WAIT IN NEW DRAFT BILL

After months of setbacks, Americans were finally getting some good news from the Pacific: U.S. warplanes operating from aircraft carriers in the Coral Sea had destroyed three Japanese aircraft carriers in the Battle of Midway. Commentators were already talking about revenge for Pearl Harbor and a possible "turning point" in the Pacific theater. But elsewhere the war news was grim. The British were on the run from Rommel's Afrika Korps in North Africa, and the Germans were at the gates of Sevastopol in the Crimea.

On the home front, the newspapers carried reports of gasoline rationing and the latest opinion poll from George Gallup, which suggested that 79 percent of Americans viewed the German government, rather than the German people, as "our chief enemy." The message that there were "Good Germans" as well as "Bad Germans" was reinforced by a new Metro-Goldwyn-Mayer movie called *Nazi Agent* starring Conrad Veidt in the dual role of a loyal German-American and his evil twin brother, a Nazi spy. "A tautly intriguing spy movie," reported the *New York Times*, noting with satisfaction that, in Hollywood at least, good always triumphed over evil.

Another news item concerned preparations for the big military parade through New York City that very afternoon. Mayor Fiorello La Guardia had urged Manhattan residents and office workers to display the Stars and Stripes as a symbol of the city's "grim determination to do the utmost in helping to defeat Hitler." He was expecting half a million people to take part in the procession, and several million spectators to line the route along Fifth Avenue. It certainly looked as if there would be a lot of American patriots in the streets by the time Dasch and his fellow saboteurs arrived in town.

THEY ARRIVED in Jamaica, the Queens terminus of the Long Island Rail Road, soon after nine. A sprawling suburb full of cheap clothing stores, it was the ideal place for the men to make themselves more presentable before their arrival in the big city. Dasch suggested that they split into pairs to avoid attention. He would stick with Burger; Quirin would team up with Heinck. They agreed to all meet at the Horn and Hardart Automat in the basement of Macy's department store in Manhattan at three o'clock that afternoon.

After storing his bag in a dime locker at the station, Dasch set out with Burger on a shopping expedition. They still had some concerns about the American money given them by Kappe back in Lorient. The fifty-dollar bills were part of the same series, all marked by the letter B on the face of the bill, so they made a rule never to cash more than one of the bills at a time.[4] That way, they would be more difficult to trace.

Dasch's first order of business was to buy a new pair of trousers. Holding the newspaper in front of his ripped pants, he walked into the first clothing store he found and bought a pair of brown slacks for $6. But the pants needed tailoring, so he went next door and purchased a pair of ready-to-wear pants for $1.69. He put them on right in the store, and walked out feeling "a little better."[5]

Next stop was the Regal Shoe Store on Jamaica Avenue, where he and Burger got shoes and socks. Feeling more confident about their spending power—they had close to $90,000 tied around their waists and in their pockets—they stopped to have their new shoes shined. Having been poor most of his life, Dasch was beginning to enjoy himself: he had always wondered what it would be like to be waited upon, rather than to wait on others. He later recalled asking "the little nigger boy" who shined his shoes whether "you could use a pair of shoes size 8½?"

"Yes sir, man," the boy replied enthusiastically, whereupon Dasch rewarded him with his castoffs.

Over the next two hours, the two saboteurs went on a shopping spree, replacing everything they had worn on the beach. At a haberdashery, they bought shirts, underwear, ties, and handkerchiefs. They then went to a clothing store next door to purchase a brown gabardine suit for Dasch and a gray flannel suit for Burger. While the suits were being altered, they obtained new underwear and shirts, and ducked into the rest room of a restaurant to wash and shave.

That afternoon, Dasch and Burger took a Long Island Rail Road train into Pennsylvania Station in Manhattan. They found a hotel opposite the station entrance, the Governor Clinton, whose twelve hundred rooms all offered "bath, radio, circulating ice water, and servidor," a trapdoor within the room door where clothes or shoes could be left for a valet.[6] Dasch registered under the name of George John Davis, of St. Louis, Missouri, at 1:15 p.m.; Burger, as previously planned, used his own name. Dasch was assigned room 1414 at a rate of five dollars a night; Burger was across the corridor in 1421.

Quirin and Heinck also acquired new wardrobes, consisting of shirts, socks, underwear, pants, and sports jackets, plus various toiletries, while they were in Jamaica. They tied their old clothes in bundles and threw them in a trash can. After eating and getting a shoeshine, they took the subway into Manhattan, getting off at Thirty-fourth Street for their rendezvous with Dasch and Burger at the Automat.

THE TWO Coast Guard intelligence officers, Nirschel and Franken, had also headed into Manhattan from Amagansett with the sabotage equipment loaded in the back of their station wagon. They took their booty to the Barge Office on the Battery, the New York headquarters for the Coast Guard, where they were directed to the office of Captain John S. Baylis, commander of the Port of New York.

Dumping the contents of the heavy canvas seabag onto the floor of the captain's office, they sorted through several pairs of sneakers, two pairs of heavy canvas trousers, five navy jackets, some with German naval insignia attached, a pair of swimming trunks, and a brown gabardine overcoat. They then ripped open the wooden crates, one of which emitted a hissing sound caused by the blocks of TNT coming into contact with air and salt water.[7] At the captain's suggestion, they completed their examination of the box at the end of a deserted pier.

By the time the officers returned, Coast Guard chiefs had decided that the FBI would have to be brought into the investigation. Back in June 1939, in an attempt to head off inevitable turf fights, President Roosevelt had ordered the heads of the FBI, the War Department, and the navy to coordinate investigations into sabotage and espionage.[8] After heated argument, the three agencies came to a working understanding: the FBI would take the lead in investigating sabotage acts on American soil, while military and naval intelligence would be responsible for infiltrating undercover agents abroad. Even though the Coast Guard had been first to learn about the sabotage plot, it would have to recognize the authority of Hoover's G-men.

It was a painful decision because the FBI under Hoover had the reputation of being the least collegial arm of the government. The FBI director was constantly standing on his dignity and fighting with other agency heads over who was responsible for investigating what. Once the FBI took over an investigation, Hoover's men shared as little as possible with other government agencies.

At 11 a.m., Baylis called the head of the FBI's New York office, Thomas J. Donegan, and asked him to come to the Barge Office to discuss "an important matter." When Donegan arrived, he discovered senior navy and Coast Guard officers assembled around the crates of sabotage equipment. Nirschel and Franken were also present.

The commandant of the Third Naval District, Rear Admiral Edward Marquart, had to rush away to lead the navy contingent in the New York at War parade, which was about to get under way. Before joining the marching bands, he told the Coast Guard to turn over the sabotage materials to Donegan, and to cooperate with Hoover's men.[9] The agreement was that the FBI should take "the lead" in the investigation, and the other agencies would "assist." But everyone present had a different interpretation of what this meant.

Nirschel and Franken were unhappy at being muscled out of the way by the F.B.I. Having spent the night chasing saboteurs and submarines around Long Island while FBI agents were still asleep, they felt they had a head start on tracking down the invaders and wanted to pursue the leads they had already developed. The FBI would later accuse the two Coast Guard officers of withholding two potentially important pieces of evidence.

One of these items was the $260 in fresh bills used to try to bribe the Coast Guard on Amagansett Beach; the other was a brown vest that had once been part of a suit. Unlike the other pieces of clothing found scattered around the beach, this one had an easily traceable identification mark: a New York dry-cleaning tag was imprinted on the lining.[10]

HORN AND HARDART was the kind of American institution that Dasch remembered fondly from his nineteen years in the United States. As the world's largest restaurant chain, serving over half a million people a day, it had pioneered the business of producing and serving inexpensive and reasonably nutritious food through a bank of glass-fronted compartments known as an Automat. The chain also boasted "the best coffee in town," brewed by a revolutionary drip filter system and dispensed from a chrome dolphin's head for a nickel a cup. Horn and Hardart was so successful that its coffee-and-pie formula was even celebrated in song by Irving Berlin, composer of "God Bless America":

> *Just around the corner,*
> *There's a rainbow in the sky,*
> *So let's have another cup of coffee,*
> *And let's have another piece of pie.*

Dasch had enjoyed his first American meal in the original Horn and Hardart in Philadelphia, back in 1922, soon after jumping ship. Penniless and speaking only a few words of English, he had cadged a fifty-cent piece from a stranger, which he promptly spent at the Automat.[11]

Dressed in their new suits, Dasch and Burger headed for the Horn and Hardart in Macy's after leaving their bags at the Governor Clinton. Dasch showed Burger how an Automat worked: change a dollar bill with the lady "nickel throwers," feed the nickels into the machine, turn the knob, and pick up your meal. After weeks without fresh food on *U-202*, Dasch chose two different kinds of salad—"my weakness, especially in the summertime"—a bottle of milk, and a piece of coconut pie. He then led his companion upstairs to a table in a cavernous chrome-and-glass eating hall.[12]

As they were enjoying their meal, they were taken aback to see two German-looking types appear in the dining hall in loud striped jackets, open sports shirts, neatly pressed pants, and shiny new shoes. The transformation was remarkable: a few hours before, Quirin and Heinck had looked like refugees on the run. After complimenting his subordinates for "looking so neat," Dasch told them to get something to eat.

"Aren't you glad to be back in the United States?" he asked with a smile, once they returned to the table with their plastic trays. They agreed that there was a positive side to life in America.

The top priority was to find the others a place to stay, and decide their next rendezvous point. Dasch recommended the Hotel Chesterfield, just around the corner. He said they would all meet again the following day at 1 p.m. at the Swiss Chalet restaurant on West Fifty-second Street. If they were unable to make this appointment for any reason, they would get together at 6 p.m. at Grant's Tomb, near Columbia University.

Quirin and Heinck paid no attention to Dasch's recommendation of the Chesterfield, and relied instead on the advice of a passerby, who suggested the Martinique Hotel on Broadway and Thirty-second Street. They checked in under the names of Richard Quintas and Henry Kaynor, sharing a double room for five dollars a night.

In the meantime, there was more shopping to do. Macy's was running its annual Father's Day Sale—leather wallets down to $1.98 from $2.98!—and was just the place to pick up a few more suits and shirts. "Today's Father is a busy man indeed," the ads proclaimed. "He's probably busier than he's ever been on his job and even some of his spare time is given over to defense activities. So this year give him clothes for his precious leisure moments."[13] The store even managed to make a patriotic slogan out of its traditionally low prices: "A Macy gift is proof of your thrift."

Dasch and Burger headed for the men's department, where they bought shirts, underwear, handkerchiefs, ties, pants, and another couple of suits, plus a Lord Elgin wristwatch for Dasch. They then purchased three suitcases to haul everything back to their hotel a few blocks away. Not long afterward, Quirin and Heinck appeared in the store on a similar mission.

WHILE THE saboteurs were shopping at Macy's, American bombers and fighter planes were roaring over Manhattan. Tanks with names like Lincoln, Ball of Fire, and Hellzapoppin' moved up Fifth Avenue, as hundreds of tons of tickertape floated down from surrounding skyscrapers and rooftops, creating the illusion of a snowstorm in the sweltering heat. The area around Penn Station, where Dasch and his companions spent most of their time, was almost deserted as New Yorkers flocked to Fifth Avenue for the big parade.

The authorities were even more vigilant than usual, mobilizing ten thousand policemen to guard against acts of sabotage by enemy agents as well as more mundane crimes, such as pickpocketing. A series of giant floats passed the reviewing stand outside the New York Public Library, including an "Axis War Monster" float in which a mechanical dictator crushed human beings to death by the thousand while loudspeakers blared "Heil Hitler!" and "Il Duce!" Another float celebrated the exploits of Lieutenant Colonel James Doolittle and a small band of American pilots who had boosted morale at home by dropping a few bombs over Tokyo two months earlier.

The soldiers and sailors were followed by war industry workers carrying banners proclaiming they were on their guard against saboteurs. Then a detachment from the merchant marine, including 150 survivors from

U-boat sinkings in the Atlantic. "The Axis Subs Don't Scare Us," read one much-applauded banner; "We Deliver the Goods." There were also loud cheers for a group of German-American trade unionists who carried an outsized figure of a worker aiming a sledgehammer at a swastika. Other slogans captured the feverishly patriotic mood:

> *I Need America, America Needs Me*
>
> *Buy Stamps to Stamp out the Axis*
>
> *Don't Talk*
>
> *Keep 'Em Sailing*
>
> *Open a Second Front Now*
>
> *Remember Pearl Harbor*

Attended by two and a half million people, one-third of the city's population, this was "the greatest parade" in New York's history, Mayor La Guardia told reporters, as he wiped the sweat off his face in the humid eighty-degree heat.[14] The only parade likely to surpass it was when the boys "came home victorious."

AMONG THE people absent from the parade was a small team of experts assembled by the FBI to examine the sabotage materials retrieved by the Coast Guard from Amagansett Beach. That afternoon, they laid out the contents of the wooden crates and seabag on the floor of the basement shooting range of the Federal Court House in downtown Manhattan, and began tagging every single explosive device and item of clothing. Cursing the Coast Guard for ripping open the boxes so unmethodically, they drew up their own meticulous inventory:[15]

1. Two small bags marked "C. Heinrich Anton Dusburg Reihanzünder" 6.1939, containing ten fuse lighters, pull wire.
2. One small paper bag containing five fuse lighters.
3. Twenty-five electric blasting caps, .30 caliber.
4. Fifty electric match heads contained in small brass tabular adapters.
5. Fifteen wooden box containers, approximately 2 × 3 inches, apparently containing five detonators each with threaded ends.

And so on down the list of seventy-three different items, ending with "coil of detonating fuse approximately 82′ in length." Assistant FBI Director Eugene J. Connelley, assigned by Hoover to head the investigation, described the haul as the "most impressive" array of sabotage equipment he had ever seen.[16] Whoever put it together must have had access to some extraordinary resources.

The FBI scientists were led by Donald Parsons, an eight-year Bureau veteran and one of the top explosives experts in the country. As he picked up each item, he marveled at its sophisticated construction. He conducted a series of tests on the explosive devices, checking the fuses against a stopwatch and firing bullets into the yellow blocks of TNT to test their explosive velocity. It did not take him long to conclude that there was enough material in the boxes to do millions of dollars' worth of damage to the American war industry.

While Parsons and his colleagues were analyzing the bomb-making equipment, other FBI agents were preparing for a night on Amagansett Beach to see if anyone returned to the empty arms cache. G-men took over the Coast Guard observation tower on the beach and accompanied the newly armed sand pounders on their patrols. Shifts of fifteen agents at a time were assigned to foxholes on the beach. Vacation cottages were commandeered as FBI posts, and agents were equipped with telephones and walkie-talkies.

Despite the evidence of a large-scale sabotage operation, Hoover and Connelley were skeptical of some aspects of the story told by Cullen and other coastguardsmen. The talk about a German submarine stranded on the sandbar seemed too fantastic to be true, an example of the "garbled stories" coming out of the Coast Guard and the navy.[17] Hoover and Connelley also found it difficult to accept the claim that Cullen had run into people on the beach burying explosives and had been allowed to tell the tale. They speculated that he might have been accepting money from whiskey runners, "and it was only when he realized that explosives were being cached that he decided to report the matter."[18]

Suspicious of Cullen, Hoover's men decided to isolate him from his comrades. They took him to the home of an FBI agent in East Hampton, where they questioned him for "hours and hours," searching for inconsistencies in his version of events.[19] It soon became obvious to Cullen that the G-men "figured that I had to be in league" with the men on the beach. But he stuck to his story.

NIRSCHEL AND FRANKEN were angry about being sidelined by the FBI. On their way back to Long Island, the two Coast Guard intelligence officers decided to do a little sleuthing of their own, beginning with the question of who owned the brown vest they had failed to turn over to the Feds.

The vest bore the dry-cleaning mark 1167-X11.[20] Knowing that most dry cleaners had their own distinctive system for identifying clothes, the two lieutenants decided to consult a Nassau County policeman recognized as "the outstanding authority in the country" for deciphering laundry marks. Without revealing the circumstances of the find, or why they needed the information, they persuaded him to provide a list of laundries in the New York area that used such symbols.

The officers also made a careful examination of the bills given to Cullen as a bribe. They noted that the bills had been issued by Federal Reserve Banks in San Francisco, Chicago, Cleveland, and New Jersey, "indicating the possibility that the pay-off men had come from California and had either cashed large bills or checks en route." This suggested "a California connection" to the plot.[21]

In the meantime, other Coast Guard intelligence officers were fanning out around Amagansett. The FBI insisted that they keep away from the beach, but this did not prevent them from trying to make themselves useful by going undercover in "strategically important jobs."[22] One German-speaking agent got himself hired as a waiter in a restaurant known to be frequented by Bund sympathizers; a second found a position at a wholesale fish business; a third went to work for a gas station at Montauk Point.

They quickly began to tire of their assignments. As the Eastern Sea Frontier war diary noted, "FBI agents were in control of the man hunt and the [Coast Guard] intelligence officers were shunted off without being given any information as to developments." The supposedly glamorous undercover life turned out to consist mainly of pumping gas and waiting on tables.

AFTER THEIR shopping expedition to Macy's, Dasch and Burger went back to the Governor Clinton for a bath and a nap followed by dinner. The hotel boasted "two delightful restaurants and a coffee shop"; they chose the Coral Room on the ground floor. Dasch ordered a couple of rare steaks and a bottle of wine, a meal virtually unobtainable in wartime Germany.[23]

Over dinner, they talked about the harsh times back home and their assignments in America. Emboldened by the wine and fine food, Dasch mentioned the hardships experienced by some of his relatives under the Nazi regime.[24] He was thinking in particular of the father-in-law of his sister Johanna—a man he had visited in Germany—who had spent nine months in a concentration camp at the age of seventy-three because of his devout Catholicism. During the time the old man was in prison, his wife had died.

Dasch's stories prompted the more reserved Burger to open up about his own experiences with the Gestapo. He described how he had got into trouble with Nazi Party officials over a report he had written for a Berlin political science institute on social conditions in occupied Poland; the party hacks were already suspicious of him because of his close association with the murdered S.A. chief, Ernst Röhm, and were not prepared to tolerate even mild criticism of their activities. As a result, Burger spent seventeen months in Gestapo prisons, first in Poland and then in Berlin, accused of "falsification of documents."[25]

While the Gestapo investigated his case, Burger was confined to a cell with sixty other inmates and no open windows. His assistant was also arrested. But the worst part, he told Dasch, was the harassment of his wife, whom Burger had recently married and who was pregnant with their first child. The Gestapo urged Bettina to file for a divorce, telling her that her husband had stolen money from the state and would be sentenced to eight years on a chain gang. As it turned out, the Justice Ministry eventually dropped the charges against Burger and ordered him to report to the army. But Bettina was so shaken by the Gestapo's tactics she had a miscarriage. In return for his freedom, Burger had to sign a declaration promising never to speak of his experiences in prison.

Although Dasch knew about Burger's prison record, he had never heard the full story, nor understood the depth of his hatred for Himmler and the Gestapo. They both sensed they were feeling each other out, dancing around a previously taboo subject.

"Boy," Dasch said finally. He habitually called anyone whom he perceived as junior to him "Boy," even at the risk of causing offense. "Boy, I have a lot to talk to you about. There's something I need to tell you, but I need to put you through some tests first."

"I know what you are going to tell me."

"If you know what I want to tell you, then you will have to kill me."[26]

Burger smiled. "I am quite sure that our intentions are very similar," he said.

By this time, the restaurant was getting crowded, and the diners at the next table could hear their conversation. They decided to leave. Dasch suggested a stroll through Manhattan to see the sights. They walked north in the direction of Times Square and Radio City.

As they joined the crowds of New Yorkers, wandering away from the tail end of the big parade along Fifth Avenue, the two men did not resume their unfinished conversation from the restaurant. Instead, Dasch began telling Burger about his political beliefs, and the "socialist ideals" inculcated in him by his mother. He was vague about what these ideals actually meant, other than a belief in the power of well-led masses to effect human progress.

By way of illustration, Dasch suggested they look at the murals in the entrance of the seventy-story RCA building in Rockefeller Center, one of the most impressive of the skyscrapers rising from the center of Manhattan. The murals depicted "The March of Civilization," and there was quite a history behind them. Originally, John D. Rockefeller Jr. had commissioned the Mexican artist Diego Rivera to paint the murals, but he became upset over Rivera's inclusion of a portrait of Lenin, symbolically clasping the hands of a Red Army soldier and an American Negro. This was unacceptable to the apostle of American capitalism, and he ordered Rivera's murals to be ripped out of the ceiling.

In place of the communist morality tale, Rockefeller commissioned a capitalist morality tale from another Mexican artist, José Maria Sert. As they looked at the soaring ceiling, Dasch and Burger could see the figures of Lincoln and Emerson in the place previously occupied by Lenin. On one part of the ceiling, planes circled in ever-tighter loops, causing spectators below to feel almost giddy. Elsewhere, oppressed slaves were rising up against their masters and well-muscled workers were building a futuristic city in the sky. The overall effect was a paean to the productive capabilities and industrial might of a free society.

The paintings, Dasch informed Burger gravely, illustrated "the history of mankind from the early days of slavery to the present."[27] The two of them were destined to be part of the never-ending struggle for a better world.

They did not get back to their hotel until nearly midnight. It had been an extraordinarily full day, beginning nearly twenty-four hours earlier on a deserted beach, and they were both exhausted. As they headed up to their rooms, Dasch said he would explain his ideas more fully in the morning.

CHAPTER SEVEN

HIGH STAKES

(JUNE 14–17)

THE FOLLOWING MORNING, Sunday, Dasch invited Burger to his room for breakfast. After they finished eating, he pushed the breakfast cart out into the hall, locked the door, tossed the key into the bathtub, and closed the bathroom door as well. Then he walked over to an open window, fourteen stories above the Manhattan street, and announced that if the two of them were unable to come to an understanding, "either I go out the window or you go out the window."[1]

"I want the truth, nothing else, regardless of what it is. If we can't agree, we will have to fight it out."

Burger, accustomed by now to Dasch's melodramatics, looked at him with the same knowing smile as the evening before. "There is no need for either of us to go out the window because we both feel very much the same way."[2]

They still had to tell each other their life stories, Dasch insisted. Only then would they find out whether they had similar opinions about the mission on which they had been sent. Ever loquacious, he launched into his own biography, beginning with his experiences as a fifteen-year-old guard at a German prisoner of war camp in northern France during World War I. In the camp, he told Burger, he became friendly with a Corporal Fensch, a man more than twice his age who, prior to the war, had been a philosophy student at the University of Munich. Fensch converted the impressionable young Dasch to communism.

After arriving in the United States in 1922, Dasch went on, he tried his hand at various jobs and became actively involved in union politics. He soon became disillusioned with the American Communists he met, despite sharing many of their ideals. He investigated various political ideologies, finally concluding that the ideology of Hitler's National Socialist Party most closely matched his own. When World War II broke out, he thought it would be "yellow" to remain behind in America, and decided to return to Germany "to find out what it was all about."[3]

It did not take him long to realize he had made a big mistake. Disenchantment began to set in on the long boat trip from San Francisco to Japan and Russia, on the first leg of his journey back to Germany. There were many enthusiastic Nazi Party members on the boat, among them Werner Thiel, now a member of the second group of saboteurs that would be landing in Florida. At first, the Nazis were relatively subdued. But after the boat left Honolulu en route to Japan, they grew bolder and started "singing German songs and boasting of the way they were going to fight the English." Dasch, whose English was better than his German, found the regimented atmosphere on board the *Tatuta Maru* "distasteful" and refrained from joining the other passengers in their enthusiastic Heil Hitlers. A self-appointed gauleiter for the rest of the group denounced him as a spy and threatened to report him to the authorities on their return to Germany.

Arriving in Berlin in May 1941—eighteen months into the war—he was dismayed by living conditions in Germany, which were much worse than he had expected. Even though the German army had won some spectacular military victories, Berliners seemed "suspicious and afraid" of each other.[4] Food shortages were already quite noticeable and graft and terror were rampant. Dasch told Burger about an accountant friend who worked in a bank and was reprimanded when he raised questions about the bank accounts of high Nazi Party officials.

He went on to describe how he had got a job monitoring American propaganda broadcasts for the German Foreign Office. He was amazed to find out how many people listened to these broadcasts, despite the risk of imprisonment if they were caught. It was an important lesson in the power of propaganda. At the same time, he felt that American propaganda to Germany could be much more effective. Instead of trying to win over ordinary Germans disillusioned with the hardships of life under Hitler, American broadcasters insulted them by lumping all Germans together as "Nazis." Dasch's dream, he told Burger, was to "lick the Nazis with their own weapons" by persuading the Americans to employ more sophisticated propaganda techniques.

The mention of propaganda techniques struck an immediate chord with Burger, who had been working for the Nazi Party's propaganda bureau when he was arrested by the Gestapo. He readily agreed that the German people were thirsting for the "right type" of foreign propaganda that would create conditions for the downfall of the Nazi regime.

Dasch told Burger about observing Walter Kappe recruit German-American returnees for "special missions" to the United States. At first, Kappe had kept him in the dark about the nature of the work in America, but eventually let him in on the secret. Dasch had then helped Kappe recruit the other saboteurs, including Burger. In fact, he had been planning to sabotage the sabotage mission all along.

He reminded Burger of their first meeting, at Quenz Lake back in April, when Burger cursed Himmler and the other "dirty bastards who beat me up." Sensing that the conversation was headed in a dangerous direction, Dasch had cut Burger short. He now encouraged him to finish the story.

There was a silence as Burger gathered his thoughts. Outside in the street, New Yorkers were going to Sunday morning church services, travelers were streaming to and from Pennsylvania Station, news vendors were shouting the latest headlines from Russia and the Pacific. Unlike Dasch, Burger spoke in slow, halting sentences. But once he began talking, his hatred of the Nazis and the Gestapo came tumbling out.[5]

When World War I ended with Germany's humiliating defeat, Burger had been even younger than Dasch—just twelve years old—and even more disoriented politically. By the age of fifteen, he had been swept up in the politics of the extreme right, rushing off to fight the Poles in Upper Silesia. He joined the National Socialist Party in February 1923, nine months before the ignominious Munich beer hall putsch that ended with Hitler's arrest and imprisonment. While he was an admirer of Hitler, he owed his true allegiance to Ernst Röhm, a former army officer and organizer of the paramilitary groups that paved the way for the Führer's eventual seizure of power.

After moving to the United States in 1927, Burger had let his Nazi Party membership lapse; he had to apply for readmission when he returned to Germany in 1933. Back in Munich, he was assigned to the office of Röhm's chief of staff, a job that offered a ringside seat to the Nazi fratricide that broke out the following year. Many Röhm supporters were murdered in the Night of the Long Knives, but Burger had an incredible piece of luck. A few days earlier, he was transferred to the staff of one of the few S.A. men who still had Hitler's confidence. Over the next few years, he had kept his head down as old comrades stood to attention at Nazi Party meetings, shouted "Long live Röhm," and then shot themselves in protest. Like many former storm troopers, Burger had held on to a ceremonial dagger presented to him by Röhm with a few words of dedication, despite orders to hand the dagger back or scratch Röhm's name off the inscription.

Burger told Dasch he had been planning his escape from Germany for a long time. He had thought about organizing former storm troopers scattered around the world into a volunteer corps to fight the Nazis. His hatred of the S.S. had been strengthened by his encounters in prison with Jews, Catholic priests, and other opponents of the Nazi regime. He desperately wanted to get out of Germany, but it was difficult to leave in a way that would not expose his wife to retribution. When he found out that he could travel to America as part of a group of Nazi saboteurs, he leapt at the chance.

"I never intended to carry out the orders," he said.

Burger described how he had scattered bits of evidence on the beach, including a pack of cigarettes, bathing trunks, shirt, socks, and a vest. These items had probably already led the American authorities to the buried arms cache, making it impossible for any member of the group to carry out Kappe's orders for a large-scale sabotage campaign.

By now, the two V-men had worked themselves up into a state of high emotion, and were sobbing and hugging each other for support. Instead of commenting directly on Burger's actions, Dasch reached out and patted him on the arm.[6] Burger told Dasch he had long suspected him of being an American agent: how else to explain his remarkable lack of interest in the details of sabotage training at Quenz Lake? Dasch's Nazi posturing had also seemed very artificial.

As he listened to Burger's tales of Nazi Party intrigues and repression of political opponents, Dasch decided that his companion was "made to order" for "the setup which I hope to be able to create to fight that rotten gang."[7] In his mind, the two of them would play starring roles in the anti-Hitler propaganda campaign, using as their weapons the knowledge they had gained of the inner workings of the Nazi system and the wads of American dollars supplied to them by Kappe. Together, they would open up the eyes of the German people to the truth about Nazism.

"Kid, you are a godsend," he said, putting his long, gangly arms around the stolid Burger. "God brought us together. We are going to make a team."[8]

It was getting on toward 1 p.m., and suddenly both men realized that they would be late for their planned meeting with Quirin and Heinck at the Swiss Chalet. In order to head the others off, Dasch called the Hotel Chesterfield, only to discover that they had never checked in there, as Dasch had recommended. He and Burger interpreted this as a sign that their two companions "did not trust us" and were going to be difficult to control.[9]

Having established that they had similar views, Dasch and Burger now had to formulate a plan of action. Beyond wanting to hit Hitler "where it hurts," neither man had a very clear idea of what to do next. They were both afraid to go to the New York office of the FBI because Kappe had told them that it was under constant observation by the Gestapo. On the other hand, they also had to be careful not to be caught by the American authorities before they could turn themselves in voluntarily.

The solution they eventually agreed upon was to telephone the FBI in New York, provide a code word and a rough outline of their mission, and announce that one of them would travel to Washington to meet with J. Edgar Hoover "on a very important matter."[10] Since it would be easy to trace a call from their hotel, they decided to look for a more discreet place to make the call. Burger jotted down the number of the FBI's local office from the telephone directory, and handed it to Dasch.

They were still talking and making plans when they realized they might be late for their second rendezvous with Quirin and Heinck at 6 p.m. Rushing out into the street, they jumped into a taxi and headed uptown to Grant's Tomb.

STANDING ON a bluff overlooking the Hudson River, the monument to America's Civil War hero was one of New York's most celebrated landmarks. Built at the end of the nineteenth century using eight thousand tons of granite, it was an American version of the great European monuments that the saboteurs had been gazing at just a few weeks before, the Brandenburg Gate and the Arc de Triomphe—a little ugly and crass, but exuding power and strength. Across the front of the tomb, above the Ionic columns, were the words of Ulysses S. Grant following the deadliest war America had ever fought: LET US HAVE PEACE.

The great chunks of polished white marble, the American eagles with their wings outstretched, the sheer size of the monument—"the tomb of all tombs," in the words of Theodore Roosevelt—all combined to create an image of a resurgent America after a great national catastrophe. Over 600,000 Americans died in the Civil War, compared to 100,000 in World War I; American deaths in World War II would eventually total around 200,000. The country had bounded back from these earlier crises, as it appeared to be recovering from the devastating setback of Pearl Harbor. It was this self-confidence that Dasch and his men had been sent to America to destroy.

When Dasch and Burger pulled up in a cab on Riverside Drive, the sun was already beginning to go down, sending flashes of light through the panoply of trees along the Hudson River. Quirin and Heinck were sitting on a bench in front of Grant's Tomb, nervous and angry about the missed lunchtime meeting, and almost ready to leave. When they saw their companions arrive, twenty minutes late, they showed no sign of recognition. Instead, they got up from the bench and walked along 120th Street toward Columbia University. Dasch and Burger trailed behind.

As they crossed Broadway, the four men finally came together. Quirin and Heinck were full of recriminations, saying they were about to leave New York because they feared something had happened to Dasch and Burger. Quirin reminded Dasch of Kappe's orders to move to Chicago as soon as possible, and set up a sabotage cell there. Neither he nor Heinck felt safe in Manhattan, he complained.

Dasch tried to calm them down. He told them he had many matters to attend to as group leader, such as making sure their identity papers were in order and contacting various people about their future work. They would all have to stay in Manhattan until he was ready to leave. In the meantime, they should try to remember the formulas for homemade explosives they had studied at Quenz Lake.

Quirin and Heinck were themselves divided over whether to go back to collect the boxes of explosive materials in Amagansett. Quirin, who had always shown the greatest enthusiasm for the sabotage mission, wanted to return immediately. Heinck, by contrast, was nervous, and helped persuade his friend that Dasch's encounter with the coastguardsman made it too dangerous to try to pick up the gear. As they walked away from Grant's Tomb, Heinck told Burger, "I guess the job is all over now."[11]

Although they agreed to meet again the following Tuesday at 11 a.m. at the Horn and Hardart in Macy's, the two pairs of saboteurs were deeply suspicious of each other. When Dasch asked Quirin and Heinck the name of their hotel, they replied, "The Chesterfield." Dasch knew this to be false because he had called the hotel a few hours before and was told they had never registered there. Dasch told Heinck that he and Burger were staying at the New Yorker Hotel, another lie.

Quirin and Heinck wandered off by themselves, frustrated and disappointed. Dasch and Burger caught a bus in the direction of Penn Station. They got off at Fifty-second Street, and walked across town to Madison Avenue, looking for a phone booth with a little privacy. They eventually found one in the lobby of a hotel. Burger waited outside the booth as Dasch picked up the phone.

ON THE evening of Sunday, June 14, Dean F. McWhorter was manning what was known around the New York FBI office as the "nutters' desk": fielding telephone calls from concerned, outraged, and just plain crazy citizens. At 7:51, as he meticulously noted down in his logbook, a call came through that he could remember for a long time.

The caller was nervous but persistent, with a slight foreign accent. He began by saying he wanted a record made of the call, as he had a statement to make of the utmost importance to the nation's security. The agent was skeptical, but it was his job to hear people out. He asked the caller his name.

The caller gave an unintelligible foreign name.

"Can you spell that, sir?"

"Franz. F-R-A-N-Z. Daniel. D-A-N-I-E-L. Pastorius. P—"

As his own personal code word for the FBI, Dasch had decided to use the title of the sabotage operation. But either he got it garbled or McWhorter made a slip in writing the name of America's first German settler. It went down in FBI records as "Postorius."[12]

"What type of information do you want to give?"

The caller became even more conspiratorial. He told McWhorter he was a German citizen who had arrived in America from Europe the previous morning. His case was "so big" that the right place to "spring it" was Washington, and the "person who should hear it first" none other than J. Edgar Hoover.[13]

McWhorter replied with the practiced spiel of a bureaucrat dealing with an unwanted caller. The director was an exceptionally busy man. There was no need to go to Washington. The Bureau had men in New York who could interview Mr. Postorius at any time.

This seemed to irritate the caller, who told the agent to take down a simple message. "I, Franz Daniel Postorius, shall try to get in touch with your Washington office this coming week, either Thursday or Friday, and you should notify the Washington office of this fact." The caller said he was about forty years old and could easily be recognized by a streak of gray that ran through his dark hair. He then insisted that McWhorter read back the whole message, and specify the exact time and date.

After McWhorter got off the phone, he typed out "a memorandum for the file" recording the contents of the conversation and concluding, "This memo is being prepared only for the purpose of recording the call made by POSTORIUS."

The memorandum duly made its way to the file room, then to the desk of a supervisor, who handed it to his assistant, with the remark "Napoleon called yesterday."[14] The assistant decided the caller was "crazy" and there was therefore no need to relay his message to Washington.[15]

The message went back to the file room.

AFTER PRYING itself off the sandbar at Amagansett, submarine *U-202* headed out into the Atlantic en route to the Caribbean, the latest hunting ground of German U-boats. "The crew needs a little rest," Linder noted in his log, soon after his seemingly miraculous escape. "Dive and continue under water. The stress of the last couple of hours was too great. But morale of entire crew is great."[16]

The medical crisis over the appendicitis case came to a head early on Monday morning. Linder sent a message to U-boat headquarters asking for a doctor from one of the supply ships that were circulating off the American coast. All attempts to relieve Zimmermann's pain had failed, and it looked as if an emergency operation would be necessary. There was no opium left on board *U-202*. Twenty hours later, another small miracle occurred. The patient was "feeling considerably better," Linder reported. The crisis was over.

Linder also reported that he had successfully completed his part of Operation Pastorius. His message was relayed by U-boat command to Abwehr headquarters in Berlin, where Colonel Lahousen noted in his diary that "the task force consisting of four persons was put on land during the night of June 13–14 at the ordered place near East Hampton on Long Island, New York State."[17]

As far as the Abwehr spymasters were concerned, everything was going according to plan.

DASCH MAY have announced his intention of turning his comrades in to Hoover and the FBI, but actually doing the deed was another matter entirely. He felt edgy and unsure of himself, a "mental and nervous wreck," his mind "all tied in knots."[18] He struck Burger, the one person he had taken into his confidence, as a man in the throes of a nervous breakdown. He now resorted to a tried-and-tested method of calming his nerves: playing cards.

Known as Mayers after its manager, Joseph Mayer, the waiters' club on West Forty-ninth Street at the back of Rockefeller Center was one of Dasch's favorite haunts. Everybody there knew him, and there was nothing he loved better than to drop by for a game of pinochle. Mayer considered him to be "a Communist through and through," but other waiters could not figure out whether he was a Communist or a Nazi.[19] In fact, Dasch appeared to see little difference between the two ideologies, remarking at one point that Nazis and Communists were "striving toward the same ends."[20] He often talked about how wonderful everything was in Russia, hinting that he had a brother high up in the Russian Communist Party. When he left New York in a hurry to catch the boat from San Francisco, he told his friends he was going not to Germany, but to Russia. A few weeks after his departure, Mayer received a postcard from Dasch, postmarked Japan, with the message, "Regards to the boys."

Since it was practically impossible to travel from either Russia or Germany to America, the "boys" were surprised to see Dasch walk through the door of Mayers, around nine o'clock on Monday evening. He seemed reluctant to say where he had been since they last met, and instead insisted on immediately starting a two-handed pinochle game. He boasted that he had plenty of money, adding, "Thank God, I don't have to work as a waiter anymore."

His principal opponent was a German Jew named Fritz Muller, an old waiter buddy. Aware of Dasch's constant financial problems, Muller was stunned to hear him say he would not mind losing some money at cards, as he had $83,000 in reserve. He would have put this down to bragging, but he saw Dasch break open several large bills. While Muller played for his usual two-dollar stake, his opponent placed side bets of $30 and $40 a game with other people in the club.

As the game became more and more intense, other waiters gathered around the table, urging Dasch to tell them about life in Russia and joking about his sudden reappearance. To the persistent questions about how he got back, he would only reply, "I'm here—what difference does it make how I came?" One friend speculated that he must have come by plane; another said the only way of getting to the United States from Europe these days was by submarine. At this, Dasch's face went white, but he brushed the remark aside: "Never mind the wisecracks."[21]

By the second day, he was exhausted, and could be heard mumbling to himself, "If I talk, it means death." But he seemed addicted to the pinochle table. A "pinochle fiend," in the phrase of one of his fellow waiters, he was fascinated by the game's seemingly infinite variations. Win a trick, meld, watch the points pile up. He could play for hours in search of the holy grail of pinochle players, the magic combination of two Queens of Spades and two Jacks of Diamonds, the three-hundred-point "double pinochle."

The marathon game finally sputtered to a halt around 8 a.m. on Wednesday when Dasch, by now several hundred dollars richer than when he arrived, announced he would pay everyone's bill for food and drink. He told one of the waiters he was in the United States on a mission for the Russian secret service, and had an appointment with the Russian embassy in Washington. To Mayer, on the other hand, he said he had to go to Washington "to see Mr. Hoover," as "I've got something to explain to him."[22]

On his way out the door, he gave a five-dollar bill to a waiter with a hard-luck story about losing all his money at cards and repaid an old ten-dollar debt to another waiter, known as Johnny the Polack. He then disappeared into the morning rush-hour crowds. The card-playing binge had lasted for almost thirty-six hours.

Calming his nerves was certainly one explanation for Dasch's bizarre behavior. But if his own account of his actions is to be believed, he was guided by another, equally important, motivation: he wanted to give the second group of saboteurs a chance to turn themselves in to the FBI rather than be arrested on the spot, as soon as they landed in Florida. He thought in particular of the young Chicago boy, Herbie Haupt, who seemed to see the sabotage mission as his best chance of going home to his family. As Dasch later put it, "To be a real decent person I had to wait, to give every person a chance to say what I had to say."[23]

From his conversations with Linder aboard U-202, Dasch knew that the second party of saboteurs under Edward Kerling was likely to land in America around June 17, the very day he staggered out of Mayers.

AFTER ESCAPING the depth charge attack from the British plane on its first day out of Lorient, *U-584* had had a fairly routine Atlantic crossing. One day, it accidentally met another German submarine traveling on the surface. Later Kapitänleutnant Joachim Deecke tried to chase a 20,000-ton Allied freighter, but it was traveling too fast, and its zigzag tactics made it impossible to get close enough to fire his torpedoes.

The landing of the V-men from *U-584* went much more smoothly than the landing from *U-202* just four days earlier. Even so, there were some anxious moments. As he navigated the shoreline south of Jacksonville, Deecke had to dodge an American patrol boat and a barrage of zeppelin observation balloons monitoring the coast for enemy submarines.[24] The little zeppelins were particularly tiresome creatures, very difficult to shake off.

Eventually the submarine got within several hundred feet of a wide sandy beach near Ponte Vedra. Deecke ordered the bow tanks to be flooded, so that his boat nudged against the sand, its decks peeking out of the water. A thin sliver of moon glowed in the sky, making the night a little less impenetrable than the mist-shrouded obscurity that had enveloped *U-202*, but dark enough nonetheless. Unlike their counterparts from *U-202*, the men from *U-584* were dressed only in bathing suits and German marine caps as they came ashore in a rubber dinghy.[25] They assumed that the Nazi swastika insignia on the caps would be sufficient to give them prisoner of war status as German soldiers if they were captured on landing. Their civilian clothes were zipped up in waterproof bags.

After depositing their passengers on the beach, the two crewmen from the submarine scooped up a can of American sand to take back with them to Germany. They could hear some girl bathers chatting and giggling a little to the north of the landing spot. They used flashlights to signal Deecke that the landing had gone according to plan and returned to the U-boat almost immediately.

A slender man with wavy brown hair and heavy jaw, Kerling made a quick tour of the beach to make sure there were no inhabited houses nearby and that nobody had seen his men land.[26] He then selected a place to hide the four boxes of explosives and other sabotage gear, all practically identical to those brought ashore by Dasch's group. The spot he chose was easy to remember: a grove of palm trees on a little hill next to a wire fence, halfway between the beach and the road. The saboteurs buried the boxes just as a gray dawn was breaking, and threw the spade into the sea, where it would be taken out by the tide.

Dressed in swimsuits and carrying their clothes in bundles under their arms, they then walked north from Ponte Vedra Beach in the direction of Jacksonville Beach. For the next four hours, they lounged around on the beach, swimming and relaxing like vacationers. While still in their bathing suits, they gave a cheery wave to a passing police patrol car, and received a wave in return.[27] At around eleven, they put on their clothes and caught a bus into Jacksonville, some forty-five minutes away.

Like Dasch's group, they decided it was safer to split up into pairs. Kerling and Neubauer, the injured soldier with the American wife, checked into the Seminole Hotel in downtown Jacksonville under the names of Edward Kelly and Henry Nichols.[28] Haupt and Thiel found rooms in the Mayflower Hotel, just a block from the bus station. As an American citizen, Haupt registered under his own name: if questioned about where he had been over the last year, he planned to claim he had just returned from a long trip to Mexico. Thiel signed as William Thomas.

That afternoon, they went on a shopping expedition, just like their comrades from *U-202*. Haupt, who had the most expensive tastes and felt deprived of consumer goods in Germany, felt particularly at home in American stores. He had his hair cut and got something to eat, and then proceeded to make a string of purchases: a three-piece tan suit from a fashionable New York tailor, a pink-gold Bulova wristwatch, some neckties and shirts, underclothes, a tan leather suitcase, silk handkerchiefs, and several pairs of shoes.[29] The others limited themselves to the basics.

In the evening, they all met for drinks at the Mayflower Hotel and agreed on a plan of action. Kerling and Thiel would travel to Cincinnati and New York, Neubauer to Chicago. Haupt was adamant that he also be allowed to return to Chicago, despite warnings from Kappe about contacting his family. Even though Kerling knew of Haupt's fondness for money, and doubted his loyalty to the Nazi cause, he decided to entrust him with a canvas zipper bag containing $10,000 in a false bottom, to be left for safekeeping with his uncle in Chicago. His reasoning was that a Haupt running around with plenty of spending money posed less of a threat than a financially strapped Haupt who might be tempted to turn everyone in to the FBI for a cash reward.[30]

The plan was for the saboteurs to meet again on July 6, two days after the planned July 4 rendezvous between Kerling and Dasch in Cincinnati. Even though gasoline rationing was in force along the East Coast for owners of private automobiles, Kerling and Haupt would somehow find a way to return to Florida and retrieve the explosives.

IN NEW YORK, meanwhile, the other saboteurs were wondering what had become of their leader. Neither Quirin nor Heinck had seen Dasch since the tense meeting at Grant's Tomb. To their dismay, he failed to show up at Horn and Hardart on Tuesday morning.

Burger tried to telephone Dasch in his room at the Governor Clinton around 10 a.m. on Tuesday to remind him about the rendezvous. There was no answer. Since Dasch had previously told him to keep an eye on the other two, he went to the Automat by himself. Quirin and Heinck were both in a bad mood, saying they wanted to get out of town as soon as possible and expected Dasch to give them suggestions about their trip to Chicago. They had felt exposed in their downtown hotel and had moved to a more modest rooming house on Seventy-sixth Street. Although Burger did his best to smooth things over, he got the impression that the pair were getting "more and more suspicious."[31]

When they were not arguing with each other, the saboteurs spent most of their time in Manhattan shopping. They bought watches and cuff links, perfume and leather belts, bathrobes and slippers, sports coats and top-coats, shirts and neckties, shoes and shoe trees, hats and cigars, scissors and keychains, and still more suits, which had to be taken in and taken out. The slow, phlegmatic Heinck seemed incapable of making up his mind about anything, so Burger took him to Rogers Peet clothing store on Fifth Avenue and Forty-first Street to measure him for a suit. Burger, who was an enthusiastic photographer, also spent around $180 on a new Leica camera with various filters, lenses, and exposure meters.[32] He later explained that he had owned a Leica in Germany but his wife had been forced to sell it because of financial difficulties while he was in the hands of the Gestapo. It seemed only right that he should buy a new camera at Nazi government expense.

When Dasch finally returned on Wednesday morning, from his

marathon pinochle game, he told Burger he was exhausted and needed to go to bed. He could not face another meeting with Quirin and Heinck. To Burger's complaint that this was hardly the right time to disappear for so long, Dasch replied, "You should be glad I played pinochle because I'm now more or less my old self again."[33] Burger had to admit that his friend seemed less high-strung than before his disappearance: his hands were no longer trembling uncontrollably.

Around noon, Burger visited Quirin and Heinck in their new lodgings, a nondescript brownstone house. He asked the "colored woman who came to the door" to speak with a Mr. Quintas, Quirin's assumed name. She told him she had never heard of a Mr. Quintas, but a Mr. Albany had checked in the day before. This turned out to be Quirin.

Quirin and Heinck were infuriated to learn that Dasch had spent the last thirty-six hours playing pinochle. They exhausted their stock of expletives denouncing his irresponsibility. Finally, Quirin told Burger he intended to "have it out" with Dasch and take over leadership of the group himself.[34] Burger tried to calm him down, saying that George had already made preparations for everyone to move to Chicago but needed to leave New York City for a couple of days to make some "important contacts."

That afternoon, Heinck and Quirin took the subway out to Astoria in Queens to make a call on a former German-American Bund member. Before leaving Lorient, Heinck and Dasch had quarreled over whether to renew such contacts, with Dasch saying they would take place "over my dead body." Although Kappe was in favor of recruiting former Bund members, he had left the final decision to the group leaders. Now that Dasch was being so erratic, Heinck thought he had nothing to lose by looking up one of his oldest friends in the United States.

The friend, Hermann Faje, had been working as a steward aboard Vincent Astor's luxury yacht when Heinck first met him in 1934. He was now employed as a hairdresser. He was still at work when Heinck and Quirin first called, but his wife invited the two men back for dinner. Faje showed up around 11 p.m. They all proceeded to get a little drunk, particularly Heinck, who was never very good at handling alcohol.[35]

Naturally, Faje was interested in how his friend got back to the United States. After first claiming that they had returned to America on a neutral Portuguese ship, Heinck eventually blurted out that they had come back on a German submarine, and hinted that he was involved in intelligence work. He added that he was authorized to promise the Iron Cross, Second

Class, to any German-Americans who assisted him in his mission. Anxious to get rid of potentially incriminating evidence, Heinck then gave Faje his money belt for safekeeping. It contained $3,600 in fifty-dollar bills; Heinck had previously removed $400 as spending money for himself.

Heinck had one final request before he left. He had taken a liking to a fountain pen he had seen in Faje's pocket. He asked his friend to use one of the fifty-dollar bills to buy another pen just like it and give it to him when they next met. Faje was welcome to keep the change.

As Heinck and Quirin were getting drunk with Faje in Astoria, Burger and Dasch were dining together at Dinty Moore's, an Irish restaurant near Broadway and Forty-sixth Street, which specialized in corned beef and cabbage. Dasch was still "damn tired," but he was determined to introduce Burger to the culinary delights of New York City, from classic American to Scandinavian smorgasbord.[36]

"Just forget you are Dutch for once," he told Burger, using the slang word for "German."

Despite his pinochle-playing binge, Dasch was still in a state of anxiety, wondering how the FBI would react to his revelations and whether they would accuse him and Burger of being part of the sabotage plot. Burger tried to cheer him up, arguing that they were doing everything in their power to prevent the others from blowing up American factories.

AROUND THE time the saboteurs from *U-584* were heading into Jacksonville, and Burger was preparing for his meeting with Quirin and Heinck at the Automat, J. Edgar Hoover was sitting fuming in his wood-paneled office on the fifth floor of the Justice Department in Washington. The FBI director was furious with the Coast Guard for its amateur handling of the events in Amagansett. Coast Guard officials had failed to seal off the beach, they had allowed a stranded submarine to escape, and they had delayed alerting law enforcement agencies to the presence of suspected German agents.[37] Now, it seemed, they were "withholding" important evidence from the FBI.

Built like a bulldog, with a heavy torso, spindly legs, and a pugnacious face, Hoover had already become an American legend for his single-minded rebuilding of the country's top federal law enforcement agency. In 1924, at the age of twenty-nine, he had taken over a corrupt and ineffective division of the Justice Department and turned it into a feared and respected crime-fighting force. The new agency—renamed the Federal

Bureau of Investigation in 1935—reflected Hoover's own image of himself as a young lawyer with a reputation for professionalism, hard work, and an extraordinary eye for detail. Hoover and the FBI were almost synonymous in the public mind: its successes were his successes; when it messed up, it was the director who got the blame.

Brought up by a stern mother, Hoover imposed a strict code of behavior on his agents and demanded their total loyalty. They had to dress and conduct themselves at all times as eager young executives. The G-men, or "Government men"—the term originated with the criminal underworld and was later popularized by Hoover's supporters in the media—all came in a standard shape and size. Hoover insisted that his agents wear dark suits, white shirts, sober ties, and snappy hats. They could be neither too heavy nor too short. The agents were all men and, with a few exceptions, such as the director's personal driver, all white. Above all, they must do nothing to "embarrass" the Bureau, which meant doing nothing to embarrass Hoover personally.

One key to Hoover's success was his genius for public relations. He understood that a favorable public image for the Bureau and himself would lead almost automatically to more generous congressional funding, which could then be used to further strengthen the Bureau. With the aid of some very skillful publicists, he set out to turn the G-man into a popular hero, whose exploits were chronicled in newsmagazines, comic strips, radio programs, and, most important of all, Hollywood movies. Journalists and writers deemed "friendly" to the FBI were given plenty of material; those who declined to see stories the same way as Hoover were frozen out. The Bureau's spokesman and symbol, needless to say, was Hoover himself, energetic, incorruptible, and plainspoken. He depicted himself as the sworn enemy of an unholy alliance of "human rat" gangsters and their "dirty, filthy, diseased women," "the miserable politicians who protect them," and the "sob-sister judges" who always sided with the criminals.[38]

The news that Nazi agents had come ashore on Long Island, and might already be plotting acts of sabotage, was made to order for Hoover's talents and political needs. His enemies and even some allies, such as President Roosevelt, had long suspected that the director was much more enthusiastic about pursuing Communists than Nazis. Hoover had done his best to correct this impression, sending a memo to FDR in early June listing the Bureau's accomplishments in combating the "pro-Fascist element," including the "apprehension" of 8,827 German, Italian, and Japanese subversives.[39] But he felt under pressure to do more, particularly since Russia was now a valued ally of the United States, doing most of the actual fighting against the common Nazi enemy. By vigorously going after suspected Nazi saboteurs, he could once again prove his indispensability.

Hoover had reported the landing of the saboteurs to the White House in a memorandum dated June 16, which also mentioned "widespread rumors" of additional landings of German agents along the coastal areas of Georgia and Massachusetts.[40] He had alerted all coastal offices of the FBI to be on their guard for "additional enemy activity," and also kept in close touch with his nominal boss, Attorney General Francis Biddle, who marveled at his "imaginative and restless energy . . . stirred into prompt and effective action."[41] As Hoover talked about the hunt for the Nazi agents, Biddle noticed sparks of excitement flickering "around the edge of his nostrils." His eyes were bright, his jaw firmly set. "He was determined to catch them all before any sabotage took place."

In order to catch the saboteurs, Hoover decided to rely on Assistant Director Eugene Connelley. When the director needed someone to handle an exceptionally important or delicate investigation, he invariably picked Connelley, a man known throughout the Bureau as a slave driver, albeit a very capable one.[42] By chance, Connelley had been in the New York office on an inspection tour at the time of the Amagansett incident: Hoover ordered him to drop everything else and take "complete charge" of the case.[43]

Connelley called Hoover from New York at 10:23 a.m. on Wednesday, according to the office log kept by the director's personal secretary, Helen Gandy. He had a long list of criticisms of the Coast Guard, beginning with what he saw as their inadequate patrols of coastal areas.[44] Beach patrols were unarmed, patrol posts too far apart, and communications with Coast Guard stations practically nonexistent. There was no system for reporting incidents to other government agencies. The fact that Cullen had run into German intruders on Amagansett Beach was sheer coincidence: there were long periods when the beach was not patrolled at all. In Connelley's opinion, the entire system of beach defense needed to be revamped and upgraded. Hoover told him to put his criticisms in writing: if there were similar incidents in the future, the FBI would be able to say, "I told you so."

Of even greater concern to Hoover was Connelley's complaint that Coast Guard intelligence officers were giving the Bureau "the runaround." Connelley had heard through the police grapevine that the Coast

Guard was mounting its own investigation into a vest found on the beach: laundry marks showed that it had been handled by a dry cleaner in Yorkville, a German neighborhood of Manhattan. Without telling the FBI, the Coast Guard intelligence officers had traced previous ownership of the vest to a German-American plumber suspected of Nazi sympathies.

To the hypersuspicious Hoover, this information was further demonstration of the need to aggressively defend FBI prerogatives. He considered the behavior of the intelligence officers "outrageous" and "reprehensible," and immediately telephoned the director of Naval Intelligence to demand that they be court-martialed for "insubordination."[45] He was not appeased later that afternoon when the two lieutenants, Nirschel and Franken, finally handed over the vest to Connelley. He continued to fume about Coast Guard "incompetence" for years afterward.

For all Hoover's criticisms of the Coast Guard, the FBI's own performance had hardly been stellar. The truth was that nobody, including the FBI, took the first reports of Nazi saboteurs landing in Amagansett very seriously. Although the Bureau claimed it was not "officially" informed about the case until 11 a.m. on Saturday morning, other records show that the FBI's New York office received preliminary reports of the landing within two hours of the saboteurs' coming ashore, but took no immediate action.[46] Hoover and Connelley were initially skeptical of Cullen's claim that a German-speaking man on the beach had offered him a bribe. When the leader of the saboteurs called the FBI office in New York with a personal message for Hoover, he was, perhaps understandably, dismissed as a crank.

The laundry marks on the vest—seen by both the Coast Guard and the FBI as an important break in the case—soon turned out to be a false lead. The plumber had no connection with any of the saboteurs: the numbers used to identify clothes were recycled year after year.

The investigation had reached a dead end.

CHAPTER EIGHT

A STORY TO TELL

(JUNE 18–19)

BY THURSDAY MORNING, Dasch decided he could wait no longer. He was nervous about going to the FBI, but even more nervous about being arrested before he could blow the whistle on Operation Pastorius. He had already called the Bureau to announce his intention of traveling to Washington to see Mr. Hoover on either "Thursday or Friday." Over breakfast in the Governor Clinton Hotel, he told Burger he would leave for Washington that afternoon. While he was away, Burger would have the job of keeping the other two saboteurs distracted.

There were a few logistical details to take care of first. He had to pick up a new suit from a tailor. He also had to decide what to do with the money he had been carrying around with him ever since his arrival in America. He thought about putting it in a safe deposit box, and visited a bank on Seventh Avenue to make the necessary arrangements.[1] After escorting Dasch down to the vault, the bank officials explained that deposit boxes could only be rented by the year. And they could only offer one kind of box: a long, thin box that would not be large enough for the thick bundles of bills he had been keeping in his Gladstone bag.

Perhaps, after all, it would be more sensible to take the money to Washington. Dasch headed back to a store near Pennsylvania Station, where he purchased a large, tan leather briefcase for $38. In another store, he bought some large manila envelopes, rubber bands, and metal clasps. Returning to the hotel, he removed the money from under the false bottom of his bag, and carefully counted it out. He sorted the fifty-dollar bills into bundles of a hundred, each bound by a rubber band, and stuffed the bundles into the envelopes. He then wrote a note for himself in pencil on hotel stationery:

Content $82,350
Money from German government for their purpose, but to be used to fight them Nazis.

George J. Dasch
alias George J. Davis
alias Franz Pastorius[2]

He packed a leather suitcase with enough shirts, neckties, pajamas, and suits, all brand-new, to last him through the weekend. The rest of his belongings he wrapped in laundry bags, which he put into the water-damaged Gladstone. He left this bag in the closet of Burger's room across the hall, after letting himself in with a key borrowed from the maid.

In the meantime, he had asked the manager to book him into a good hotel in Washington. After a couple of hours, a telegram arrived from the Mayflower Hotel, a venerable establishment in the center of the city popular with government officials and members of Congress, confirming a reservation. Dasch was lucky to get a room: hotel accommodations were in desperately short supply in wartime Washington. He settled the Governor Clinton bill, and then wrote a short note to Burger, which he left at the front desk.

Dear Pete!

Sorry for not have been able to see you before I left. I came to the realization to go to Washington & finish that what we have started so far.

I'm leaving you, believing that you take good care of yourself and also of the other boys. You may rest assured, that, I shall try to straighten everything out, to the very best possibility. My bag and clothes I've put into your room. Your Hotel Bill is paid by me, including this day.

If anything extra ordinary should happen, I'll get in touch with you directly.[3]

Untill Later,
I'm your sincere friend,
George

The train journey to Washington took a little under five hours. From Union Station, Dasch took a taxi to the Mayflower, checking in once again as George John Davis, of St. Louis, Missouri. The reception clerk told him he could stay a maximum of four nights and handed him the keys to room 351, a double room on the White House side of the hotel, for $6 a night. After washing up, he took a streetcar downtown to find a place to eat, and wandered into the Olmstead Grill, at Thirteenth and G Streets. To Dasch's dismay, his waiter turned out to be an old acquaintance from the waiters' club in New York, who immediately greeted him as "George."

At first, he pretended he had never met the man before. But the waiter, whose name was Louis B. Martin, reminded him of their pinochle-playing games at Mayers. Dasch sensed that Martin regarded him as a "conceited brat," too proud to talk to him.[4] As a stranger in a new city, on the verge of a turning point in his life, he also felt "kind of lonely." After a glass of whiskey, he told Martin, "Boy, you were correct in identifying the fellow you thought I was," and invited him for a drink after work.

The two men went around the corner to the Trans-Lux Café, where they began drinking heavily. By the second or third whiskey, Dasch had told his old acquaintance he was on an intelligence mission and, if anything went wrong, he would probably go to jail for a long time. The more he drank, the more he talked, and the more he talked, the more extraordinary and unbelievable his story became. He hinted that he was engaged in espionage work for Russia and had infiltrated a sabotage school in Germany for the purpose of learning as much as possible about the Nazi Party. Another group of saboteurs had left Europe at the same time as his group; their secret rendezvous point was Grant's Tomb in New York.

As Dasch spilled out his story, he became more and more excited, waving his long arms in the air. He claimed he had been in touch with "high officials" in Germany, and insisted that the only way to beat Hitler was to undermine him from within. "If the Nazis knew what I was doing in Germany, they would have shot me, my father, and my mother on the spot," he murmured conspiratorially, swinging back more whiskey.[5] But everything was fine now. "I am protected, I don't have to worry about that."

The two men finally parted around midnight. Dasch jumped into a cab, saying he was going to look for a girl. Martin went back to his apartment, where he described the strange encounter to his roommate, another waiter. He was impressed that Dasch, who had previously always been broke, was wearing a good suit and seemed to have plenty of money. On the other hand, they had both drunk heavily and Dasch's story was too fantastic to be believed. The roommate thought this was probably just a case of "another waiter blowing his head off because he had a few dollars in his pocket." Martin was inclined to agree.

WHILE DASCH was telling his story to Martin in Washington, Burger was doing his best to keep the others occupied in New York. He had found a nightclub on Fifty-second Street that offered a fine selection of music, liquor, and girls. Heinck, still nervous about being seen around New York, preferred to stay in his room at the lodging house. Burger and Quirin went to the Swing Club, where they spent most of the evening talking to a girl named Frankie, who promised to set them up with some of her friends the following night.[6] By the time they lurched out of the nightclub, it was 3 a.m. Rather than return to the lodging house on Seventy-sixth Street and wake the landlady, Quirin went back to Burger's hotel, spending the night on the spare bed in his room.

As long as he was drinking and chatting with girls, Quirin was easy enough to manage. By the following morning, however, he had become truculent again, demanding to know where Dasch had gone and accusing him and Burger of failing to obey orders. Apart from anything else, they were risking drawing attention to themselves by living much too lavishly, Quirin complained. "I won't stand for what is going on," he told Burger. "You and George will have to suffer the consequences."[7] He left the hotel without saying goodbye.

ON FRIDAY morning, Dasch had breakfast delivered to his room at the Mayflower. After eating, he took a shower, and then got down to business, telephone directory in hand. He could not decide whom to approach first, the FBI or the Secret Service, so he called the U.S. Government Information Service and asked the woman operator to explain the difference between the two agencies. She asked the nature of his business, and he explained that he had "a statement of military as well as political value" to make.[8] The operator suggested he call the War Department, and gave him the number of a Colonel H. I. Kramer, of Military Intelligence. The colonel was not in, so he left a message asking him to call back.[9]

Having drawn a blank with the army, he reverted to his original idea of calling J. Edgar Hoover. He dialed REpublic 7100, the general FBI number, asked for Mr. Hoover, and was put through to his office. The receptionist connected him to a second office, where another secretary transferred him to a third office, which shuttled him off to a fourth office. He was about to give up when agent Duane L. Traynor came on the line.

Traynor turned out to be in charge of the Bureau's antisabotage unit. A mild-mannered lawyer from Minnesota, he had joined the FBI four years earlier, at the age of twenty-eight, because it offered a good starting salary and the prospect of steady work. He spent most of his time investigating reports of suspected sabotage in factories.[10] It was not a particularly glamorous assignment: the acts of "sabotage" were often nothing more than disgruntled employees throwing something into the machinery because they were mad at their foremen. Sometimes, workers reported imaginary incidents, just to cause trouble. But each allegation had to be investigated.

A couple of days earlier, Traynor had attended a meeting at FBI headquarters at which his boss recounted a strange story about the landing of German agents on Long Island. Although the details were sketchy, Assistant FBI Director D. M. "Mickey" Ladd had mentioned a man with a streak of gray running through the middle of his hair threatening a Coast Guard patrol on the beach at Amagansett, and trying to bribe him to go away. The Coast Guard had later retrieved a trove of sabotage equipment apparently buried by the Germans. As one of the few FBI agents who knew about the Amagansett incident, Traynor was on the alert for saboteurs, real or imaginary.

When Dasch phoned to say he had just arrived from Germany with an important story to tell, Traynor was skeptical, but at least he was willing to listen. "Did New York tell you I was on my way?" Dasch wanted to know. No, Traynor replied, but he could meet with Dasch anyway. It was already 10 a.m. Would eleven be convenient? When Dasch said he would prefer to come a little earlier, Traynor suggested 10:30. Since it might be difficult for Dasch to find his way to the right office, Traynor said he would send a car to pick him up at the hotel.

The phone rang in Dasch's room almost as soon as he got off the line with Traynor. It was Colonel Kramer of the War Department returning his call. Dasch told the colonel that the FBI had already sent a car to fetch him, but he would keep in touch. He then quickly finished dressing, and scribbled out a note for Burger, which he handed to a room service waiter with the breakfast dishes, for mailing to New York. He began the letter with the greeting "My dear Friend Pete," an agreed-upon signal to reassure Burger that he was not writing under duress.

> Got savely into town last night and contacted the responsibly parties. At present I'm waiting to be brought over to the right man by one of his agent.
>
> I had a good night rest, feel fine physical as well as mentally and believe that I will accomplish the part of our participation. It will take lots of time and talking but please don't worry, have faith and courage. I try hard to do the right thing. In the meantime take good care of yourself and of the boys. Please don't go all over town. *Keep silent* to *everybody.* I promise you, to keep you postered on the future developments.
>
> Before I left you, I begged the mgr. of your hotel, Mr. Weil, to take good care of you, for you are a jewish refugee, so please act accordingly.
>
> Best regards and Wishes,
>
> Geo. J. Dasch.
>
> PS I'll forward to you my address where you reach me, via mail or phone, soon.[11]

Dasch was standing in the doorway of his room, fully clothed, when the agents arrived. He put on his hat, and accompanied them downstairs to the waiting Bureau car. On the five-minute drive to the Justice Department, down Pennsylvania Avenue, he struck his escorts as being "very highly-strung and anxious to relieve himself of some burden."[12] He said he had arrived in the country the previous weekend from Germany, but dodged a question about whether he had come in a U-boat.

"If the S.S. know what I am about to do, they will bump me off."

The agents escorted Dasch to the second floor of the Justice Department, through a rectangular archway emblazoned with the words JUSTICE IS THE GREAT INTEREST OF MAN ON EARTH. Built during the New Deal, the Justice Department was a mixture of neoclassical, Bauhaus, and Art Deco styles, with square pillars, a square courtyard, and wall murals depicting victories in the fight against organized crime. Everything seemed to be made out of aluminum, marble, and glass. The FBI occupied two floors of the seven-story building, which it shared with the rest of the Justice Department. The agents took Dasch through a wide, echoing corridor to room 2248, on the Tenth Street side of the building, near the Mall.

As Dasch entered his office, the first thing Traynor noticed was the streak of gray running through his otherwise dark hair.[13] He suddenly became extremely interested in this seemingly implausible visitor. He dismissed the escorts, and offered the man a chair opposite his desk.

"I have a long story to tell, but I want to tell it in my own way," Dasch began.[14]

As Dasch was baring his soul to Traynor, Attorney General Francis Biddle was preparing a memorandum for President Roosevelt noting the "first discovery of definite evidence" of a sabotage plot by Nazi Germany against the United States.[15] All coastal commands were on the alert for landings similar to the one that had already taken place on Long Island. In the meantime, Biddle told the president, it was essential to keep news of the landing out of the papers in order to allow the FBI to track the saboteurs without alerting their prey. The president totally agreed.

When he heard about the sabotage plot, Roosevelt was at his family home in Hyde Park in upstate New York, his lifelong refuge from the cares of the world. He had a lot on his mind, including a visit from Winston Churchill. The British prime minister had arrived in Washington on Thursday evening, after a twenty-seven-hour flight across the Atlantic by seaplane. He would spend Friday and Saturday as Roosevelt's personal guest at Hyde Park, and the two leaders would then travel back to Washington together.

After watching Churchill's plane make a spectacularly bumpy landing on a makeshift airstrip around noon, Roosevelt took the prime minister on a tour of his estate. The polio-stricken president insisted on driving the Ford Phaeton convertible himself, using an ingenious system of hand levers to replace the foot pedals he was unable to operate. Churchill had some anxious moments as Roosevelt jerked the car around the bluffs overlooking the Hudson River, in between talking business and urging his guest to admire the magnificent view. Churchill was more concerned that all the mechanical devices were working properly, without defects. To reassure his guest, Roosevelt invited him to feel his biceps, "which were amazingly strong and muscular."[16]

After lunch, the two leaders retired to FDR's "snuggery," a small room off the portico where he liked to swap gossip with his political cronies behind a green velvet curtain. Here the president showed the prime minister the latest American gadget, an RCA television set with a magnifying glass over the screen to enlarge the tiny picture.[17] After fiddling with the knobs for a while, and receiving some flickering images beamed from New York, the two politicians lost interest in the new invention and turned to matters of state.

Their discussions were dominated by three subjects. Roosevelt wanted to open a "second front" in France as soon as possible to relieve pressure on the Russians; Churchill was strongly opposed, believing that neither the British nor the American armies were ready to mount a cross-Channel invasion. They also discussed a plan to pool their scientific resources to build a devastating new weapon based on atomic fusion. Finally, they were both preoccupied by the war in the Atlantic. In Churchill's view, the heavy losses inflicted by German U-boats constituted "our greatest and most immediate danger."[18]

Charts prepared for the president by the Joint Chiefs of Staff underscored the prime minister's concern. Over the last three months alone, nearly four million tons of Allied shipping had been lost to submarine attacks and disasters at sea.[19] In the same period, the Allies had succeeded in building just over two million tons of new shipping. If the U-boats were able to continue causing such destruction, the war might be lost by default.

Two of the saboteurs from *U-584* had left Jacksonville by train for Cincinnati on Thursday. Haupt traveled on to Chicago; Thiel stayed the night in Cincinnati. Their two colleagues, Kerling and Neubauer, remained in Jacksonville until Friday morning, when they boarded the 8:30 a.m. train for Cincinnati. From Cincinnati, Kerling planned to travel to New York with Thiel, while Neubauer joined Haupt in Chicago.

As their train headed out of Jacksonville through northern Florida and southern Georgia, Kerling and Neubauer watched the little towns and railroad stations flash past the window. What they saw made them both very anxious, particularly Neubauer, who was still suffering from the shock of his narrow escape from death on the Russian front. There were men in uniform and civilian guards everywhere. Factories, bridges, and railroad sidings all seemed well protected. It would obviously not be easy to carry out the kind of sabotage mission for which they had been trained at Quenz Lake.[20]

Neubauer had mixed feelings about Operation Pastorius. On the one hand, he was a soldier of the Reich, accustomed to obeying orders. On the other, a sabotage operation seemed somehow unsoldierly. He thought of his wife, a loyal American citizen, who had stayed behind in Germany. On the submarine trip over, he had asked a crew member to deliver a letter to her, suggesting she try to return to the United States on a neutral ship as part of an authorized exchange of American and German civilians.[21] Before sealing the letter, he had shown it to Kerling, his group leader. To his surprise, Kerling made no objection, even though Kappe had forbidden them to communicate with their families.

Ever since landing in America, Neubauer had the feeling he was being watched, a sensation he felt even more strongly now as he sat in a train crowded with men in uniform. He was unnerved by ordinary, everyday occurrences. When the train reached Atlanta, he wanted to buy a newspaper, but the kiosk was just outside a gate, next to which "a couple of fellows were standing in civilian clothes."[22] In his paranoid frame of mind, he decided that the two civilians must be FBI agents, so he got back on the train without buying the paper.

As they traveled north, Neubauer steered the conversation to a previously unmentionable subject: the feasibility of carrying out the sabotage mission. Instead of dismissing his fears out of hand, Kerling seemed to be thinking along similar lines. Back in Germany, he had boasted that the American soldier was "no match" for the German soldier. Now he was not so sure. He was particularly worried by the introduction of gasoline rationing along the eastern seaboard, which he had heard about on the submarine. Without gasoline, it would be very difficult to go back to Florida to pick up the sabotage gear they had buried in the sand.

Together, they talked of various "ways out" if they were unable to go ahead with the sabotage plan. Kerling mentioned Mexico or Canada. Neubauer wondered what they should do if the American authorities heard about Operation Pastorius and sealed off the border. In those circumstances, perhaps the best solution would be to turn themselves in to the FBI?

Kerling seemed willing to consider anything. But on one point he was adamant: whatever they did, they all had to agree on a common course of action. No one would be permitted to just go to the FBI and say, "Here I am."[23]

SEATED ACROSS the desk from Traynor at FBI headquarters in Washington, Dasch was alternately animated and irritable, verbose and reticent. Smoking one cigarette after another, he announced that he had been sent to America by the German government to organize a "sabotage wave," then refused to say how he had arrived or provide the names of the men who came with him.

"I won't answer that kind of question."[24]

Having noticed the streak of gray running through Dasch's hair, just as the coastguardsman had described it, Traynor was pretty sure he had the right man. His main goal was to keep Dasch talking. This meant keeping him happy by plying him with cigarettes, playing to his vanity, and doing nothing to disturb the impression that Dasch was a free man voluntarily cooperating with the FBI.

After saying he planned to "begin at the beginning," Dasch asked for a Dictaphone to record his life story. The ever-courteous Traynor suggested that "it might be better" to bring in a stenographer. Dasch said this sounded like a fine way to proceed, and for the next six days and nights, fueled by a diet of milk, chicken sandwiches, and the occasional scotch and soda, he dictated a statement that eventually grew to 254 single-spaced typewritten pages.[25]

The statement soon became too much for a single person to handle, so a team of six stenographers was assembled, each of them taking dictation for an hour and then typing up the transcript, with multiple carbons. The copies were immediately distributed to the FBI officials responsible for tracking down the suspected saboteurs. Regular summaries of what Dasch was saying were also rushed to Hoover in his fifth-floor office.

By the time he got back from lunch, Hoover had decided that Dasch, alias Davis, alias "Franz V. Postoreous," held the key to the "whole affair." He was strengthened in this conviction by a surreptitious search of Dasch's hotel room by agents of the Washington field office. It took the agents just a few seconds to pick the lock on his briefcase and find the thick wads of fifty-dollar bills wrapped up in manila envelopes. They then went through the rest of his belongings, noting that they all appeared "brand new."[26] They were particularly intrigued by a pair of "small white metal emblems, about the size of a fifty-cent piece, which were cut in the shape of porcupines." One of the agents made a pencil tracing of the porcupines—a memento from Dasch's *U-202* trip—carefully replacing them in the pin tray where Dasch had left them.

Marshaling his troops like a military commander, Hoover called his assistant, Eugene Connelley, in New York at 2:36 and again at 3:57 to go over the latest developments. He reported that "Postoreous" was a "rather temperamental individual" who had nevertheless "taken a shine" to Agent Traynor, and was being permitted to tell his story in his own way.[27] He then reprimanded the New York office for failing to relay the message from Dasch the previous Sunday announcing that he was on his way to Washington. What disturbed Hoover most was the thought that Dasch "might have been considered crazy here and brushed off," in which case— horror of bureaucratic horrors—he might now be meeting with some rival agency, such as the Secret Service, or army or navy intelligence. He demanded a full investigation.

The next step, Hoover told Connelley, was to establish definitively that the man now talking to Traynor in room 2248 was the same man who accosted the Coast Guard patrol on Amagansett Beach.

JOHN CULLEN's life had been turned upside down since his mysterious encounter on Amagansett Beach. At first everybody had praised him for reporting the incident promptly, and turning in the money given to him as a bribe. But later, FBI agents had raised doubts about his story and kept watch over him day and night. They behaved as if he was somehow in league with the men on the beach. After failing to catch him in an obvious contradiction, they grudgingly accepted his version of events.

As reports flooded in of suspected German spies, the agents drove Cullen around German-inhabited areas of Long Island and New York to see if he could spot the man who had tried to bribe him. Sometimes, he would sit for hours in a car, waiting for a suspect to walk out of an apartment building or a restaurant.[28] But the search proved fruitless.

On Friday afternoon, Cullen was taken to the FBI office in New York to meet with Connelley and examine a photograph album containing twenty-two pictures of middle-aged men of vaguely similar appearance. Did any of the pictures look familiar, Connelley wanted to know. Cullen narrowed the selection down to three, and then stared intently at an FBI photograph of Dasch, dressed in a suit and tie. He noted the light streak of gray in the man's hair, and the thin face.

"I don't think this is him, but it's the best likeness I have seen so far," he told Connelley finally.[29]

It was hardly a positive identification, but it was enough for Connelley, who excitedly reported the news to Hoover.

. . .

HERBIE HAUPT arrived at Chicago's Union Station around three o'clock on Friday afternoon, after a thirty-hour train ride from Jacksonville via Cincinnati, blissfully unaware that at that very moment one of his companions was meeting with the FBI. It was good to be home. Prior to traveling around the world, he had lived in Chicago for sixteen years, most of his life. He had gone to school in the German-inhabited neighborhoods of the North Side, goose-stepped down Western Avenue with other Bund supporters, got his first job as a messenger boy with the Chicago office of Western Union, and flirted with girls along the shore of Lake Michigan.

Both the city and his own fortunes had changed dramatically in the year he had been away. When he left Chicago in July 1941 in a friend's rickety 1934 Chevrolet on what promised to be the adventure of his life, he had just $80 in his pocket. America was still at peace. He was returning to a city at war in smart new clothes with a gold watch around his wrist and $10,000 packed away in his suitcase. Headlines about the arrests of Nazi sympathizers in the German-American community stared out at him from newspaper stands.

In many ways, Haupt was the accidental saboteur. Had it not been for a series of chance occurrences, beginning with his girlfriend getting pregnant and Haupt fleeing to Mexico to avoid getting married, he would never have ended up in Germany. Once there, he quickly decided he did not like it very much. Athletic and good-looking, with wavy black hair that he liked to smear with brilliantine, he was a "typical playboy type," in Burger's phrase.[30] He loved having fun, a commodity in somewhat short supply in Nazi Germany. For the twenty-two-year-old Haupt, Operation Pastorius was a ticket back to the pleasant, carefree life he had once led.

From the railroad station, he took a cab to the home of his uncle, Walter Froehling, at 3643 North Whipple Street, arriving around 4 p.m. In Berlin, Haupt had agreed with Kappe that he would use Froehling as a mail drop and point of contact in Chicago.[31] The Froehlings lived in a two-room apartment on the ground floor of a two-story detached house, with a small garden out back. Froehling's wife, Lucille, answered the door. She was amazed to see Herbie. The last time anyone had heard from him, he was in Japan, working on some farm. He told the Froehlings he had come to their house first because he did not want to give his mother too much of a shock.

His parents would have to come over right away, Lucille and Walter decided. To cushion the surprise, Walter Froehling invented a cover story. He telephoned Herbie's mother and told her his wife was ill and needed

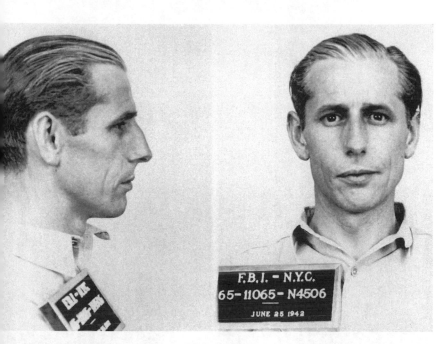

Dasch mug shots

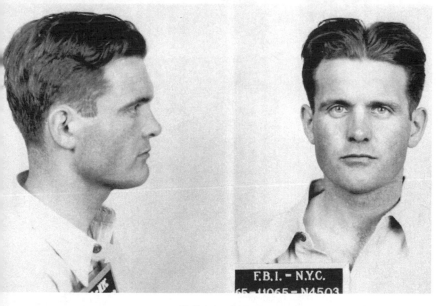

Kerling mug shots

Ernst Peter Burger

Heinrich Heinck

Herbie Haupt

Richard Quirin

Hermann Neubauer

Werner Thiel

Prewar photograph of German war ministry and Abwehr headquarters on Tirpitzüfer near the Tiergarten, where Operation Pastorius was planned

Quenz Lake

The Quenz Lake farmhouse

Burger's drawing of a pea-in-bottle detonating device

The handkerchief with secret writing that
Dasch gave to Kerling

Wartime photo of U-584, the submarine that landed Kerling and his group at Ponte Vedra, Florida, on June 17, 1942

Hans-Heinz Linder, commander of U-202

The crew of U-202, with cook Otto Wagner in the middle

*Present-day photograph of Amagansett Coast Guard post where
John Cullen was stationed on the night of June 13, 1942*

*osite page, above. Present-day
ograph of Amagansett Beach

*Present-day photograph of
John Cullen, the coastguardsman
who ran into Dasch on the beach*

*Cullen arrives for trial of saboteurs as
Heinck is escorted out of the courtroom*

FBI agent Duane Traynor, who was first to interrogate Dasch

Opposite page, ab[ove] Kerling looks on as FBI agent [searches] for buried sabotage equipm[ent] The laces on his shoes [were] removed to preve[nt] suicide atte[mpts]

Chicago Theater, a meeting place for Haupt and Neubauer

Opposite page, be[low] Sabotage boxes recov[ered] from Ponte Vedra B[each]

Dasch escorted into the courtroom

Opposite page, ab
Biddle, in white
presents evidence to
agent Charles Lann

Above: Dasch listens during the trial. Haupt is on the
other side of the soldier.

Burger listens to evidence.

Opposite page, be
Wide-angle shot of tribunal rc
The judges are at the back of the rc
next to the

Biddle and an aide, Oscar Cox, arrive for opening day of the Supreme Court session, Wednesday, July 29.

Saboteurs are loaded into a prison van at end of the tribunal session.

FBI Director J. Edgar Hoover (right) and aide Clyde Tolson arrive for the Supreme Court session.

Artist's conception of saboteur execution on Saturday, August 8, 1942

Wanted poster for Walter Kappe

Armed soldiers guard the D.C. jail as the bodies of the saboteurs are taken away.

FBI shots of Hans and Erna Haupt, parents of Herbert Haupt

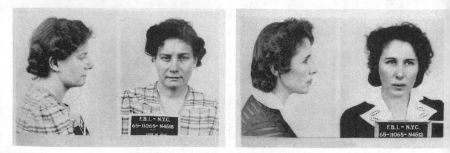

FBI shots of Hedy Engemann and Marie Kerling, mistress and wife of Eddie Kerling

help. When Erna Haupt arrived, she was escorted into the bedroom by a smiling, perfectly healthy Lucille. Her son was waiting behind the door.

"Herbie, where have you been?" she gasped.[32]

"Germany."

"How on earth did you get here from Germany?"

"Well, I'm back" was all he would say.

Suddenly she felt faint, almost "paralyzed." She had to sit down and rest. A few minutes later, Herbie talked about coming back on "a sub." The story sounded unbelievable, but she was so pleased to see him she did not press him on the details. She could not get over how well he looked, and what fine clothes he was wearing. "I made some money in Germany," he explained.

Hans Haupt showed up a couple of hours later, after returning home to find a note from his wife explaining where she had gone. He arrived as everybody was sitting down to dinner. "What would you say if Herbie were here?" Erna asked him softly, putting her hand on her husband's shoulder.

"Herbie?"

As the elder Haupt walked closer to the table, grabbing a chair for support, his son came out of the bedroom. Hans was so startled he "didn't know what to think." It was not until after supper, while his wife helped Lucille Froehling put the children to bed, that he finally confronted his son. "Now, Herbie, tell me from the beginning how you left and how you returned."[33]

It was a long story, but Herbie launched into it with enthusiasm. He had left Chicago on June 16, 1941, with a German-American friend, Wolfgang Wergin. At first they planned to spend a few weeks south of the border and then come back. But their money ran out after a week in Mexico City. After various adventures, they ran into a German-Canadian trapper named Joseph Schmidt, who suggested a way out of their predicament. The German consulate in Mexico City was recruiting laborers for a German-run "monastery" in Japan, Germany's Axis ally, and would pay their fare to Japan. Together with a dozen other young Germans, including Schmidt, Haupt and Wergin set sail for Japan on July 26.

The "monastery" turned out to be a labor camp run by German monks, with no sanitation and harsh working conditions. The two Chicago boys took one look at it and left for Tokyo, where they again threw themselves at the mercy of the German consulate. They were told that if they did not want to work in the monastery, they could sign on as seamen on a German freighter that would soon be sailing to Europe via Cape Horn. This seemed like the more attractive alternative, although they wondered if they had made the right choice as they rounded the Cape. Hundred-foot waves towered over the 8,000-ton freighter, threatening to crush it to pieces. Wergin later recalled that the boat would "go up so high, half of it would be out of the water, the propeller would spin around like crazy, and then it would crash down. We were scared. You would have to be an idiot not to be scared."[34]

The 20,000-mile trip took 107 days. They reached the French port of Bordeaux, then under German control, on December 11, the day Nazi Germany declared war on the United States. The Gestapo could not decide whether they were American or German and hauled them in for numerous interrogations, before eventually permitting them to visit their relatives. Herbie had a grandmother in the Baltic port of Stettin; Wolfgang's family was from Königsberg in East Prussia, near the border with the Soviet Union.

Herbie gave his father and uncle a somewhat romanticized account of his recruitment for intelligence work and his trip back to the United States on board a U-boat. He claimed—falsely—that they had sunk several ships on the way across. By now, Hans and Walter were beginning to think that Herbie really had been in Germany. He was using German expressions he had never used before, and seemed to know all about their relatives back home. Their remaining doubts vanished when he produced a green zipper bag with nearly $10,000 concealed beneath a false bottom, and asked his uncle to keep it somewhere safe. When they asked Herbie how he got the money, he replied, "The German Government."[35]

It was nearly eleven o'clock at night, and everyone was tired. Herbie's joy at seeing his parents was turning to testiness. He became "awfully nervous" when they mentioned that the FBI had been looking for him because he had failed to report for the draft.

"All you do is talk and talk," he snapped.[36] "Leave me alone for a while."

The Haupts took their son home, driving back toward the Loop to their apartment on North Fremont Street. As Erna prepared a bed for Herbie on the couch, he produced more wads of bills from his money belt. He counted out the money—it came to around $3,600—and transferred it to an envelope, which he hid under the rug in his parents' bedroom.

Suddenly, Erna and Hans Haupt felt very scared.[37]

In New York, Burger was trying to keep Heinck and Quirin from worrying too much about Dasch. The best distraction, he decided, was the whorehouse. Around 6 p.m. on Friday, he met the two men on the street near their lodgings, took them out for a meal, and then brought them back to his room at the Governor Clinton. From there, he telephoned Frankie, their friend from the Swing Club, who gave him an address on Eighty-sixth Street.

While Burger was in the bathroom shaving and taking a shower, he could see Heinck in the mirror rummaging through the drawer of his desk and finding a note from Dasch. Burger was alarmed to see Heinck read the letter, show it to Quirin, and then replace it in the drawer. Although the note made no mention of Dasch's intention to betray Operation Pastorius, it did talk about going to Washington "to straighten everything out." Afraid that Quirin and Heinck would do him some "bodily harm," Burger quickly finished dressing and hustled them out of the hotel.[38] Much to his relief, neither of them mentioned the note.

Instead, they piled into a taxicab and headed uptown to Eighty-sixth Street. Quirin and Heinck were still very suspicious of Dasch, and guessed he might have "run out" on them, but they were also looking forward to their night on the town.[39] As promised, there were three girls waiting for them, supervised by a madam named Anna. They stayed until three o'clock in the morning.

In Washington, meanwhile, Dasch was still talking to Traynor, pausing only for a light supper of clam chowder, ham salad, and milk. By now, he was almost on first-name terms with his interrogator.[40] He demonstrated his familiarity with American popular culture by addressing Traynor as "Pie," after the great third baseman for the Pittsburgh Pirates. The FBI man reciprocated by calling him "George." He was confident he would eventually extract enough information from Dasch to track down his accomplices.

The agents poring over the typewritten transcripts from room 2248 were still frustrated by the gaping holes in Dasch's statement. He had mentioned a second group of saboteurs who were meant to land in Florida around June 16, but did not provide a more precise location. He produced a handkerchief on which he had written a list of contacts in invisible ink, but he claimed to have forgotten the chemical needed to bring out the names. He talked about a rendezvous with the other saboteurs planned for July 4, but refused to say where it would take place.

Hoover suspected Dasch of trying to use his information as a bargaining chip, that he was hoping to be seen by the FBI as the indispensable go-between for the arrest of the other saboteurs. To some extent, the FBI director was prepared to play along. Talking with Connelley by phone that evening, he said he would like to use Dasch as "a decoy" for unraveling the entire plot.[41] If the FBI could arrest the other saboteurs and hold them incommunicado, they might be able to grab further teams of agents sent over from Germany. They would also have a channel for feeding false information to Berlin.

On the other hand, Hoover also feared that the FBI would be robbed of much of the credit for rounding up the saboteurs if news of the landings leaked out prematurely. An Associated Press reporter had already called to check a rumor about the arrest of four German agents who had landed in Florida. At first, Hoover was inclined to dismiss the story: he knew very well that there had been no arrests, at least not by the FBI. But gradually his bureaucratic paranoia got the better of him. Perhaps the navy or some other government agency had made the arrests and were waiting for the right moment to "flamboyantly announce" the nabbing of Nazi agents. It would make the FBI look bad.

By 11:30 p.m. on Friday, after more than twelve hours of nonstop talking, Dasch was hoarse and exhausted. He asked Traynor to go back to the hotel. He had one final nugget of information to pass on before they broke off for the night: his friend Peter Burger was staying in room 1421 of the Governor Clinton Hotel in New York.[42] While Dasch was unable to provide the exact whereabouts of the other two members of his group, he was confident that Burger would certainly know how to find them.

It was the break the FBI had been waiting for. With this information, they should be able to round up the remaining members of group number one, and focus their efforts on hunting down group number two. Instructions were issued to place Burger under surveillance, in the hope that he would lead FBI agents to Quirin and Heinck.

Soon after midnight, Traynor escorted Dasch back to the Mayflower, persuading him that it would be best if he spent the night with him in his room. Traynor would sleep in the spare bed. FBI agents had already commandeered the adjoining room, and had the entire hotel under observation. They had vetted anybody with the slightest connection with Dasch, including hotel guests who checked in around the same time. An FBI report noted that one of these guests acted "extremely nervously," pacing up and down the lobby.[43] The agents went through his luggage and listened to his conversations, losing interest only when it became clear he had come to Washington "for the purpose of obtaining a Federal position."

Before retiring to bed, Dasch had one more thing to show his new friend "Pie." He pulled his briefcase from under his bed, unlocked it, and took out three large envelopes, each crammed with more money than the agent had seen in his life.

Traynor did his best to feign surprise.

CHAPTER NINE

THE INVADERS

(JUNE 20–22)

T HE FBI HAD still not put a tail on Peter Burger when he stumbled back to his room at the Governor Clinton Hotel at three o'clock on Saturday morning after what he later described as a meeting with "some chance girl acquaintances."[1] But they arrived in force soon after breakfast, establishing a base of operations in the neighboring room. Since there was still no sound from Burger by 11:30 a.m., the agents made what was known in police jargon as "a mistake of identity call" to his room: when the subject answers, tell him you have dialed the wrong number.[2]

Five minutes later, Assistant Director Connelley reported to Washington that Burger was just getting up, apparently as a result of the FBI call. Agents also intercepted the letter that Dasch wrote to Burger from Washington the previous day, telling him to look after "the boys." They allowed Burger to receive the letter, calculating that it would encourage him to meet with Quirin and Heinck.

Burger finally emerged from his room at 2:40 p.m. Five FBI agents followed him as he turned right on Seventh Avenue, cutting across to Fifth Avenue along Thirty-third Street. He then walked north on Fifth Avenue for eight blocks until he reached the Rogers Peet clothing store, where he stood in the doorway, as if waiting for someone. Sure enough, he was soon joined by two other men: one slender with a long face and prominent nose, the other swarthy with a large scar running across his forehead. After picking up some packages from the clothing store, the three men entered a restaurant, where they ate a meal. As they emerged from the restaurant, FBI agents observed them shaking hands with each other and saying goodbye.

Burger walked back to his hotel, trailed by the agents.[3] Quirin and Heinck took a bus back uptown toward their lodging house, getting off at Broadway and Seventy-second Street. They were killing time. Before meeting Burger at the clothing store, they had visited a cinema to watch the latest newsreels, including one about the big New York at War parade the previous Sunday. They had no immediate plans, but thought vaguely about going to a beach or an amusement area such as Palisades Park, across the river in New Jersey, over the weekend.

Heinck told Quirin he had a few purchases to make, but would be right along. He visited a drugstore, and then a delicatessen. Quirin continued walking up Amsterdam Avenue.

The agents arrested Quirin first, at 4:30 p.m., bundling him into an FBI car and driving away at top speed. They apprehended Heinck a few minutes later as he was coming out of the delicatessen. Both men were taken to the federal courthouse in Lower Manhattan, where the FBI had its New York headquarters. There they were "processed" for arrest by being photographed, fingerprinted, and issued a set of prison clothes. They were then escorted to detention cells on the thirtieth floor of the building.

Back at the Governor Clinton, Burger tried on the new sharkskin suit he had bought at Rogers Peet. He had just sat down to read the newspaper when Connelley and several other FBI agents barged in through the open door. The expression on his face was one of immense relief: he told the agents he had been waiting for them to show up ever since Dasch went to Washington. After he was led away, the agents began looking through his belongings. Their meticulous typewritten inventory included the following items:

- 1 Leica camera #220033 and brown leather case.
- 1 letter of recommendation of Wisconsin National Guard.
- 1 lock of blonde hair.
- 1 photograph of woman with blonde hair.
- 1 pair light brown shoes 8½C with shoetrees.
- 1 leather pocket book in the inside of which appeared the following inscription: Bucyrus Erie Company Safety Contest, 1930, "ALWAYS BE CAREFUL."[4]

That evening, the three men were interrogated separately. Burger struck FBI agents as "particularly cooperative," anxious to show that "he is

100% against Germany."[5] Heinck initially tried to conceal his visit with his friend Hermann Faje three nights earlier, but ended up confessing to everything. Quirin held out the longest, at first insisting he was a Portuguese farmhand named Richard Quintas. But his denials quickly broke down once he realized that the FBI already knew all about Operation Pastorius. When the agents showed him the vest the Coast Guard had found on Amagansett Beach, he admitted it belonged to him.

His interrogators asked if he considered himself a "German agent."[6]

"Well, something like that."

"When you left Germany wasn't it your intention to come to the United States and carry out your instructions?"

"Yes, it was."

"Would you have carried out your instructions in the event you had not been apprehended?"

"I might have."

Later, when shown the transcript of the interrogation for his signature, he added the words "I am not sure."

BACK IN Washington, in room 351 of the Mayflower Hotel, Dasch and Traynor had slept in late after their draining, fourteen-hour session of the day before. At 9:20, the inquisitor and the informant ordered breakfast from room service: orange juice, cereal, toast, and coffee. They did not leave the hotel until 11:10, stopping off at Hummel's Restaurant to allow Dasch to down a quick scotch and soda on the way to FBI headquarters.[7]

Traynor's gentle treatment of his subject was beginning to pay off. After initially refusing to answer certain sensitive questions, Dasch was now providing information on all aspects of Operation Pastorius. He was eager to demonstrate his willingness to cooperate, hoping to be rewarded with an important role in the fight against Hitler. He told his interrogators he would do anything he could to shorten "this lousy war." If he was allowed to direct propaganda operations against the Third Reich, he would rally millions of Germans to the Allied cause.[8]

"Do you think I shall have the opportunity of meeting your superior, Mr. Ladd?" he asked Traynor, referring to the head of the FBI's internal security division. "And Mr. Hoover perhaps?"

Traynor was noncommittal. Anything was possible, but he would promise nothing.

Dasch persisted. He wanted to meet the people in charge of American propaganda, to point out their errors. "I am sure they are making mistakes. I know this by listening to their propaganda. It's weak."

Traynor just nodded.

The more Dasch talked, the more "eloquent and oratorical" he became, FBI agents observed.[9] His manners were "very polished, similar to those of a head waiter." He spoke with a slight German accent, frequently using phrases like "by Christ" and "Christ sakes." The agents noted the "snappy" way he wore his clothes and his peculiar habit of "placing his index finger along his nose or up the center of forehead while speaking."

HAVING DEFUSED the threat from the first group of saboteurs, the FBI now needed to focus on the others. Although Dasch obviously knew much less about Kerling's group than about his own, he did provide some important leads. He had revealed Kerling's true name on Friday afternoon, and the FBI was able to dig up its old files about his adventures on the yacht *Lekala* in 1939 when he tried to slip out of the country with several other Hitler supporters. On Saturday afternoon, Dasch gave Traynor a full description of Kerling—blond hair, good dresser, thirty-four or thirty-five, worked mainly as a chauffeur in the United States, paid-up Bund member—and also revealed the names of Herbie Haupt and Hermann Neubauer.

Haupt, Dasch told Traynor, was "a very shrewd boy," the type "generally known in the United States as a drugstore cowboy."[10] Dasch had helped Kappe recruit Haupt back in March because he thought he possessed the "necessary qualifications" for a sabotage mission. When Haupt came over from Japan on a German freighter, he had been awarded the Iron Cross, Second Class, for spotting a British steamer while at his lookout post. He was strong, street-smart, and could be "very dangerous." But he also had a "romantic" streak, as demonstrated by his love of adventure and obsession with girls. He was a "clean-cut boy" who liked "flashy things," such as a big silver ring with Indian signs that he had picked up in Mexico. Both Haupt and Neubauer were likely to go to Chicago, Dasch disclosed.

Dasch was finally willing to reveal the place where he was to meet again with Kerling so they could begin their sabotage campaign. Before doing so, however, he wanted a promise to be allowed to "exercise some of my thoughts" about how to "grab those guys."[11] If the others suspected that he had given them away, not only his life might be in danger, but also the lives of his parents back in Germany. He asked Traynor to seal the understanding with a handshake.

The request seemed fairly innocuous to Traynor, so he gave Dasch his hand. After the handshake, Dasch revealed the time and place of his scheduled meeting with Kerling: the grill of the Hotel Gibson in Cincinnati, between noon and two o'clock on July 4.

The fourth of July was still two weeks away, however, and the FBI wanted to get on with its investigation. As Ladd went through the transcripts of Traynor's interrogation of Dasch, he decided that Chicago should become the next focus of the FBI manhunt. That evening, he called the head of the Bureau's Chicago office and ordered twenty-four-hour surveillance on all known relatives of both Haupt and Neubauer.

"Assign your best agents to this case," Ladd instructed. "This is one of the most important things the Bureau has done for years."[12]

NAZI LEADERS had high hopes for Chicago. America's second-largest city was one of the great centers of German immigration to the United States and German-American culture. One in five Chicagoans, seven hundred thousand people, could trace their ancestry back to the Fatherland. German journalists returning to Germany after Hitler's declaration of war on the United States in December 1941 had depicted Chicago as the American city "most tired" of the war, and most receptive to German propaganda.

These hopes were much exaggerated. It was true that prior to Pearl Harbor public opinion in the Midwest was more isolationist than on the East Coast, and less inclined to go to war against Nazi Germany. The *Chicago Daily Tribune,* which styled itself the "World's Greatest Newspaper" under the eccentric Colonel Robert McCormick, had excoriated Roosevelt for attempting to involve the United States in yet another European conflict. But now that the nation was actually at war, its editorial policy had undergone a 180-degree turn. On Saturday morning, on Haupt's first full day back in Chicago, the *Tribune* ran a front-page cartoon attacking Roosevelt and Churchill for not doing enough to defeat the Axis immediately. The cartoon was captioned "Too Little, Too Late."[13]

Even so, the government still had doubts about the loyalty of the German-American population in Chicago and elsewhere. A secret survey commissioned by the White House estimated that one in ten German-born Americans (as opposed to Americans of German origin) was disloyal to the United States. By this calculation, the saboteurs had some thirty thousand potential accomplices. The report also noted that the Bund had some twenty thousand members, that uniformed storm troopers had marched through the streets of large American cities, and that many German-American publications had become "vigorous advocates of Fascism."[14] In addition to outright Nazi sympathizers, there was another sizable group of German-Americans who could be classified as "opportunists ready to leap on the Hitler bandwagon . . . if it appears that the Axis is going to win the war."

As a community, the German-Americans were treated more kindly than Japanese-Americans, who were already being rounded up and sent to internment camps. They also fared better than in World War I, when jingoistic politicians demanded "100 percent Americanism" and German immigrants suffered from job discrimination and beatings. The anti-German sentiment was particularly strong in cities like Chicago, St. Louis, and Cincinnati that had a large German minority. By the end of the war, hundreds of German newspapers and periodicals had been banned and many states had passed legislation restricting German-language education and even the use of German books in school libraries. A campaign to rid the American language of German words resulted in sauerkraut becoming "liberty cabbage" and frankfurters being turned into "hot dogs."

While there was no comparable wave of anti-German hysteria in America in World War II, German-Americans were feeling an ever increasing burden of suspicion and mistrust by the spring of 1942. The newspapers were full of reports of Bund offices being closed down and leaders of German-American organizations being hauled in for questioning. "Chicago Bund Chief Admits Spy Charges," declared the front-page headline in the *Tribune* on the morning of Saturday, June 20.

Haupt's parents were typical of the group labeled "opportunists" by the government, but who nonetheless thought of themselves as decent Americans. Their ties with Germany were more cultural than political. A soldier in the German army during World War I, Hans Haupt started a grocery business in Stettin in 1921, but had to close it during the left-wing political upheavals that wracked the country soon afterward. Unable to find work in Germany, he came to the United States in 1923, and worked as a bricklayer and contractor, becoming an American citizen in 1930. A passionate amateur singer, he belonged to various German music groups and cultural organizations in Chicago, and was also a member of the German war veterans association. He never joined the Bund.

When Herbie reappeared in their lives after a year's absence, Hans and Erna were caught between conflicting loyalties. They wanted to help their son, but they also worried he was up to no good. The elder Haupts tried to resolve this conflict of loyalties by insisting that Herbie register for the draft and report to the FBI first thing Monday morning to clear up questions about his status. If he refused to go to the FBI, Hans told his son, he would not be able to stay in their home.

"Don't you like me any more, Father?"[15]

"Yes, Herbert, I like you, but do me this favor and do what I told you."

AFTER GETTING up late on Saturday morning, Herbie spent the rest of the day lounging around the house. In the evening, he decided he wanted to see the parents of Wolfgang Wergin, the friend who had accompanied him on his round-the-world adventures. Back in February, Herbie had suggested Wolfgang to Kappe as a possible recruit for Operation Pastorius. Wolfgang had gone to Berlin for an interview with Kappe, but showed no interest in a scheme he considered "idiotic." He had seen the FBI's successes in dealing with gangsters in Chicago in the thirties and was "in awe" of Hoover's G-men. He thought that Herbie was likely to meet the same fate as John Dillinger and Baby Face Nelson. Wolfgang tried to talk his friend out of joining the sabotage mission, but Herbie said he could not take Germany anymore. There was nothing to eat and nothing to buy in the shops. Besides, he added confidently, he would not get caught.

Previously, Wolfgang had always looked up to Herbie, his senior by two years. Herbie had always been the leader, Wolfgang the follower. But during their final meeting, at the home of Herbie's grandmother near Stettin, their roles switched and Wolfgang found himself trying to comfort his friend. Six decades later, he would still have a vivid memory of that emotional night. "All of a sudden, he was the younger one, and I was the older one. Something overcame him, and he started crying. We were in the kitchen, and we were staying up late after everybody else had gone to bed. We didn't go to bed, we just kept talking. He was terribly homesick."[16] Before saying goodbye, Wolfgang had asked Herbie to deliver a message to his parents.

Now Herbie was back in Chicago, while his friend was headed for the Russian front, the graveyard of millions of young Germans. Knowing that the Wergins would be upset when they discovered that he had returned home without Wolfgang, Herbie asked his mother to find a pretext for calling on them after dinner.

All three Haupts showed up at the Wergins' around midnight. Wolfgang's father, Otto, was out late, playing in a band at Haus Vaterland, a German-American social center. As he expected, Kate Wergin was "very much upset" that Wolfgang was still missing. Along with the message from her son—which amounted to little more than "I'm fine, I love you"—Herbie gave Mrs. Wergin a fifty-dollar bill from his money belt. He told her it was a present from Wolfgang. Considering the size of the gift and the fact that it was in dollars, which Wolfgang had no means of acquiring in Germany, this was an implausible story, but she accepted it gratefully: "It's the first time I have ever seen such a large bill."[17]

When Otto Wergin finally returned home, around three in the morning, Herbie gave him an excited account of his adventures with Wolfgang in Mexico and Japan. He described how he had been awarded the Iron Cross after he and Wolfgang succeeded in running a British naval blockade in a German freighter. "Did Wolfgang get the medal too?" Wergin senior wanted to know. Herbie confirmed that he had.

As the Haupts were leaving the Wergins', Herbie remembered he had to be at his uncle's house on Sunday morning, in order to receive a telephone call from Neubauer, who would soon be arriving in Chicago. His parents dropped him off at the Froehlings' as dawn was breaking.

HERBIE HAUPT spent the remainder of the night sharing a couch with a male cousin of the Froehlings who was visiting from Minneapolis. At eleven, he received a call from a very nervous Hermann Neubauer, who had just arrived in Chicago, and was staying at the LaSalle Hotel. They agreed to meet at 1:30 p.m. outside the Chicago Theater, one of the city's best-known landmarks.

At the theater, Haupt suggested they see a newly released movie, *The Invaders*, recommended by his aunt Lucille because of its uncanny similarity to his own adventures. It was showing a few blocks away at McVickers, another of the city's great Jazz Age auditoriums. Starring Laurence Olivier and Leslie Howard, the movie was about six German submarine men who are stranded in Canada after their ship is destroyed by the Canadian air force.[18]

If Haupt and Neubauer were hoping for a piece of upbeat escapism, or clues about how they could merge into American society, they were disappointed. For the next ninety minutes, they sat through a morality tale of good against evil, democracy against dictatorship, good Germans against bad Germans, in which the "invaders" were all killed, exposed, or defeated.

Some of the dialogue sounded like the rants they had heard from Kappe at Quenz Lake. "You are the first Germans to set foot on Canadian soil," the fictional U-boat captain told the six men who went ashore on a reconnaissance mission, thereby escaping the destruction of the submarine. "Today Europe, tomorrow the world. Heil Hitler."

Other characters poked fun at Nazi ways:

FRENCH-CANADIAN TRAPPER *[played by Laurence Olivier with an atrocious French accent]*: Do you really march around Berlin doing this? *[Mimics Heil Hitler salute and Nazi goose step.]*
NAZI INVADER: Yes, we do.

Far from helping the two real-life saboteurs feel more relaxed, the movie deepened their already strong sense of isolation and paranoia. One scene depicted the leader of an ethnic German community providing food and shelter to his compatriots from the U-boat while denouncing their Nazi ideology. Another showed the fictional invaders trapped in a crowd of civilians as a Royal Canadian Mountie read their descriptions over a loudspeaker. "Look closely at your neighbor," the stern voice urged, as thousands of eyes bore into the faces of the fugitives. "Sooner or later, their nerves will crack and they will give themselves away."

After the movie, Haupt and Neubauer went to a restaurant next door for a meal, but soon felt uncomfortable. "Let's get away from here," said Haupt. "We may be watched by the FBI."[19] As they walked to Grant Park by the side of the lake, Neubauer said he was so nervous he was unable to sleep. He had to force himself to eat. "I don't see how we are going to go through with this," he murmured.

There was little Haupt could do to help Neubauer. They agreed that any decision about Operation Pastorius would have to wait until after July 6, when Kerling arrived in Chicago, following his meeting with Dasch in Cincinnati. In the meantime, Haupt and Neubauer would meet again on Wednesday at 1 p.m., outside the Chicago Theater.

Haupt spent the evening at the Froehling house, avoiding an FBI stakeout of his parents' place at 2234 North Fremont Street.[20] By the time he got home, it was nearly ten o'clock. After a wasted day outside the Haupt apartment, the G-men had left for the evening.

EDDIE KERLING and Werner Thiel arrived in New York around noon on Sunday, about the time that Haupt and Neubauer were making arrangements to meet at the Chicago Theater. They had taken a roundabout route. From Jacksonville, they had traveled separately inland to Cincinnati because they believed that the FBI was keeping a much closer watch on direct trains up the East Coast. After meeting in Cincinnati on Saturday afternoon, they had taken the overnight train to New York.

From New York's Grand Central Terminal, they walked across the street to the Commodore Hotel, an ugly hulk named after the steamboat and railroad king Cornelius Vanderbilt.[21] Among other attractions, the hotel boasted "the world's most beautiful lobby," which looked like a drawing room in the middle of the Amazon jungle, full of ferns and palm trees. Kerling registered under the name of Edward Kelly, while Thiel gave his name as William Thomas. Exhausted by the all-night train ride, they went up to their shared ninth-floor room, lay down on their beds, and immediately fell asleep. They did not awake until early evening.

Of all the saboteurs, Kerling was the most enthusiastic Nazi. He professed to like Americans, but he was scathing about their fighting abilities. America, he felt, was a weak, deluded nation that had been tricked into going to war with Germany by "a small group of Jews."[22] Kerling expanded on these ideas in a letter to an American girlfriend, Miriam Preston, written two weeks before Pearl Harbor:

> To us it does not matter what Mr. Roosevelt intends to do. We are prepared for everything. You have no idea in America what your soldiers would have to put up with. I know America well. I know what you can put against us, but please believe me, Miriam, I feel sorry for the American soldier, for your brother, if he should have to fight against the German army. Russia had an army which had been trained for at least 10 years to fight us. Look what happened. I don't underestimate the courage of the American boy by no means, but against tactics, training and invasion of the kind you have never seen—he is a helpless child. Miriam, we are in for a struggle for life or death. We know it—that is why our spirit can't be beaten and why we are winning.[23]

But now that he was actually back in New York, what most preoccupied Kerling was not Nazi Germany's struggle for survival, but his exceptionally complicated personal situation. For the past ten years he had been married to a woman named Marie; they had worked together as a chauffeur-and-cook couple for wealthy Americans like Ely Culbertson, the contract bridge expert. But Marie was unable to bear children, and Kerling had a wandering eye.[24] He was a handsome man with a strong physique, heavy jaw, wavy brown hair parted in the center, and a boyish enthusiasm that struck some women as romantic. While in Florida, on the yacht *Lekala*, he had met a Miami waitress named Hedwig Engemann, who became his mistress.

Marie Kerling did not object to this arrangement. She regarded her husband as a friend rather than a lover and, after his return to Germany in June 1940, she began seeing another man. She encouraged Eddie to divorce her and marry Hedy, so he could have children of his own. Kerling, however, was not so sure. He felt "carefree and content" when he was with Hedy, but he had belatedly come to realize that he loved his wife. She had a "heart of gold," and he wanted to make things up with her.[25] The truth was he needed both Marie and Hedy.

The man who could help him resolve this conundrum—or at least put him in touch with both women—was an old Bund comrade, Helmut Leiner. Leiner, who had worked as a gardener on Long Island, lived in the Queens neighborhood of Astoria. On Sunday evening, after he woke up from his nap, Kerling took a subway to Astoria with Thiel. Since Kerling did not want to be seen by Helmut's parents, and risk embarrassing questions about how he got back from Germany, he sent Thiel on ahead to contact his friend. Thiel arranged for Kerling and Leiner to meet on the street.[26]

Leiner was a sick man. He was recovering from a bad bout of tuberculosis, and had only been released from the hospital three days earlier. But he agreed to accompany Kerling and Thiel back to Manhattan, and have dinner with him at the Blue Ribbon, a German restaurant just off Times Square. After dinner, all three men went to the Tavern Inn, a few doors down the street, where they spent the next three hours downing a succession of Tom Collinses, gin and sour mix with ice and a splash of soda. Leiner gave Kerling an update on Marie, who was working as a cook for a wealthy family in Midtown, and Hedy, who was running a grocery store on Second Avenue. He promised to arrange meetings with both women.

Kerling trusted Leiner completely. He trusted him so much that he had selected him as a possible point of contact with Dasch. Exactly one month earlier, on May 21, in the Abwehr laboratory in Berlin, Dasch had written Leiner's name and address on a handkerchief in invisible ink, in case he needed to get in touch with Kerling in an emergency. Although Kerling had no means of knowing it, that handkerchief was now in the possession of the FBI.

WHILE KERLING was looking for his old friend Leiner in Astoria, Dasch was having an early dinner with Duane Traynor at a Washington seafood restaurant called O'Donnells, a favorite haunt of FBI men. He was feeling "rather depressed," he told Traynor. He feared that the U.S. government would not permit him to undertake his "main mission," which was to aid the German people in overthrowing Hitler.[27] If he could not accomplish this goal, he might as well be "shot as a traitor and a spy." Otherwise, he would find a way to take his own life. The next day, Traynor wrote a memo analyzing the split personality of the saboteur-turned-informant.

> As an egomaniac, he likes to picture himself in two characters, one of George John Dasch and the other of George John Davis. George Davis is a stool pigeon, an informer and a traitor to the German government. [This] is the individual who is furnishing all the information in this case and who immediately reported his landing to the FBI in order that no sabotage would occur and no lives would be lost. On the other hand, George Dasch is the individual who is fighting for the German people, the true people of Germany who are opposed to the things that Hitler stands for. He believes these people to be in the majority in Germany at the present time but feels they are coerced into following Hitler's methods and program. This is the individual who will take part in the reconstruction of Germany after the war.

Dasch could be exasperating. Asked to describe the formulas for explosives that he had studied at Quenz Lake, he told Traynor he had not paid much attention. "If I like something, I learn it; if I don't like it, I don't learn it." On the other hand, he continued to provide useful information that could be used to track down his fellow saboteurs. At first he could not remember the real name of the fourth member of Kerling's group, who used the alias William Thomas, even though they had both traveled back to Germany together on the *Tatuta Maru*. Traynor tried to jog his memory by reading names beginning with "Th" from a telephone book, on the theory that the saboteurs used the same initials for their assumed name as for their real name. When he got to "Thiel," Dasch stopped him.

"Thiel! That's his real name. Werner Thiel. If you look through the records of the Nazi Bund, you will find him."[28]

On Sunday evening, Dasch suddenly remembered the name of the "smelly" chemical that would bring out the secret writing on the handkerchief he had shown Traynor during their first meeting. "Ammonia," he said excitedly. "I passed the handkerchief over a bottle of ammonia . . . It shows red until it dries. You read it slowly and then it goes away again. You have to do it slowly. Just pass it over ammonia water."[29]

By Monday morning, the FBI laboratory had deciphered four names and addresses, and concluded that the ink used for the secret writing was "undoubtedly phenolphthalein, a constituent of the most common laxatives."[30] Traynor and Dasch were soon poring over photographic enlargements of the handkerchief, trying to figure what the cryptic words meant.

"What the hell is 'Bingo'?" Dasch wracked his brain or, as he affectionately called it, his "noodle." "Now wait a minute. 'Bingo' is the name of this little kid Haupt. That is the name under which he is known in the German High Command."[31]

Next to "Bingo" was the name Walter Froehling, Haupt's uncle and contact person. "This is to be used in case we decide at our headquarters to find a farm, a hideout where we put the boxes. This Walter Froehling is either a relation of his or a friend or something to do with the Bund."

On the next line, Dasch found the name Helmut Leiner, with an address in Astoria, Queens. "He is a very good friend of Kerling . . . We agreed that any time I lost track of this Kerling guy, I should always get in touch with Leiner. He would tell me where this Kerling is to be found."

By lunchtime, Traynor's superiors had sent messages to FBI offices in New York and Chicago, ordering surveillance of everybody named on the handkerchief. In the meantime, Hoover prepared a memorandum for President Roosevelt reporting that the FBI had "apprehended all members of the group which landed on Long Island," who were being held "secretly and incommunicado."[32] He emphasized his own personal role in cracking the case, even though he had not yet spoken to any of the saboteurs:

I have taken detailed statements from each of the persons arrested and the story is a startling and shocking one. Long and extensive training is being given by the German authorities to specially selected men who in turn are being placed on board German submarines to be landed on the shores of the United States. The group which landed at Amagansett, Long Island, on June 13, 1942, was the first group to arrive in this country. The second group were landed approximately the same time on the coast of Florida. I expect to be able to have in custody all members of the second group. I am definitely informed that additional groups will be sent from Germany to the United States every six weeks to initiate a wave of terror within the United States by the commission of acts of sabotage against many of our key industries, factories, electric power systems and waterworks. I have been able to secure a list of these facilities that were to be included in the first acts of sabotage.

What Hoover failed to mention in the memorandum was that far from being "apprehended," the leader of the saboteurs had turned himself in to the FBI voluntarily after being dismissed initially as a "crank." That was the kind of extraneous detail that would only serve to "embarrass" his beloved Bureau.

THE FBI had been unable to find Herbie Haupt over the weekend, despite placing his parents' home under surveillance. On Monday morning, Haupt made the Bureau's job a lot easier.

At his parents' insistence, he registered for the draft. After visiting the local draft board and formally receiving a draft card, he took a taxi to the Chicago headquarters of the FBI. He told the receptionist he had just returned from Mexico and wanted to clear up questions regarding his draft status. The receptionist referred him to the complaint desk, where he explained that he had run away from home to avoid getting married.

Haupt's statement to the FBI was a mixture of truth, lies, and concealment. He omitted any mention of his trip to Germany, saying he had spent most of the last year in the mountains of southern Mexico living with Indians and prospecting for gold. His biggest problem was how to explain away the cable he had sent his parents from Japan while on the way to Germany. His mother had told FBI agents about the telegram the previous December, when they came looking for him, so he could hardly deny its existence. Instead he claimed that he himself had never been in Japan: the telegram had been sent by a friend acting on his behalf. He had wanted to convince his former girlfriend that he would not be returning home for a very long time. In order to deceive her, it had been necessary to deceive his parents as well.

The FBI agent seemed to accept this explanation, asking merely if Haupt would fight for the United States if drafted. "I would rather not fight against the German people," he replied coolly.[33] "But if I have to go to war, I will go." To Herbie's relief, he was then permitted to leave. "We have no further interest in you," the agent told him.

In the meantime, Assistant FBI Director Connelley had arrived in Chicago, charged by Hoover with ensuring "proper coverage" of the friends and relatives of Haupt and Neubauer.[34] Hoover was unhappy with the performance of the Chicago office and wanted Connelley to "straighten out the matter." Connelley assigned more agents to watch the Haupt residence, and was soon rewarded: at 12:25 p.m., the agents reported "a man fitting the description of the subject get out of a Yellow taxi" and enter the house.[35] Herbie had returned home following his visit to the FBI.

Rotating teams of agents proceeded to follow him for the rest of the day, as he visited bars, old friends, and his former boss at Simpson Optical Company, where he had worked as an optician before going to Mexico. The agents were under instructions not to arrest Haupt: they hoped he would lead them to Neubauer and perhaps to other members of his group.

ALTHOUGH HEDY ENGEMANN had not seen Kerling for over two years, her feelings toward him were as strong as ever. She had a vivid memory of their first meeting in Miami, at a time when he was being chased by the Coast Guard on suspicion of planning to sail his yacht *Lekala* to Germany illegally. A friend had arranged a double date, telling Hedy she had come across someone "very exciting." They had spent the day "fooling around" onshore, and he had then taken her back to the *Lekala* for the night. It was a lot of fun.

When Hedy discovered that Eddie was married, she was shocked, as if "the sky fell down on me."[36] She decided she never wanted to see him again. But he was very insistent, and they went out with each other for the next three months "because I loved him so and could not find the strength to leave." As time went by, she decided it did not matter that he was married. She moved to New York, and Eddie insisted on introducing her to his wife. After he left for Europe, the two women became "very good friends as we both had the same heartache," in Hedy's phrase. Marie Kerling even encouraged Hedy to join her lover in Germany. Hedy also became friendly with many of Eddie's friends from the Bund, including Helmut Leiner.

On Monday afternoon, Leiner appeared at Hedy's grocery store, and said he had a "big surprise" for her. He persuaded her to come with him to Central Park, where Eddie was waiting. As Hedy and Eddie fell into each other's arms, Leiner discreetly excused himself. Hedy was "dumbfounded" to see her lover. Her eyes told her that Eddie was there before her: the engaging smile, the slender physique, the twinkling look in his eye. But she found it difficult to accept "the fact that he was back." It was like living a dream.

Initially, Kerling refused to tell Hedy how he got back from Germany, saying coyly, "Ask me no questions and I will tell you no lies."[37] When she remarked that the only way he could have traveled across the Atlantic was by submarine, he smiled enigmatically. They talked for an hour, chatting about old friends as they walked hand in hand through the park. When Hedy finally said she had to get back to the grocery store on Second Avenue, Kerling invited her to join him and Leiner for dinner.

They met around nine at a German steakhouse near the Commodore Hotel. After a drink or two, Eddie began to open up, and soon he was telling Hedy about the submarine trip. He described how they had to man the bilges and pump water, just like in the old days aboard the *Lekala*. He also told the story of their landing in a rubber dinghy.

Speaking with his usual infectious enthusiasm, Kerling now proposed another adventure. He would buy a car and they would travel together to Cincinnati, Chicago, Florida. She was also enthusiastic about this idea, even though it would mean finding someone else to look after the grocery store. She would do almost anything to be with him.

They spent the rest of the evening in a Cuban nightclub, talking and drinking until well after midnight.

CHAPTER TEN

WIVES AND GIRLFRIENDS

(JUNE 23–27)

Eddie Kerling woke up on Tuesday morning to read a small but alarming item in the *New York Mirror* gossip column. FBI agents, the newspaper reported, were "swarming through the Florida swamps because of stories that Nazi submarine crews in civilian clothes are at large in that state."[1] Kerling showed the item to Thiel. Having just arrived from Florida, the two saboteurs naturally assumed that someone must have heard about their landing.

"I think we had better forget the whole thing," Kerling muttered.

That afternoon, he met Leiner at Pennsylvania Station. They took a train across the river to New Jersey to look for the Lutheran pastor whose name Kerling had written down in invisible ink on a handkerchief as a useful contact in America. The expedition proved futile—Father Emil Krepper was evidently out of town—and Kerling and Leiner returned to Manhattan without accomplishing anything.

They had dinner together at the Crossroads Inn on Times Square. Having arranged Kerling's reunion with his mistress, Leiner agreed to act as the go-between to his wife. He called Marie Kerling from the restaurant, and suggested they get together later that evening, without telling her Eddie was in town. After some discussion about the best place to meet, they finally settled on Hedy Engemann's grocery store around 9:15 p.m.

When they finished dinner, Kerling and Leiner went their separate ways. The plan was for Leiner to bring Marie to a restaurant on the corner of Lexington and Forty-eighth Street. Before he could see his wife, Kerling had one other engagement. He had promised to meet Thiel and one of Thiel's old Bund friends for drinks in a bar on Forty-fourth Street. Around

10:30, he would excuse himself and join Marie at the Brook Restaurant, four blocks north.

The Engemann grocery store was located in the heart of Yorkville, at 1653 Second Avenue, beneath a modest awning advertising "Everything for the Table." Marie had still not arrived when Leiner pulled up in a taxi, so he was able to spend a few moments conspiring with Hedy about the logistical arrangements for the evening, which were beginning to resemble a French farce, with multiple entries and exits of wives and lovers from adjoining bedrooms. They agreed that Hedy would pretend that she knew nothing about Eddie's return.

When Marie finally showed up, Leiner joked that he had arranged a "blind date" for her.[2] "But I don't want to go on a blind date," Marie complained. Leiner then took her aside and told her the "startling news" that her husband had returned from Germany and wanted to see her that very evening. She was so shocked she started to cry. She had so many questions: How had he come to the United States? Where was he living? What did he intend to do here? When was he going back? Leiner replied that Eddie would explain everything.

Marie could not believe that her husband was really back in New York. "You're crazy," she told Leiner.[3] She talked to Hedy, who said she could not believe it either, even though she had seen Eddie twice the previous day. But Leiner insisted it was true, and promised to take them both to see Eddie immediately. Marie asked Hedy to come along. At first she was reluctant, but eventually she agreed—after changing into a more flattering dress.

Shortly after 10:30, they all climbed into a taxi, and headed down toward Forty-eighth Street, where they entered the Brook Restaurant. They found a private booth and ordered drinks. There was no sign of Eddie, but Leiner kept on saying he was not far away, and would certainly show up in the next few minutes.

They waited for half an hour, an hour, ninety minutes. Leiner was unable to explain what had happened. At midnight, a very irritated and very confused Marie announced she was going home.

TUESDAY WAS Herbie Haupt's fifth day in Chicago. He had resumed what his mother called his usual "lively routine": visiting friends, hanging out at bars and restaurants, and playing cards and dice.[4] He spent the morning shopping for a snap-brim straw hat, and then took in a matinee performance of a new Marlene Dietrich movie, *The Lady Is Willing,* at the local cinema.

The future of the sabotage mission was unclear—it made him nervous just thinking about it—but he had made two important decisions about his own future. He wanted to make things up with his old girlfriend, Gerda Stuckmann, and he wanted to buy a new car.

Before leaving for Mexico, he had owned a 1941 Plymouth that was being used by his father for construction work and was beginning to look "quite shabby."[5] In the early evening, he went with his father to a local dealership to inspect late-model used cars.

A 1941 black six-cylinder Pontiac sports coupe caught his eye, with a sticker price of $1,045. Herbie agreed to put up $100 of the $410 down payment for the car; his father said he would withdraw the remaining $310 from his saving account. They would pay off the balance in monthly $50 installments. It would take a day or so to get the car properly registered, and to make arrangements with the finance company. Herbie asked the salesman to attach an American flag emblem to the car before delivery.[6]

In the meantime, his mother had arranged a date for him with Gerda, a slim brunette with big brown eyes and a pretty face who had worked as a model and beautician. It was their first meeting since he rushed off to Mexico when she was five months pregnant. The baby had died mysteriously a few days after its birth. At least that was her story: there were also suspicions that she might have secretly given it away.[7]

Gerda showed up at the Haupt apartment around eight, excited and nervous. For the next two hours, she and Herbie sat together awkwardly on the settee in the front room, as his parents sat in the kitchen, wondering what was going on next door. Occasionally, Erna Haupt brought in drinks of whiskey and ginger ale.

Herbie did not tell Gerda about going to Germany, or his trip back on the U-boat. Instead he said he had been to Mexico and the "West Coast," and had returned to Chicago by train. He seemed "very nervous" to her, and she was at a loss to understand the reason.[8] Around 10:30, Herbie offered to drive her back to her apartment on Albion Avenue, in a northern section of Chicago, near Loyola University. They took his old Plymouth, stopping a block from her home, on a darkened, dead-end street leading to a railway embankment. Herbie explained that he did not want to go up to her apartment: her parents might be angry with him for walking out on her. But he had something important to tell her.

"Will you marry me?"

Gerda was stunned. She had been married once before, at the age of twenty, to a man named Herbert Melind, who had subsequently died. She was now nearly twenty-five, more than two years older than Herbie. She had been desperate to marry him when she was pregnant with his child. Now she was not so sure. Although she liked Herbie, she was bewildered by the sudden turn of events. Apart from a single card, postmarked St. Louis, she had not heard from him at all during the year he was away.

Not only did Herbie want to marry her, he wanted to marry her the very next day. He pulled out an engagement ring, and pressed ten dollars into her hand, so she could get the blood tests required by Illinois state law. He insisted he had changed his ways, and planned to get his old job back at the Simpson Optical Company.

"Why the rush?" she asked. But she promised to think it over, and give him an answer by the following Saturday. In the meantime, she would get the blood work done.

Parked inconspicuously around the corner were two black Hudson sedans belonging to the FBI with six agents inside. They watched as "a young lady" got out of the Plymouth "alone" at 12:05 a.m. and walked to "what was believed to be her apartment" at the end of the tree-lined street. They then followed "the subject" as he did a quick U-turn and drove home.

"I'VE BEEN working like hell from daybreak until dawn," Dasch wrote Burger midway through his interrogation in a letter intercepted by the FBI. "What I have thus far accomplished is too much to describe here. I can only tell you that everything is working out alright. Have faith and patience. You will see and hear me in the near future. Please stick to your job and keep the other boys content and please don't lose their sights."[9]

By the time Dasch wrote this note, Burger and the "other boys" in his group were all being questioned at FBI headquarters in New York. Dasch, by contrast, had the illusion of being a free man. Although he was accompanied everywhere by FBI agents, he still lived at the Mayflower Hotel, ate breakfast in the coffee shop, and dined at a different Washington restaurant every evening. Traynor was doing his best to keep his prize witness happy, even though he suspected that he would later have to "crucify him."[10] For his part, Dasch felt fine, apart from some "constipation," which he attributed to the nervous tension of the past few weeks.[11]

By Tuesday morning, the fourth day of Dasch's interrogation, Traynor and the other agents had squeezed out of him most of the details directly relating to the plot. They listened intently as he described plans to send over more teams of saboteurs. One such team, scheduled to arrive in "September or October," would probably be led by Dempsey, the pugnacious little boxer with the squashed-in nose who dropped out of sabotage school early on. But Dasch could provide few details about what these groups would do.

He was much more expansive when asked questions about his favorite topic, American propaganda to Germany. He described how he would get "mad as a dog" listening to American radio broadcasts that "called the German people Nazis."[12] The way Dasch saw it, American broadcasters were playing into the hands of Nazi propagandists who continually accused America of seeking the destruction of the entire German nation, not just the Nazi regime.

Occasionally, Dasch veered off into a subject that was of little interest to his interrogators, who were focused almost exclusively on the nuts and bolts of the sabotage plot. Before leaving Berlin, he had been sitting in Kappe's office when a German intelligence officer gave a vivid, harrowing account of the mass execution of 35,000 Jews in the Ukrainian capital, Kiev. According to the officer, the Jews were rounded up in groups of two or three hundred people, ordered to dig a huge pit in the ground, and then shot in the back of the head by S.S. officers so that their bodies tumbled into the pit. Dasch recalled that the officer "laughingly remarked that the trigger finger of the executing officers [often] became tired," in which case they were replaced by fresh executioners.

"I sat there on my little chair in the corner, my stomach turned. I didn't know what to do for a moment. I thought they were the dirtiest bastards on earth."[13] After the intelligence officer left the room, Dasch said he turned to Kappe, and remarked, "For Christ sake, this is an awful war and this is an awful way to kill people." Kappe rebuked him for being "chicken-hearted." "What kind of a German are you? We Germans have one mission, which is to kill all the Jews."

The FBI agents changed the subject. They had little time for Nazi atrocity stories. In retrospect, it is evident that Dasch had just given them an accurate description of the early days of the Holocaust.

. . .

FBI AGENTS had been following Kerling since Tuesday afternoon, when he met Leiner at Pennsylvania Station. They had obtained Leiner's name and address from Dasch's handkerchief, so it was a simple matter of waiting to see if he would contact anyone answering Kerling's description. They were soon rewarded.

That evening, the G-men followed Kerling to Lexington and Forty-fourth Street, where he entered a bar. He was soon joined by two other men. One of these men was Werner Thiel, who had been named by Dasch as a member of the Florida group of saboteurs. The other was Thiel's closest friend in the United States, Anthony Cramer, a longtime Bund member devoted to the Nazi cause. Later the FBI found letters written from Cramer to Thiel around the time of Pearl Harbor, while Thiel was back in Germany, denouncing the "Jewish cabal" that ran America and poking fun at Americans for thinking "too little with their brains and too much with their spinal cords."[14]

The agents watched Kerling as he chatted with Thiel and Cramer and then left the bar, at around 10 p.m., heading north on Lexington Avenue, apparently in preparation for his meeting with his wife. They allowed him to pace up and down for a few minutes, and then arrested him, bundling him into a Bureau car and driving him downtown to the federal courthouse in Foley Square.

Back at the bar, Thiel was observed passing a money belt to Cramer which, the agents later learned, contained about $4,000. The G-men permitted Thiel and Cramer to spend another hour and a half together, following the two men as they walked down the street for coffee and pie. They arrested Thiel shortly after he said goodbye to Cramer.

THE INTERROGATION of the two saboteurs began soon after midnight and continued all night. In Connelley's absence, the interrogations were supervised by the acting special agent in charge of the New York office, Thomas J. Donegan, a tough Irish cop with little patience for prevarication. Donegan summoned Kerling to his office at 1:55 a.m., and sat down with him on the settee.

"Tell us where the explosives are buried," he demanded, pointing at a large map of Florida he had with him in his office.

Kerling denied any knowledge of explosives.

"Tell us about the submarine you came in."

Kerling said he did not come to America in a submarine. He had come overland from Mexico.

"You dirty Nazi rat," Donegan exploded. "I know you came in a submarine. You are a fool if you think that I am going to sit here and listen to that kind of story from you."[15]

What happened next is disputed. Kerling later claimed that Donegan reached across the settee, pulled his hair down until his head was in his lap, and punched him several times on the left side of the face. After a few minutes, a doctor came in and asked him how he was being treated. When Kerling complained that he had been struck in the face, Donegan took him outside the room, and asked in a menacing tone of voice, "Did I hit you?" Fearing another beating, Kerling replied, "No, you didn't." He then told the doctor that he wished to withdraw his complaint. The doctor pronounced him "fine."

Thiel, who was interrogated after Kerling, would later tell a similar story. The only difference was that when the doctor asked whether he had been mistreated, he said right away that he had no complaints. "I thought there was no use telling the doctor that I was mistreated." Donegan acknowledged using "strong language" with both Kerling and Thiel, but denied any physical abuse.

Neither saboteur got any sleep that night. Whenever it looked as if they were about to drop off, an FBI agent was in their face, asking questions and demanding answers. At first, Kerling replied with monosyllabic grunts, refusing to talk about Thiel until he knew that he was also in police custody. He also did his best to protect his wife and mistress. Slowly, however, they dragged the details out of him.

"What were you meant to do in the United States?"

"Let me answer those questions tomorrow."

"We want to get this in general, not in detail. Just a few of these things now."

"I gave you enough. That was the arrangement. You said you'd let me sleep for a while and talk later."

"We must get a little more amplification than we have now."

"I can't think. What's the use?"

"You want water or a cup of coffee?"

"No."

"Where did you go to school then?"

"Brandenburg."

"How many were in the school?"

"Nine. No, eleven."[16]

HERMANN NEUBAUER felt so lonely cooped up in his hotel room that he bought himself a bottle of rum for company, even though he did not much care for alcohol. Like Haupt, he had relatives in Chicago, including his father-in-law, a Republican precinct captain on the North Side. But he steered clear of his wife's family, fearing that they might be under FBI observation.

On Tuesday evening, on the spur of the moment, Neubauer decided to take a chance and visit some old friends of his wife. Although he had never met Harry and Emma Jaques, he had seen quite a bit of Emma's sister and brother-in-law in Germany. He trusted them not to give him away. They were simple people, first-generation German-Americans who had arrived in the United States in the mid-twenties. Harry worked as a painter and decorator.

"I guess it looks kind of funny for me, a stranger, to drop in on you when you don't know me," he told them, before announcing that he was the husband of Alma Wolf.[17] Emma was dubious, as she had heard that Alma's husband was in a hospital in Stuttgart, having been seriously wounded on the Russian front. To prove his identity, Neubauer displayed the scars on his leg and cheek.

The couple sat Neubauer down in a chromium chair in the living room and offered him beer and cigarettes. They talked about various shared friends, including Eddie Kerling and his wife, Marie. While Emma was in the kitchen fixing sandwiches, Neubauer told Harry that he had arrived on a submarine on a mission for the German government. Jaques cut him off, saying he did not want to hear any more.

He did, however, agree to look after two envelopes containing around $3,600, which he placed on the coffee table in their living room. After Neubauer finally left, around two in the morning, Harry and Emma carefully placed the money in a five-pound coffee can, hid it on a shelf in the pantry, and went to bed.

BY THE morning of Wednesday, June 24, the FBI had six of the eight Nazi saboteurs in custody. Only two remained at large: Haupt and Neubauer.

Agents were keeping a twenty-four-hour watch on Haupt, and could arrest him at any time. The only reason for waiting was the belief he would lead them to Neubauer. Connelley reported to Hoover that he had fifteen places in Chicago under observation, including the home of Neubauer's in-laws. That afternoon, the FBI would get its best chance of grabbing Haupt and Neubauer in one swoop.

The only sign of activity in the Haupt household that morning had been the 7:05 a.m. departure of Hans Haupt, dressed in a blue shirt and suspenders. Herbie was inside the house, sleeping off his marriage proposal to Gerda the night before. He emerged from the ground floor apartment at precisely 1 p.m. The surveillance team noted that he was wearing a light tan suit with a red V-for-Victory pin in the lapel, dark brown tie and matching pocket handkerchief, brown and white sports shoes, and the light brown straw hat he had purchased the day before. After "loitering" in front of his front gate for a few minutes, he entered a Checker cab, and headed toward the Loop, Chicago's downtown district.[18]

Haupt got out of the cab at the State-Lake Building, on the corner of State and Lake Streets opposite the Chicago Theater, and entered Liggett's drugstore on the ground floor. FBI agent John Lynch supervised the surveillance operation from the lobby of the State-Lake Building, directly adjoining the drugstore. He could see "the subject" reflected in the shiny marble walls of the lobby: Haupt was sitting at the wooden lunch counter of the drugstore munching a sandwich. A second agent, James Berg, stood by the soda fountain, nonchalantly sipping a cup of coffee and stealing occasional glances at Haupt in a mirror. Agent Frank Meech stood on an elevated train platform with a commanding view of State Street. A fourth agent, Elmer Fletcher, sat in the FBI pursuit car around the corner on Lake Street.

At 1:35 p.m., Haupt came out of the drugstore's revolving wooden door and walked slowly down State Street, which was lined with wooden huts and construction equipment for the building of a new subway. Lynch followed closely behind, and watched Haupt enter the Oxford Shirt Shop, two doors down from the drugstore. In accordance with standard FBI procedures, Lynch then checked to see if there were any rear exits from the shirt shop. He asked Berg to relieve him in front of the store to watch for Haupt's reappearance. After Lynch established that there was only one way out of the store, he returned to his previous post.

Berg dropped into the store to check on Haupt on the pretext of purchasing a tie clasp. Although he could not see Haupt, he could hear a store clerk conversing with someone in a back room. An hour passed, then two hours. More agents arrived to reinforce Lynch and his men, but nobody resembling Haupt came out of the store. The subject had vanished.

Exactly how Haupt performed this disappearing act only became clear much later. In the few seconds that Lynch left the front of the shirt shop unobserved to confer with Berg, Haupt walked out the front door and crossed Lake Street to the Chicago Theater. As this was happening, Meech left his post on the El platform to take up a new one under the theater's light-studded marquee. During the thirty seconds it took Meech to walk down from the El platform and reach the front of the movie palace, Haupt must have slipped into the theater.

Haupt met Neubauer inside the theater's vast lobby, with its marble pillars, red-carpeted stairways, Louis XIV–style tapestries and drapes, and enormous chandeliers suspended from the five-story-high ceiling. When the theater was opened in 1921, with seats for five thousand people and a stage big enough for an opera, *Billboard* magazine proclaimed it "perhaps the most magnificent theater in the world," a piece of Versailles transported to Chicago.[19] The front of the house was decorated by a stained-glass window and dozens of laughing joker faces that seemed to mock the hapless FBI agents frantically looking for their quarry.

After the show—a Bob Hope movie featuring a gang of evil Nazi spies—the two saboteurs sat down on the faux Louis XIV furniture in the lobby. Neubauer was still a bundle of nerves.[20] That morning, he told Haupt, he had jumped out of bed in a cold sweat when someone knocked at the door of his hotel room unexpectedly. It turned out to be an electrician checking a broken light fixture, but Neubauer found it difficult to stop his hands from shaking violently. In addition to his fear of the FBI, he was afraid of running into someone he knew, as he had worked in the Chicago hotel industry before the war. He had decided to move to a hotel with a predominantly Negro staff, who, he reasoned, would be less likely to recognize him.

Haupt tried to boost Neubauer's morale by describing how he had sauntered into the Chicago office of the FBI to clear up his draft status. Nothing had happened to him, and he had walked right out again. To Neubauer, this sounded foolhardy. Nevertheless, he agreed to meet with Haupt again on Sunday night at the Uptown Theater.

After leaving Neubauer, Haupt phoned Gerda Stuckmann. She had completed her blood work for the marriage license, and wanted to know if he had also taken the test. He lied and said yes. They arranged a date for Saturday.

FBI agents stationed outside the Haupt apartment on North Fremont Street observed the "subject returning to his residence" at 5:30 p.m. Surveillance of the Oxford Shirt Shop was discontinued. Half an hour later, Herbie drove to the Warner Motor Sales Agency with his father to pick up his new car. At 6:30 p.m., the agents observed the younger Haupt leave the dealership in "a black 1941 Pontiac five passenger coupe having red wheels, a radio aerial on the left front side and red sticker on the right side of the windshield." They spent the rest of the evening chasing him around various Chicago nightspots. It was not until 1 a.m. that he finally returned home.

By Wednesday evening, Kerling was cooperating with his interrogators, having concluded there was no point in holding out any longer. He agreed to accompany FBI agents to Florida to locate the spot where he had buried the explosives when he first came ashore. Hoover called Connelley in Chicago, and ordered him to fly to Jacksonville to oversee the recovery of the arms cache. This was a "mighty important" operation and Hoover worried that someone else might mess it up.[21]

Kerling arrived in Jacksonville on Thursday morning on the overnight train from New York in the company of his FBI escorts. Connelley flew in by plane. In order not to attract any attention, they set off for the beach in a lone automobile. Four miles south of Ponte Vedra, Kerling told the driver to stop. He walked up and down the beach, carefully examining each clump of trees, without recognizing any of them. After about an hour, he had the FBI men drive him up and down Highway 140, until he spotted a fence next to an abandoned building.

He led the FBI agents along the fence to the tip of the sand dunes, where there was a grove of palm trees. "This is the place," he told them. By this time, he was exhausted, and could hardly stand. He had not slept for the past two nights, was sick with dysentery, and in a state of shock.[22] He was dressed in an open-neck shirt and dark pants; his guards had removed the laces from his shoes to prevent any suicide attempt. As the agents began digging into the sandy soil, the cocksure Nazi Party member who once boasted that the American soldier was no match for the German slumped to the ground, clutching his head between his knees.

There were four boxes buried in the sand. Connelley had arranged for the FBI's top explosives expert, Donald Parsons, to carefully examine each box. The contents were virtually identical to the sabotage materials recovered twelve days earlier at Amagansett.

As KERLING was scouring Ponte Vedra Beach for the buried boxes, Dasch was completing his marathon, 254-page typewritten statement. "My mind is all upside down," he told his interrogators, as he signed each page separately, making the occasional correction.[23]

The time had come to rid Dasch of the notion that he would play a starring role in the arrest of the other saboteurs. As gently as possible, Traynor explained that his plan assumed that the U.S. government was unaware of the landing on Amagansett Beach. In fact, the FBI had been making extensive inquiries of its own, long before Dasch came to the Washington office, beginning with the questioning of the young coast-guardsman, John Cullen. If the Coast Guard knew about the events on the beach, then other government agencies also knew. There was a danger that the newspapers would get hold of the story, causing members of the second group "either to go into hiding or immediately begin their wave of sabotage." Five saboteurs had already been arrested. Since Dasch was worried about the fate of his relatives back in Germany if it became known that he had betrayed Operation Pastorius, it seemed to make sense to arrest him as well.

By inventing a clever cover story, Traynor told Dasch, the FBI could make it appear that he had been betrayed by either Quirin or Heinck. In order to make the story convincing, the FBI could not merely pretend to arrest Dasch. It would have to treat him exactly the same as the other arrested saboteurs. While the Bureau would examine ways to allow Dasch to contribute to the propaganda war against Nazi Germany, Traynor would make no promises.

This was not at all what Dasch had had in mind when he walked into Traynor's office six days before. "If I am not treated fairly and squarely," he told Traynor, "I will lose all faith in human nature. I might as well be dead. And if I have to die, I might just take another life to avenge myself."[24] He then began to cry.

At 12:15 p.m., Traynor informed Dasch he was under arrest, and would be sent to New York to join the other saboteurs. Agents went through his pockets, and confiscated all his personal property, including his gold wristwatch, Schaeffer pen, gold tie clasp, and brown fedora hat. They catalogued his stash of money, which came to a total of $82,710.17, and had him sign a receipt. Before escorting him to the railroad station, they took him to see Mickey Ladd, the assistant FBI director in charge of internal security. Ever since he arrived, Dasch had been pestering Traynor to allow him to meet with Hoover, but had to settle instead for a ten-minute meeting with Ladd.

"Have you read my stuff?" was Dasch's first question on entering Ladd's office.[25]

"I have only managed to read part of it so far."

"Have you read the part about propaganda?"

"Not yet."

Dasch was crushed.

He was taken by train from Washington to Jersey City, and then by car ferry to Manhattan, in order to avoid running into crowds of travelers at Pennsylvania Station. After treating him to a final dinner at a restaurant around the corner from FBI headquarters, his escorts took him to a sixth-floor conference room where they told him to change into his prison clothes. He was then photographed with a prisoner identification tag around his neck and examined by the same doctor who had asked Kerling and Thiel if they had any "complaints" two nights before.

From this point onward, there was no longer any pretense that Dasch was a free man. FBI agents chronicled his every move. They noted in a logbook that the prisoner "urinated at exactly 11:40 p.m.," while en route to detention cell number three on the thirtieth floor of the federal courthouse, next to the cells of Burger, Quirin, Heinck, Kerling, and Thiel. "Appears a little depressed."[26]

THURSDAY WAS the day that Herbie Haupt was meant to start work at his old job at the Simpson Optical Company. But that morning he complained to his mother of pains in his hip and heart and said he could not report to work.[27] He had something more important than work on his mind. Having registered for the draft the previous Monday, he needed to find a way to avoid being drafted.

He knew just the person to help him: an old Bund acquaintance named William Wernecke. The Wernecke family owned a horse farm outside the city where Herbie liked to take his girlfriends riding. Wernecke had amassed a large collection of rifles, shotguns, dueling pistols, and several thousand rounds of ammunition. Before Haupt left for Mexico, he and Wernecke used to practice their marksmanship at the farm dressed in the Bund uniform of black trousers, brown shirts, and black ties. Wernecke's ambition was to be a storm trooper following a Nazi victory in the United States, but his views were so extreme that he was expelled from the Bund for factionalism.

A draft dodger himself, Wernecke was more than willing to help other Nazi sympathizers escape compulsory military service, which had been introduced in the United States in November 1940, more than a year before Pearl Harbor. His techniques included feigning deafness, rheumatism, and heart trouble, and joining an obscure religion, the "Allied Christian Management Army," whose guiding tenet was a refusal to go to war for reasons of conscience.

The alliance between Haupt and Wernecke was largely one of convenience. Wernecke considered Herbie a "gigolo" and a "showoff," and was jealous of his success in picking up girls.[28] For his part, the fun-loving Haupt had little interest in the kind of political fanaticism espoused by Wernecke. His own attraction to Nazism was more aesthetic than political: he looked good in a Bund uniform. Since he did not fully trust Wernecke, Haupt avoided any mention of his trip to Germany. But he did say that he had been in Mexico City, and that he had put in a good word for his friend with the German consulate. This pleased Wernecke, who was afraid that his services to the Nazi cause had gone unnoticed in the Fatherland.

Trailed by an FBI car, the two men went first to the office of Wernecke's doctor, a Nazi sympathizer named Fred Otten. "We'll fix him up," Otten declared cheerfully, after Wernecke introduced his "sick" friend. The doctor immediately diagnosed high blood pressure, "probably due to nervousness," and agreed that Haupt should get a cardiograph. He gave him some pills to help him sleep and then wrote out a prescription, advising against "any undue physical exertion."[29]

That evening, Wernecke invited Haupt for a drive in the country. Wernecke's car was a black Hudson sedan virtually identical to the model used by the FBI. As they drove along a deserted country road, they noticed another car just like theirs a few hundred yards behind. When they stopped, the other car also stopped. They turned around and drove back alongside the other Hudson. Two men in dark suits were sitting in the front. Soon afterward, the second car turned off the road. Haupt and Wernecke breathed a sigh of relief. They decided they were mistaken. Nobody was following them.

The following day, Friday, Haupt resumed his draft-dodging quest. The doctor's prescription was only a temporary solution. He needed something more definitive to get a deferment. Wernecke suggested nitroglycerin pills, three of which would cause the heart to beat rapidly for a few minutes, long enough to mislead a cardiograph. Herbie ordered six pills from a pharmacy on the way to Grant Hospital, and was taken aback to discover that they were only sold in batches of a hundred. The good news was that a hundred pills only cost thirty-nine cents. A worthwhile investment, he decided.

By themselves, the pills were sometimes insufficient to significantly affect the results of the cardiograph, Wernecke explained. As Haupt was undergoing his examination, Wernecke stood behind the door, making frantic hand motions to signal his friend to hold his breath and beat his chest. Herbie was unable to beat his chest without alerting the nurse administering the cardiograph, but he did succeed in holding his breath. He paid his five-dollar fee and made arrangements to pick up the results the following day.

That left the religion option. Wernecke explained that founding one's own religion was easy: with three or four like-minded people, you could even appoint your own ministers. Alternatively, Haupt could join the Allied Christian Management Army.[30] While Herbie was in the bank changing some money, Wernecke went across the street to his church. He returned a short while later to say the "head man" was willing to help. His reasoning was simple. Since Roosevelt was "against God," it was the church's duty to help anyone who wanted to stay out of Roosevelt's army. For a donation of $100, it would even be possible to ordain Haupt as a Bible student dating back to 1941. While not as cheap as nitroglycerin tablets, Wernecke's religion was certainly worth considering.

BY SATURDAY morning, Hoover and Connelley decided that Haupt had been enjoying himself in Chicago for long enough. It was time to reel him in. They would deal with Neubauer later.

FBI agents had established a command post at 2231 North Fremont Street in a rented room on the first floor, with a view of the Haupt apartment directly opposite. They were waiting for Haupt as he came out of the house at 9:08 and climbed into his Pontiac sports coupe. They allowed him to drive one block south, in the direction of the Loop, and then one block west on Webster Avenue. As his car passed under the elevated station, they pulled him over.[31]

At first, Haupt denied all knowledge of Operation Pastorius, although he admitted knowing Hermann Neubauer. He later conceded that he had arrived in America by U-boat, and had been part of a sabotage plot, but claimed he was planning to turn his seven comrades in to the FBI. "What took you so long?" the agents wanted to know. Haupt said he feared one of the other saboteurs might try to kill him if he betrayed the plot, so he decided to wait until they were all "in one place" where they could be easily rounded up by the FBI. Now that he was under arrest, it seemed obvious to Haupt what had happened.

"Peter Burger beat me to it," he said bitterly. "I knew all the time he would turn us in."[32]

Burger, Haupt went on, had never hidden his hatred of the Gestapo for mistreating his wife and causing her to lose her baby. "He hates the Gestapo more than anything else on earth. He told me about the horrors he suffered in a concentration camp and the horrors he saw other people suffer."

Haupt told the FBI agents about his meeting with Neubauer at the Chicago Theater, and said he believed Neubauer was registered at the Stevens Hotel, "under the name of Smith."[33] G-men promptly raided the luxury hotel overlooking Grant Park and Lake Michigan, but there was no sign of the eighth saboteur. Haupt then recalled that Neubauer had said something about moving to either the Sheridan Plaza or Edgewater Beach on the North Side. Dispatched to these hotels, agents immediately focused on "an individual using the name H. Nicholas" who had checked in to the Sheridan Plaza the day before.[34] A search of his room turned up numerous items purchased in Jacksonville, Florida, and a Jacksonville–Chicago rail ticket.

Neubauer was arrested as he returned to his hotel room at 6:45 p.m. after watching yet another movie. He struck his captors as exceptionally nervous. He had changed hotels twice in three days, and was planning to move again on Saturday. The previous evening, he had paid another visit to Harry and Emma Jaques, who had mentioned hearing a radio report of the landing of German agents in the United States.[35] Neubauer did his best to brush the report aside, saying he had read something similar in the newspapers. But he was seriously rattled.

An FBI doctor noted that Neubauer's pulse was "very rapid, being approximately 125 beats," and that he complained of continual headaches, caused by a head wound received on the eastern front.[36] By the following morning, he had calmed down somewhat, although his nerves remained "twitchy."

After eleven days of freedom, it was a relief to be in captivity.

PART THREE

CAPTIVITY

(JUNE 27–AUGUST 9, 1942)

CHAPTER ELEVEN

"AS GUILTY AS CAN BE"

(JUNE 27–JULY 4)

GEORGE JOHN DASCH posed a difficult dilemma for Hoover's G-men. On the one hand, there was no denying that he had performed a valuable service for the United States by betraying an ambitious, and potentially deadly, Nazi sabotage operation. On the other hand, his megalomaniac personality, tendency to ramble, and refusal to do what was expected of him were all likely to make him a poor witness in court. In this particular production, there could be only one starring role. The more credit Dasch received for exposing Operation Pastorius, the less would redound to J. Edgar Hoover and the FBI.

After being left to ponder his predicament in a solitary detention cell for some thirty-six hours on the thirtieth floor of the federal courthouse in Manhattan, Dasch was permitted to change out of his prison clothes into a suit. He was then taken to meet the head of the FBI's New York office, Thomas Donegan. With Donegan was Dasch's original interrogator, Duane Traynor. Together they played "good cop, bad cop": Traynor the solicitous lawyer doing his best to look after the interests of his client, Donegan the tough policeman warning Dasch of the consequences of noncooperation.

"I am very upset. I didn't expect to be left all this time alone in a cell. It seems you don't believe me," Dasch began.[1] He felt that he had already played his part by allowing himself to be led in prison clothes past the cells of the other saboteurs, in order to dispel any suspicion that he was the traitor. Looking at Traynor, he said he hoped he would now be taken "out of here."

Donegan made clear this would not be possible, as the saboteurs were likely to be brought before some kind of court, and everything would then "come out in the newspapers." He gave Dasch a choice. One option was for the FBI to acknowledge his contribution in rounding up the other saboteurs, in which case he would be given "appropriate consideration" by the attorney general. The drawback was that news of his betrayal would rapidly make its way back to Germany, endangering the lives of his parents and relatives. The second option was for Dasch to plead guilty, in which case he would be treated the same as the other saboteurs, and be sentenced to a long prison term. After a "period of time," say six months, Director Hoover would recommend a presidential pardon.[2] If he followed this course, "everything would appear in order to the Germans" and he would not be singled out as the traitor. The choice was entirely up to Dasch.

It was clear from the way Donegan spoke which option the FBI preferred.

Dasch felt trapped. He told the two FBI agents that his information about conditions in Germany would go "stale" if he spent too long in prison, and he would no longer be able to fulfill his dream of leading a propaganda offensive against the Nazis. He wanted to know exactly how long he would be in prison. He was also frightened that the Nazis would take revenge on his parents, particularly his mother. At times, he broke down crying. By the end of the ninety-minute session in Donegan's office, he had come around to the FBI's point of view, and agreed to plead guilty and be sentenced to prison, on the understanding that he would be released from prison sooner rather than later.

Traynor explained that in order to deter future sabotage operations, it was necessary to convince Nazi leaders that the American coastline was impenetrable, even though this was obviously not the case. Hitler should be led to suspect that Operation Pastorius had been betrayed from within his own intelligence service, thereby creating distrust at the highest levels of the German government. Much of the propaganda and deterrence value of rounding up eight Nazi saboteurs would be lost if the real reason for their capture became known.

"You will have to become an actor, and a damn good one," Traynor told Dasch. "You will have to steel yourself to play the part, particularly since there will be many occasions when you feel downhearted and depressed."[3]

Dasch promised to do as Traynor and Donegan asked. After being taken to the bathroom to change into his prison clothes, he was escorted back to his cell.

WHEN DASCH first walked into FBI headquarters in Washington, Hoover's immediate inclination was to use him as a decoy to channel misinformation to Hitler, and arrest any future teams of Nazi saboteurs. This was a tactic he had already employed successfully with William Sebold, a German-born naturalized American recruited by the Abwehr to operate a clandestine shortwave radio station on Long Island. Sebold reported what had happened to the American authorities and, for the next sixteen months, supplied his masters in Berlin with bogus information fed to him by the FBI. As a result, Hoover had rolled up an entire network of thirty-three Nazi agents in July 1941, effectively shutting down Abwehr espionage operations in the United States. In return, the FBI helped Sebold begin a new life under an assumed identity after he testified against his fellow agents at their trial.

Hoover quickly decided that Dasch's case was very different from Sebold's. He did not believe it would be possible to keep the Dasch affair out of the newspapers for very long. Other government agencies knew about the saboteur landings, and people were bound to talk. There was already speculation in the newspapers about a hunt for Nazi saboteurs in Florida. A reporter from the Associated Press had been asking questions about a rumor that the FBI had arrested some German agents who landed on the East Coast. Although the reporter had been warned off the story, the news was sure to get around.

"This thing can blow up in our faces at any moment," Hoover told Eugene Connelley on June 24.[4] "If the AP has the story, we can be sure that some of the columnists will have it within a few days." Although his men were keeping a close watch on Haupt, Hoover was afraid they might "lose" Neubauer if the news broke prematurely.

Hoover was paranoid about leaks from other government agencies. At one time or another, he suspected the army, the navy, and the Coast Guard of talking to the press about the Dasch case. In fact, some of the leaks may well have come from within the FBI itself. Bureau documents show that reports of the Amagansett incident were widely disseminated within the organization, particularly in Florida, where they were discussed at a law enforcement conference attended by dozens of people.[5]

In addition to the danger of leaks, there was also "the danger facing our coasts," in Hoover's phrase. The landings in Long Island and Florida had demonstrated the lamentable state of the nation's coastal defenses. Coast Guard patrols were untrained and unarmed, and there were not enough of them to mount anything approaching a permanent vigil. Kerling's men had reached Jacksonville without arousing anyone's suspicions. The fact that a Coast Guard patrol had run into Dasch on the beach at Amagansett was sheer coincidence. The FBI director was angry with the Coast Guard for allowing a stranded U-boat to escape, and doing nothing to prevent the intruders from taking the Long Island Rail Road into Manhattan.

Mixed up in all these calculations was the question of who would get the credit for rounding up the saboteurs. Already embroiled in a furious argument with the Coast Guard and navy intelligence over who had responsibility for investigating the case, Hoover feared that some other agency would "flamboyantly announce" a major breakthrough. The only way to prevent this from happening was for Hoover to make a flamboyant announcement of his own. He wanted the Nazi saboteur case to be recognized as a major FBI triumph, an important contribution to the war effort. Which meant a triumph for Hoover personally, since the Bureau was his creation and he was its public face. In Hoover's mind, the national interest, the Bureau's interests, and his own personal reputation were inextricably intertwined.

The press conference at which Hoover would break the news was planned like a military campaign. The director brought a large entourage to New York, having already decided that Haupt would be arrested as soon as he left his house on Saturday morning. He waited all day Saturday for news from Chicago of Neubauer's arrest, which finally arrived at 6:45 in the evening. Journalists were then told to come to the FBI's New York office at 8:30 for an important announcement.

The rest of the government had been left in the dark about Hoover's intentions. A few minutes before 8:30, his aides began phoning senior government officials to tell them what was about to happen.[6] Hoover himself called his nominal superior, Attorney General Francis Biddle, to say he had seized "the last" of the saboteurs, and was about to inform the press. Biddle, who was dining with the Yugoslav ambassador when the call came through, felt an immediate "flood of relief."[7] "I had had a bad week trying to sleep as I thought of the possibilities. The saboteurs might have other caches hidden, and at any moment an explosion was possible. Would it not have been better to alert the country, even if we lost our quarry?"

Hoover's aides told the War Department that the FBI was compelled to go public because "the newspapers became aware of the story" as a result of the arrests of Haupt and Neubauer in Chicago.[8] This was untrue. FBI memos show that Hoover had been planning to break the story for at least three days, and was simply waiting for the right moment.

"I have a very important statement to make," the FBI director began, once the reporters were all assembled. "I want you to listen carefully: this is a serious business."[9]

The story that Hoover told the press was a dramatic one, and emphasized the central role played by the FBI in cracking the case. There was no mention of Dasch, and no mention of Dasch's encounter with the Coast Guard on Amagansett Beach. An amused Biddle later recalled that Hoover's performance and the accompanying press reaction created the impression that "a particularly brilliant FBI agent, probably attending the school in sabotage where the eight had been trained, had been able to get on the inside, and make regular reports to America. Mr. Hoover, as the United Press put it, declined to comment on whether or not FBI agents had infiltrated into not only the Gestapo but also the High Command, or whether he had watched the saboteurs land . . ."[10]

The *New York Times* came out with a front-page banner headline of the type normally reserved for major events of the war, such as Pearl Harbor and the Japanese defeat in the Battle of Midway:

FBI SEIZES 8 SABOTEURS LANDED BY U-BOATS HERE AND IN FLORIDA TO BLOW UP WAR PLANTS

INVADERS CONFESS

Had TNT to Blast Key
Factories, Railroads and
City Water System

USED RUBBER BOATS

Carried $150,000 Cash
—All Had Lived in U.S.
—Face Death Penalty

The *Times* story quoted Hoover as saying FBI agents had been pursuing the saboteurs "almost from the moment the first group set foot on United States soil," and had recovered enough sabotage equipment for "a two-year campaign of terror."[11] It recalled the infamous Black Tom explosion in World War I, and accused former German diplomats in the United States of recruiting German-Americans for use as saboteurs prior to the outbreak of war. But it added reassuringly: "Before the men could begin carrying out their orders, the FBI was on their trail and the round-up began. One after another, they fell into the special agents' net. Each confessed fully, providing information that will make repetition of the sabotage invasions difficult."

A few more details were provided by Walter Winchell, the most widely read gossip columnist in America and beneficiary of frequent leaks direct from Hoover, including a fair amount of misinformation. In his weekly radio broadcast, Winchell reported that the saboteurs had "spent a lot of time in Broadway stores" and well-known Manhattan restaurants and nightclubs. "The apprehension of the spies by the G-men, based on the slightest of tips, will take your breath away," he told his listeners.[12] Although the full, incredible story could only be told after the war was over, Winchell was already in a position to reveal that "FBI agents are not only in the United States, but are even in the Gestapo and the border of Berlin." He hailed the arrest of the saboteurs as "the most exciting achievement yet of John Edgar Hoover's G-men."

PRESIDENT ROOSEVELT was entertaining European royalty at Hyde Park, his ancestral home, when he learned about Hoover's latest exploit. Just why a wartime leader of the United States would want to spend so much time with dethroned monarchs was a mystery to his advisers, but they were willing to indulge him. It was one of FDR's foibles, a way of relaxing, like mixing martinis or going through his stamp collection. But sometimes even kings and queens got on his nerves.

The royals "are driving the P to distraction," Roosevelt's seventeen-year-old goddaughter, Margaret "Roly" Hambley, wrote in her diary, after being roped into entertaining King George of Greece. To her great disappointment, the king turned out to be a very ordinary sort of person, not at all "the kind of man Churchill is . . . It is just awful trying to remind oneself that he is a king and should be treated as such . . . If only he had some kind of monocle or something on!"[13] Other guests at Hyde Park that weekend included Princess Martha of Sweden, FDR's alter ego Harry Hopkins and his fiancée, Louise Macy, who, Roly commented tartly, had "a very lifeless way of talking" in an affected "English accent." The formidable Queen Wilhelmina of Holland was expected shortly.

The president had just returned from taking his guests for a ride through the Hudson Valley countryside when Biddle called with news of the arrest of the saboteurs and the seizure of $175,000, a huge sum by 1942 standards. "Not enough, Francis," he joked.[14] "Let's make real money out of them. Sell the rights to Barnum and Bailey for a million and a half—the rights to take them around the country in lion cages at so much a head."

As an aficionado of spy stories and tales of subversive enemy activity, Roosevelt was "delighted" by the latest turn of events, and chuckled at the thought of the embarrassment inflicted on the Nazis.[15] Biddle thought the president really believed in the Old Testament principle "a tooth for a tooth." Like Hoover, Roosevelt was concerned that America's coastline was insufficiently protected: he wanted to use the case to send a very clear warning to Hitler to refrain from similar stunts in the future. He summed up his thinking in a memorandum to the attorney general three days later, outlining his ideas for making an example of the saboteurs, and deterring any others who might follow them.

1. The two American citizens [Burger and Haupt] are guilty of high treason. This being wartime, it is my inclination to try them by court martial. I do not see how they can offer any adequate defense. Surely they are just as guilty as it is possible to be and it seems to me that the death penalty is almost obligatory.[16]

2. In the case of the other six who I take it are German citizens, I understand that they came over in submarines wearing seamen's clothes— in all probability German Naval clothes—and that some of them at least landed on our shores in these German Naval clothes. I think it can be proved that they formed a part of the German Military or Naval Service. They were apprehended in civilian clothes. This is an absolute parallel of the case of Major André in the Revolution and of Nathan Hale. Both of them were hanged. Here again it is my inclination that they be tried by court martial as were André and Hale. Without splitting hairs, I can see no difference.

Biddle did not need reminding that Nathan Hale had been a spy for George Washington captured by the British behind their lines on Long Island and hung the very next morning, on September 22, 1776. Major John André was a British officer caught by Washington's army behind American lines in civilian clothes after returning from negotiations with Benedict Arnold for the surrender of West Point. He too was found guilty of espionage and executed by hanging, on October 2, 1780. Like Hale and André, the Nazi saboteurs had violated the customary rules of war and should be dealt with accordingly. That, at least, was how Roosevelt saw it.

"I want one thing clearly understood, Francis," he told Biddle the next time they discussed what should be done with the saboteurs. "I won't give them up . . . I won't hand them over to any United States marshal armed with a writ of habeas corpus. Understand?"

NOT EVERYONE in the government was happy with Hoover's handling of the case, and particularly his decision to go public. The secretary of war, Henry Stimson, was "very, very angry" with the FBI for failing to consult with the military before announcing the arrests of the saboteurs.[17] A patrician Republican lawyer recruited by Roosevelt to give a bipartisan character to the war effort, Stimson felt that an extraordinary chance had been lost to destroy Nazi sabotage networks once and for all.

Stimson's chief of intelligence, Major General George Strong, was informed about Hoover's press conference a few moments before it began, and given no opportunity to object. "The premature breaking of the story has wrecked our plans for seizing two additional groups of four men each who apparently are scheduled to land on our shores in August," Strong complained the following day.[18] "In consequence, the only benefit to National Defense that can be obtained is the deterrent effect upon possible sabotage by the prompt trial and execution of the eight men now in the hands of the FBI."

At least Strong was informed in advance. Other officials received their information from the press. The head of naval intelligence in New York, whose men had dug up sabotage material on Amagansett Beach, was "incensed" by the "entire absence of any reference" to his department in the materials released by the FBI. Captain R. C. MacFall described the failure to keep him informed of developments as "rather shoddy" and "not conducive to full cooperative effort."[19] "Our operatives were made to appear stupid when they were informed by local police and radio broadcasts that the enemy agents had been picked up. In view of the fact that they had been sitting in company with FBI agents in fox holes on the beach during rain and fog, and were being bitten with sand fleas, they do not feel very happy being treated this way."

The sniping went both ways. Hoover was furious with naval intelligence for allegedly "concealing" evidence from the FBI. He delighted in shooting down attempts by other government agencies to muscle their way into the investigation. He accused the Justice Department of making "amateurish suggestions" and blasted a senator who called on the FBI to employ "strong arm tactics" against the saboteurs as "a cheap politician trying to get some publicity."[20] When the Office of Strategic Services asked for access to the transcripts of the interrogations of Dasch and the other saboteurs, Hoover ruled that "none of this material is to be plowed over until we are definitely through with it." By contrast, when other agencies refused the FBI access to their materials, he was always quick to complain.

Some of this bureaucratic bickering percolated up to an exasperated FDR. The chief of the president's Secret Service detail, Mike Reilly, complained that "Hoover's boys hogged all the credit for running down the culprits."[21] A branch of the U.S. Treasury, the Secret Service had played a peripheral role in the investigation, tracing the dollar bills that Dasch used to try to bribe the coastguardsman on Amagansett Beach to a shipment of currency sent to Germany in 1939. Reilly complained that the nation's oldest federal law enforcement agency always received "fullest cooperation from Army and Navy Intelligence . . . but never the slightest recognition from FBI."

IN THE meantime, Dasch was having second thoughts about his agreement to plead guilty. Escorted back to his cell from Donegan's office on the afternoon of June 27, he had "ample time" to brood over his situation. At 10:25 that evening, he asked his FBI guard for another meeting with Donegan. The guard promptly relayed the message to Donegan, who said he would see the prisoner in the morning.

An obviously distraught Dasch then asked the guard for a cigarette and a cup of cold water. As he sipped the water, pacing up and down his tiny cell, he began talking incoherently to the guard. "I've been a coward, but tonight I found myself."[22] He said he had read a newspaper account of the sufferings of American soldiers on Corregidor, which had helped him find his courage. "I cannot cause an innocent man's death. Young people should live. People who have already lived their lives can die. That's the way my mother and father would want it."

The guard had no idea what Dasch was talking about, and was under strict orders not to engage the prisoner in conversation. He just listened, waiting for him to hand back the empty cup.

Dasch had a sleepless night, tossing and turning on the hard planks that served as a bed. The following morning, he peeked through the peephole of his wooden cell door and saw another guard reading a newspaper story about Hoover's press conference. His own picture was splashed across the front page under the headline "CAPTURED NAZI SPY."[23] He felt confused and betrayed. His brother and sister lived in the United States. What would they think when they saw the story? What would his friends think? What right did they have to use his picture anyway?

When Donegan finally dropped by to see him, Dasch said he had changed his mind. Instead of pleading guilty, he would take his chances in court, and provide a full explanation for his behavior. The meaning of his disconnected remarks of the previous evening now became clear. He was willing to risk Nazi retribution against his parents in Germany ("people who have already lived their lives") for his own reputation and the well-being of his brother and sister in the United States ("Young people should live").

FBI officials were furious. Donegan reported to Hoover that the prisoner was "behaving like an opera star."[24] Connelley said he was in favor of "shooting Dasch" because he "backs in and out," "stands on his dignity," "gets up and waves his arms," and throws a fit "when there is no reason for it at all." Even the patient, solicitous Traynor admitted to having "doubts" about Dasch's veracity. He found it almost impossible to figure his star informant out. First Dasch had expressed great concern about the fate of his parents in Germany, insisting that the German government must never be permitted to learn of his role in betraying Operation Pastorius. Now he was saying his parents would have to look after themselves.

Dasch signaled his dismay at the way he was being treated by becoming surly and uncooperative. Hoover felt that his initial 254-page "confession" was too candid and unwieldy to be used in court, and wanted him to agree to a summary prepared by FBI agents. But Dasch refused to sign the new document, saying it was "too cold and bare" and left out many important details.[25] Instead, he penned a rambling twelve-page letter, depicting himself as "little Geo. J. Dasch" battling impersonal, bureaucratic forces on both sides of the Atlantic.[26]

"I came to this country not as a foe, but as an ally, ready and anxious to do my very best in helping to defeat the present government of Germany," he wrote. "One thing I could not foresee was the way I was to be received after arriving in the U.S.A. I had all reason to believe that I would be greeted with open arms, befriended as an ally." Instead, "I was not only thrown into jail but also photographed like a criminal." He explained his change of heart by arguing that he did not want to expose his relatives in the United States to the "risk of losing their jobs" if he was convicted as a Nazi spy. Above all, he refused to be party to "a lie."

> Any good soldier carries his flag proudly to the battle. I always wanted to be a good soldier, a soldier that carries his flag openly, unashamed into a battle for rightfulness, into the battle to free these poor people of Europe regardless of race, religion, or nationality. Just because I'm so deeply convinced that the battle I pray to take part in is for a just cause makes me proud to carry my flag into the open. Let them rotten gangsters [the Nazis] know that poor little me was able to beat to the punch by not only exposing their rotten plans to the people of the U.S.A. but by coming out in the open and fight with all my knowledge, all that I've observed, all the trickeries I've learned from them. I do not fear the loss of my beloved ones over there, for mother told, to go right ahead. Their lives rest in the hands of God . . .

Dasch "wants to be a martyr," Connelley complained.[27]

FRANCIS BIDDLE had the reputation of being the liberal ornament in FDR's war cabinet. He was descended from a long line of Philadelphia aristocrats, and was married to a well-known poet, Katherine Garrison Chapin. His friends included writers, intellectuals, foreign diplomats—a representative cross-section of the Great and the Good. Some Roosevelt intimates regarded him as too effete and soft to make an effective attorney general during a time of war. The saboteur case was his opportunity to prove them wrong.

The president himself enjoyed ribbing Biddle for his commitment to civil liberties. A few months earlier, over lunch in the cabinet room of the

White House, he had played a practical joke on his chief law enforcement officer. Putting on his most serious and solemn face, he said he planned to suspend freedom of speech for the duration of the war, and wanted Biddle to draft a suitable proclamation. "It's a tough thing to do, but I'm convinced it's absolutely necessary and I want to announce it in this speech we are working on now."[28]

The other people in the room, who were in on the presidential joke, sat silently as Biddle rose to the bait and passionately defended the right of Americans to express themselves freely, even in a time of war. As he paced back and forth, the attorney general got more and more worked up, making a fervent plea for Roosevelt to reconsider. Biddle's tirade went on for some five minutes before the other lunch guests burst out laughing.

Now that the Nazi saboteurs were under lock and key, Biddle was as eager as any of his colleagues to make an example of them. Like Roosevelt, he felt they should be tried by military tribunal. It would be difficult to prove a case of attempted sabotage in a civilian court: Dasch and his colleagues had not even gone back to collect the bomb-making equipment cached on the beaches, much less blown anything up. According to civilian law, "if a man buys a pistol, intending murder, that is not an attempt at murder."[29] Legal experts at the War Department believed that a U.S. district court would sentence the saboteurs to a maximum of two years in prison and a fine of $10,000 for "conspiracy to commit a crime against the United States."[30] Under military law, they could be charged with violating the rules of war by crossing the front line in civilian clothes with hostile intent, an offense that carried the death penalty.

Not only was Biddle prepared to hand the saboteurs over to the military authorities; he wanted to prosecute the case himself, a highly unusual step for an attorney general. He was afraid that lawyers for the saboteurs might invoke the ancient tradition of habeas corpus, a procedure that could send the case to the Supreme Court. If this happened, there was a serious risk of army prosecutors messing things up. He was worried that the judge advocate general of the army, Major General Myron Cramer, had limited legal experience and had never appeared before the Supreme Court.

"We have to win in the Supreme Court, or there will be a hell of a mess," Biddle warned Roosevelt.[31]

"You're damned right, Mr. Attorney General."

Biddle's desire to prosecute the case himself was strongly opposed by the secretary of war. A stickler for regular procedures, Stimson thought the trial should be handled as a "routine matter" by the military, with as little fanfare as possible. He had a low opinion of his cabinet rival, whom he regarded as both weak and vain. Already upset by Hoover's headline-grabbing news conference, Stimson suspected that Biddle had also fallen victim to "the bug of publicity."[32] He told him it was "infra dig" for the attorney general to appear in a case of "such little national importance."

But Biddle insisted on leading the prosecution team at the trial. Reluctantly, Stimson let him have his way.

NEWS OF the saboteur debacle reached Hitler at the Wolf's Lair in eastern Prussia as he was preparing a new offensive in the Crimea. In the early morning hours of Sunday, June 28, Berlin time, American radio stations started carrying reports of the arrest of all the participants in Operation Pastorius. The detail contained in the reports—accurate descriptions of the bomb-making equipment, the names of the V-men, as well as an account of how they had received extensive training at a sabotage school outside Berlin—left no room for doubt that the operation had been a complete fiasco.

The Führer was livid. He summoned the Abwehr chiefs, Canaris and Lahousen, to appear at Wolfsschanze the following Tuesday. Once again, they took a military plane from Berlin to Rastenburg, and then a staff car through the woods to Hitler's military headquarters. That afternoon, Hitler subjected them to one of his most withering tirades, complaining that the Americans had achieved a huge propaganda victory. The only possible quibble with the American account was that some of the sabotage objectives, such as the targeting of the Hell Gate Bridge in New York, had been misrepresented or exaggerated.

Canaris tried to shift the blame onto the Nazi Party, arguing that the saboteurs had not been "trained Abwehr agents," but Nazi loyalists selected by the party. This only made Hitler more angry.

"Why didn't you use Jews for that?" he yelled at the stocky admiral.[33] Even though the Holocaust was already well under way, Hitler still thought he could force Jews to do his dirty work. Canaris, who was beginning to doubt the Führer's sanity, would later use Hitler's remark as an excuse for recruiting a few Jewish agents into the Abwehr, thereby saving them from the death camps.

The commander in chief of the submarine fleet, Admiral Dönitz, was also infuriated by the news from America. He had little confidence in either the Abwehr or the Nazi Party's Ausland Institut, which had screened the agents in the first place. He had opposed the use of his U-boats for transporting saboteurs, and had only agreed to Operation Pastorius after being assured by the Abwehr that the V-men were all "high-class intelligence agents."[34] This was obviously not the case, and Dönitz angrily withdrew his consent for follow-up operations.

FROM THE German point of view, the only glimmer of light from the whole affair was the havoc submarine *U-202* inflicted along the eastern seaboard following its miraculous escape from Long Island.[35] But even that was marred by controversy.

In the early morning hours of Monday, June 22—nine days after landing the saboteurs on Amagansett Beach—Linder had spotted a 4,900-ton steamer 150 miles southeast of New York. He fired a torpedo at the ship, hitting the boiler room just above the water level on the starboard side. One of the boilers immediately exploded, killing five crewmen. The ship sank in eleven minutes, as the survivors scrambled aboard lifeboats.

When *U-202* surfaced to survey the damage, it turned out that the steamer, the *Rio Tercero,* had been flying the Argentine flag. In theory at least, it should have been off-limits to German submarines as a neutral ship, although Linder maintained that it had not been properly identified. He invited the captain and surviving crew members on board and, in a conciliatory gesture, offered them some glasses of cognac and a pair of shoes, which they accepted. After the Argentineans got back into their lifeboat, four German sailors appeared on the deck of the U-boat armed with submachine guns. The Argentinean captain feared a massacre, but at that moment an American plane appeared overhead, and *U-202* immediately crash-dived. The sinking of the *Rio Tercero* prompted a strong diplomatic protest from Argentina to Nazi Germany.

Eight days later, on June 30, Linder struck again. This time, he sank a 5,900-ton American vessel, the *City of Birmingham,* off Cape Hatteras, a favorite stalking ground for German U-boats. The ship, which was packed with 381 passengers and crew, went down in just four minutes, but only nine persons were killed. On his way back to Europe, Linder refueled from one of the large supply submarines cruising around the Atlantic and intercepted an outbound American convoy near the Azores.

FROM HIS bedroom on the second floor of the Hyde Park mansion, Franklin Roosevelt looked out onto an idyllic scene of parkland, rolling hills, and the Hudson River glinting through a forest of maple and white pine. An apple tree brushed against the stone wall outside the room, so close that the president could lean through the hospital-green shutters of the window and pluck the fruit. Below the window was a steep hill that descended to a wooden bluff above the river, where, as a boy, Franklin had loved to go sledding in the snow.

Now that he was preoccupied by the affairs of the world, Roosevelt loved the "peacefulness and regularity" of Hyde Park, and the life of the country squire that went with it.[36] Paralyzed from the hips downward, he would replay his boyhood adventures over and over in his mind until he eventually fell asleep. Because of his infirmity, his bedroom had become a second office. A black telephone on the wall above his heavy mahogany bed provided a direct line to the White House. In the morning, he would eat breakfast in bed and go through piles of papers sent up from Washington.

Thursday, July 2, was a big document-signing day at Hyde Park. The president's aide, William Hassett, brought in an "unusually fat" pile of papers for him to sign, including what Roosevelt described as "the biggest appropriation bill in the history of the world" and documents setting up a military tribunal to try the Nazi saboteurs.[37] "The Boss" signed the papers in bed, scrawling his name in the proper place with a heavy stroke of a pen. Then Hassett spread the documents out on every flat space in the room, including the rest of the bed, the chairs, and much of the floor, to wait for the ink to dry. "I've done half a day's work, and I'm not yet out of bed," FDR boasted to his wife, Eleanor, when she phoned him from Washington. "Having a grand time."

The previous evening, Biddle had sent up a packet of papers to Hyde Park explaining the difficulties of trying the saboteurs in civilian court and the legal basis for establishing a tribunal. He pointed out that a military trial was likely to be "much swifter" than a civilian trial, and would side-step the cumbersome rules of evidence demanded by civilian courts.[38] Furthermore, he proposed trying the saboteurs by a military commission rather than by court-martial because of its "greater flexibility, its traditional use in cases of this character and its clear power to impose the death penalty." Courts-martial were subject to the Articles of War, a military code dating back to 1775 and the War of Independence against the British. A military commission was ad hoc, and the president could draw up his own rules. He could stipulate, for example, that the death penalty could be imposed with the agreement of only two-thirds of the members of the tribunal rather than the unanimous vote required by a court-martial. All this would "save a considerable amount of time," in Biddle's view.

At this point, Roosevelt was still unaware of the assistance provided to the FBI by Dasch and Burger, and believed all the saboteurs to be equally guilty. As far as he knew, the Bureau had broken the case through its own investigative brilliance. Hoover had discussed the case with Biddle, and together they decided to keep the information about Dasch's betrayal of his colleagues to themselves for the moment. As long as FDR was at Hyde Park, Biddle told Hoover, "it would be very unwise to speak to the president over the telephone concerning Dasch."[39] They would tell him later, when they could get him on his own.

The president signed two documents relating to the saboteurs.[40] The first was an order establishing a military commission to try the eight invaders, giving the chairman of the tribunal the right to admit any evidence that would have "probative value to a reasonable man." The tribunal's verdict and sentence would be transmitted directly to the president for action, rather than being subject to the normal review procedures contained in the Articles of War.

The second document was a presidential proclamation denying the defendants access to civilian courts. Biddle was worried that lawyers for the saboteurs might try to invoke a "troublesome" Supreme Court decision that dated back to 1866, just after the Civil War, restoring liberties suspended by Abraham Lincoln while he suppressed the Confederate rebellion. The Supreme Court had ruled in *Ex parte Milligan* that civilians could never be brought before a military tribunal at a time when civilian courts were "open and properly functioning." It was unclear whether the saboteurs were civilians or not: only two of them, Burger and Neubauer, were formally enrolled in the German army. It was also unclear whether the Supreme Court decision applied to foreigners. Roosevelt's advisers hoped to avoid this legal controversy with a presidential order carving out an exception to the *Milligan* ruling:

NOW, THEREFORE, I, FRANKLIN D. ROOSEVELT, President of the United States of America and Commander in Chief of the Army and

Navy of the United States, by virtue of the authority vested in me by the Constitution and the statutes of the United States, do hereby proclaim that all persons who are subjects, citizens or residents of any nation at war with the United States or who give obedience to or act under the direction of any such nation, and who during time of war enter or attempt to enter the United States or any territory or possession thereof, through coastal or boundary defenses, and are charged with committing or attempting or preparing to commit sabotage, espionage, hostile or warlike acts, or violations of the rules of war, shall be subject to the law of war and to the jurisdiction of military tribunals; and that such persons shall not be privileged to seek any remedy or maintain any proceeding, directly or indirectly, or to have any such remedy or proceeding sought on their behalf, in the courts of the United States . . .

All this was very satisfactory to Roosevelt, who wanted to dispose of the saboteur case as swiftly and efficiently as possible. Hassett was faithfully echoing his master's opinions when he noted in his diary, "Hanging would afford an efficacious example to others of like kidney. There's no doubt of their guilt, but we are always too soft in dealing with spies and saboteurs."

THE ESTABLISHMENT of a military tribunal meant that the saboteurs would have to be transferred to the custody of the army. After some discussion with Hoover and Biddle, army leaders decided that the Justice Department building in Washington offered the best location for the trial, including security, easy access, and plenty of space. In between court sessions, the prisoners would be held at the Washington, D.C., jail, one wing of which was transferred to the authority of the army.

Stimson summoned the provost marshal of the Military District of Washington, Brigadier General Albert Cox, to make the necessary arrangements. "In the last war a man named Grover Cleveland Bergdoll got away," Stimson growled.[41] "In this war nobody is going to get away. See Edgar Hoover and arrange for the transfer of the prisoners."

The FBI director went to New York to supervise arrangements and get a firsthand glimpse of at least some of the saboteurs. He ignored Dasch, who was still bitter about the way he was being treated, but spent ten minutes with Peter Burger in his cell. When Hoover called on him, Burger had just finished a ham and egg sandwich, and was lying on his bed reading a historical novel set in the time of the American Revolution.[42] His whole demeanor was one of passive resignation. He remained expressionless as one of Hoover's aides formally charged him with attempted sabotage and violating the rules of war, crimes that carried the death penalty. Burger had been very helpful throughout the investigation, returning with FBI agents to Amagansett to point out things they might have missed on the beach. The plan was to rely on his evidence as much as possible at the trial, thereby avoiding emotional outbursts from the "wild" and unpredictable Dasch.

Late that evening, agents escorted all eight saboteurs in handcuffs to Pennsylvania Station, where an entire carriage had been reserved for them on the overnight train to Washington. At 6:55 the following morning, the train arrived at Union Station, where the prisoners were formally handed over to the army.

Another train was traveling toward Washington on the same railroad track, an hour or so behind the train carrying the saboteurs. Aboard the second train was the president, returning to the capital after a week at Hyde Park. For Roosevelt's devoted companion, Daisy Suckley, it had become a familiar ritual. She noted in her diary that the president's black Scottish terrier, Fala, jumped on the sofa next to FDR and snuggled up beside him. Orange juice and "delicious canapés" were served. Then "the usual bad night listening to the wheels go round."[43] At 8:30, everybody appeared for breakfast in Roosevelt's stateroom. "The president said he had a bad night."

"A tense Fourth of July," Hassett noted in his diary. "War not going well."

CHAPTER TWELVE

MILITARY TRIBUNAL

(JULY 6–28)

K ENNETH C. ROYALL had been working in the legal affairs office of the War Department for less than a month when a White House messenger hand-delivered an order direct from President Roosevelt. The message instructed him to serve as defense counsel for the German saboteurs arrested by the FBI a few days before. Attached to the order was the presidential proclamation denying the defendants access to civilian courts.

As he mulled over the message, Royall quickly realized that he was caught in a quandary. He felt bound by the *Manual for Courts-Martial,* which stated that defense counsel "will guard the interests of the accused by all honorable and legitimate means known to law."[1] In order to defend his new clients properly, he knew he had to do everything in his power to get their case transferred to the civil courts. But this meant defying the wishes of his commander in chief, who had expressly forbidden any such move. After a brilliant career that included editing the *Harvard Law Review* and serving as a trial lawyer in his native North Carolina, he had joined the army as a colonel. He was now confronted with a choice between conscience and discipline.

He talked the matter over with the other military lawyer named in Roosevelt's order as his co-counsel. Unlike the forty-eight-year-old Royall, Colonel Cassius M. Dowell was a regular army officer who had risen from the rank of private and was nearing the end of a spotless if unexceptional military career. He had little trial experience, but was an expert on court-martial procedures, about which he had written a book. Dowell listened carefully as Royall argued they had a duty to ensure that their clients got as fair a trial as possible. It was difficult to square this with a closed military tribunal with few of the usual procedural safeguards for the accused.

"So what do we do about it?" the older man asked.[2]

Royall was in favor of writing a letter to the president, asking him to waive the restriction on appealing to the regular courts. He said he was prepared to sign the letter alone, as he did not want to get Dowell into trouble with the army. Since Royall would be returning to civilian life after the war, his own situation was different. To be kicked out of the army "for defending a client, no matter who the client was, would be about the best advertisement I could get," he joked.

Dowell, however, wanted to sign the letter as well. As drafted by Royall, the missive was polite but firm, questioning the "constitutionality" of the order denying their clients "any civilian remedy." The defense attorneys requested Roosevelt's authorization to mount a full legal challenge to his own presidential proclamation.[3]

The ball was now back in the president's court. Short of backing down and withdrawing his order, he had three choices. He could summarily reject the defense counsels' request. But as Biddle pointed out in a memorandum, this might "give the public the impression that the prisoners are not being given a fair trial."[4] He could authorize an appeal to the Supreme Court. Or, finally, he could say nothing, leaving the two colonels to wrestle with their consciences alone.

He decided to keep silent. He had his secretary, Marvin McIntyre, inform the colonels that the July 2 proclamation remained valid but that they should decide for themselves how to perform their duties.

"Is there anything else we can do?" Dowell asked Royall after the telephone call from McIntyre.

"I don't know but one thing."

"What's that?"

"Write another letter."

So they wrote another letter to the president, announcing their intention to challenge "the constitutionality and validity" of his order establishing military tribunals "at the appropriate time." They concluded with a curt, one-sentence paragraph: "Unless ordered otherwise, we will act accordingly."

The tribunal hearing was scheduled to begin the following day. Since they never heard back from the White House, the two colonels proceeded to "act accordingly." First they had to get to know their new clients.

GENERAL COX had arranged for his prisoners to be held in the empty women's section of the District of Columbia jail. Strict measures were taken to ensure that they were kept isolated from the outside world and from one another. The cell on either side of each prisoner was kept vacant so they would not be able to communicate through the wall. Guards watched them constantly through peepholes, and their cell lights were never dimmed. In order to prevent any attempts at suicide, they were given paper plates and cardboard spoons with their meals.

Pretrial meetings with defense attorneys took place in a reception area down the corridor from the cells. The saboteurs were isolated from the outside world, and had little idea what kind of case the FBI had been able to build against them. The defense lawyers did their best to explain the charges of espionage and sabotage and go over each one's story, looking for weaknesses in the prosecution's case.

Excitement mounted outside the District jail on the morning of Wednesday, July 8, as the army prepared to transport the saboteurs to the Justice Department, where the military proceedings would take place. This was the first time most Americans had a chance to see the Nazi enemy up close. It was quite a show. As the *Washington Times-Herald* reported breathlessly that afternoon, "All the drama, action and thrills that go with war, death and intrigue were written into a rapid-moving two hours today as eight Nazi spies were rushed from the Army-guarded District Jail to the Department of Justice building."[5]

Steel-helmeted guards with fixed bayonets had been posted at the gates of the jail since early morning. At 8:40 a.m., six policemen on motorcycles roared out of the gates, followed by a car bearing General Cox. Then an army transport truck full of soldiers, sirens blaring, machine guns pointed in all directions. Next, two black marshal's vans, with soldiers mounted on the running boards, followed by another transport truck and more motor-cycle outriders.

As the procession sped through Washington, from the Anacostia River to Independence Avenue, and across the Mall to Constitution Avenue, shouts of "There go the spies" and "Nazi rats" went up from the thousands of office workers lining the streets. From Constitution, the cavalcade turned right onto Ninth Street, and then made a left through the heavy iron gates of the Justice Department building, where Dasch had come to make his confession less than three weeks before.

As they sat in handcuffs inside the black vans, the eight saboteurs were shocked by the ferocity of the public reaction.[6] Heinrich Heinck would later complain to his wife that "we are watched more carefully than vicious criminals. Handcuffs, machine guns, and so forth. The sirens scream loudly when we ride through Washington. You know what I think of America but now my dream and ours has been destroyed." Eddie Kerling railed against American hypocrisy. When men like Nathan Hale in the Revolutionary War or Douglas MacArthur in the battle of Vera Cruz risked their lives going behind enemy lines, he wrote his friend Miriam Preston, they were hailed as "heroes." But Germans on a similar mission for their country were denounced as "rats."

The vans deposited the prisoners in the Justice Department basement, from which they were taken, by elevator, to a heavily guarded corridor on the fifth floor, screened from nearby offices by boarded-up glass doors. After reviewing several possible sites for a closed military trial, Hoover had persuaded the army that this one offered "the best set-up as far as safety and comfort of any in Washington."[7] The corridor could be sealed off from the rest of the building. During noon recess, the prisoners could be kept in cells in the basement. The hearing itself would take place in a long, narrow room previously used as a classroom for new FBI recruits. Everyone who entered room 5235 required a pass personally signed by both Hoover and Cox.

At precisely 10 a.m., the chairman of the tribunal, Major General Frank R. McCoy, gaveled the session to order, declaring, "The Commission is now open for the trial of such persons as may be brought before it."

"Bring in the prisoners," ordered General Cox.[8]

Uniformed soldiers escorted the saboteurs to their seats along the wall closest to the corridor, between square pillars. On the wall opposite, heavy blackout curtains had been hung on the windows overlooking the court-yard of the building, preventing any daylight from filtering into the room. McCoy and his six colleagues—three major generals and three brigadier generals—sat on a slightly raised podium to the left of the accused, under-neath an American flag and a green velvet drape that concealed a motion picture screen. Two small tables, for exhibits and court reporters, were placed directly in front of the judges, along with a chair for witnesses. The rest of the room, which measured about 100 by 20 feet, was taken up by two long tables, one for the prosecution, the other for the defense. The bright artificial lighting and sparse government-issue furniture gave the room an impersonal, even garish feeling.

While in jail, the prisoners wore striped pajamas, but they were allowed to change into their civilian clothes for their appearances before the tribunal. On trial days, they were shaved by a prison barber, and got dressed in their new double-breasted suits, snap-brim hats, two-tone shoes, and other fashionable items they had bought on shopping expeditions in New York, Chicago, and Jacksonville. As soon as they returned to the jail, they had to change back into their pajamas.

Government lawyers had combed the archives to find a precedent for a military commission, as opposed to the much more common court-martial, which was the way the military administered justice to its own members. They discovered that Andrew Jackson had used military commissions during the War of 1812, when he was in command of American forces at New Orleans. Military tribunals had been used frequently by both sides in the Civil War to punish such offenses as blockade-running, engaging in partisan warfare, or unauthorized trading with the enemy. In 1865, a military commission convicted Mary Surratt of conspiring with John Wilkes Booth to assassinate Abraham Lincoln, and sentenced her to death by hanging. After the Civil War, military commissions fell into disfavor in the continental United States, although they were reintroduced in Hawaii after Pearl Harbor.

GENERAL McCOY had hardly begun to swear in the officers of the court when Royall rose to challenge the authority of the military commission, preparing the ground for a later appeal to the Supreme Court. He described the president's proclamation setting up the tribunal as "invalid and unconstitutional," and quoted directly from *Ex parte Milligan*. As long as civil courts were "open in the territory in which we are now located," they should have jurisdiction.

Biddle quickly rose to his feet. Dressed in a white linen suit and white dress shoes, the attorney general stood out sharply against the background of khaki uniforms. Sketching the government's case in the simplest possible terms, he said the defendants were in "exactly and precisely the same position as armed forces invading this country." As such, they had no "civil rights" worth considering.

After a long discussion about the proper role of military tribunals, McCoy called a recess. He and his fellow judges excused themselves for half an hour, "about the time it takes to smoke a good cigar," in the phrase of Lloyd Cutler, a junior member of the prosecution team.[9] On his return, the general announced curtly, "The Commission does not sustain the objection of the defense. Proceed."

A distinguished soldier-diplomat, McCoy was the epitome of the "reasonable man" standard established by the president for the conduct of the tribunal. Like most of his fellow judges, he had no legal background. But he had impeccable military credentials. He served in the Spanish-American War with Theodore Roosevelt and was wounded in the Rough Riders' charge up San Juan Hill. TR later described his protégé as "the best soldier I ever laid eyes on."[10] Determined to prevent the saboteur case from getting bogged down in technical legal wrangling, McCoy even objected to Royall's use of the term "court" to describe the proceedings.

"This is a military commission," he lectured. "Please use that term."

An officer proceeded to read the charges against the eight saboteurs, beginning with "Charge One: Violation of the Law of War." The defendants were "enemies of the United States acting for and on behalf of the German Reich," who had passed through American defense lines "in civilian dress contrary to the law of war . . . for the purpose of committing acts of sabotage, espionage, and other hostile acts." They were also charged with violating the eighty-first and eighty-second Articles of War. The first of these articles dealt with "relieving or attempting to relieve enemies of the United States with arms, munitions, supplies, money, and other things"; the second punished "lurking or acting as spies in or about the fortifications, posts and encampments of the armies of the United States." The final charge was criminal conspiracy.

As they listened to the accusations, Dasch and the other saboteurs finally understood the seriousness of their situations. There could now be no doubt in their minds: if convicted, they faced the death penalty.

The defense lawyers objected that the accusation of "relieving" enemies of the United States was designed to be used against U.S. citizens who aided the enemy. Furthermore, their clients had never "lurked" about U.S. army encampments. McCoy overruled the objections in his usual brisk manner, causing Royall, who had been born and raised in the South, to think of an old saying from Reconstruction days: "Give the nigger a fair trial and hang him quick."[11]

Each defendant was required to respond to the charges, beginning in alphabetical order with Burger. They stood up one after another to plead "not guilty" to all charges. The trial proper could now get under way.

THE GOVERNMENT'S first witness was John Cullen, the coastguardsman who ran into the saboteurs the night they landed on Amagansett Beach, newly promoted to coxswain from seaman second class for his vigilance. After leading Cullen through his story, Biddle asked if he recognized the man who had walked toward him through the fog.

"I think so, sir."

"Will you stand up and identify him, if you see him in court? Stand up please. Now do you see the man?"

"Yes, sir."

"Which is he?"

"Right here, sir."

"Go and point to the man you have in mind. It won't hurt you. Just go and point at him. Point at him. Which is he?"

From the witness chair, Cullen walked over to the defendants, pointing at Dasch. In his well-cut suit and highly polished shoes, the defendant looked very different from his scruffy appearance on the beach, when he was dressed in sodden pants and a black fedora. But he was easy to recognize from the gray streak running through his hair. To make sure there would be no mistake, FBI agents had taken Cullen to the D.C. jail the evening before. He had stood in front of each cell door, examining the saboteurs in turn, before picking out the man who had introduced himself as George John Davis.

Biddle asked Dasch to stand up. He did so, taking a couple of steps toward Cullen, so they were barely inches apart.

"Is that the man you remember seeing?" Biddle asked the witness.

Cullen wanted to make doubly sure. He asked the accused to say "a few words." Dasch obliged with the first phrase that came into his head: "What is your name?"

"That's the man." Cullen sounded very confident now.

Cullen ran through the rest of his testimony quickly: how Dasch had pretended to be a fisherman stranded in the fog, how he refused to go with him to the Coast Guard station, the attempt at bribery, the menacing phrase "I wouldn't want to have to kill you."

The defense lawyers allowed most of Cullen's testimony to stand without objection. Royall interrupted on one point only, when Cullen talked about other coastguardsmen digging up four boxes of sabotage equipment. This was "hearsay," Royall argued, and should be stricken from the record. Since Cullen was not present when the boxes were dug up, he had no direct knowledge of what had happened and was relying on second-hand accounts. McCoy was unimpressed. He pointed out that the presidential order establishing the commission gave extraordinary latitude to both sides to introduce any evidence that would have "probative value for a reasonable man." As chairman of the tribunal, he would rule on what was "reasonable" or not.

It was left to the prosecution to speak for the defense. Biddle said he would call other witnesses later to establish how the boxes had been found, and there was therefore no need to rely on Cullen. He agreed that the witness's assertion should be struck from the record. Faced with this common front, McCoy grudgingly accepted Royall's objection. It was the first time he had ruled in favor of the defense.

Cross-examining Cullen, Royall established that the saboteurs would have had little difficulty overpowering him, as there was no one else on the beach and the Coast Guard station was not visible through the fog.

"No one was in your vicinity, no member of the Coast Guard?"

"No, sir."

"And no one attempted to injure you in any way?"

"No, sir."

Dasch's defense counsel, Colonel Carl Ristine, joined in the cross-examination of Cullen. A lawyer in the office of the army inspector general, Ristine had been pressed into service at the last moment to represent Dasch, whose role in going to the FBI put him in a different category from the others. He barely had time to talk with his client or review basic court documents. Dasch would later complain that the pleasant, soft-spoken Ristine lacked forcefulness; he wished his defense had been entrusted to a man like Royall, who "fought like a lion" for his clients.[12]

At the end of the session, Dasch asked Ristine if he could arrange a meeting with Cullen, as he wanted to refresh his memory about events on the beach. Ristine brought the young coastguardsman over to the defendants. Although Dasch was polite and very friendly, he was also upset with Cullen for not standing up for him.

"I was supposed to kill you, but I didn't," he told the coastguardsman. "Now it's your turn to help me."[13]

Dasch said he had never used the phrase "I wouldn't want to kill you" when talking to Cullen on the beach, but instead something like "You want to live, don't you?" He asked Cullen to change his testimony. But Cullen insisted that he had clearly heard the word "kill."

Hoover, who was seated next to Biddle at the prosecution table, was alarmed to see the government's lead witness chatting with one of the defendants. He walked over and told them brusquely to break it up. Soldiers escorted Dasch out of the room.

PRACTICALLY NOTHING of what was happening inside room 5235 was known to journalists assigned to cover the trial. The secrecy was intensely frustrating. This was one of the biggest stories of the war, and it was taking place behind closed doors. Instead of real information, the journalists were fed irrelevant scraps, such as the detail that the prosecution team included a lawyer named George Washington, "the nearest living collateral descendant" of America's first president.[14] The most that Biddle would say when he emerged from the barricaded corridor was that the trial would continue "tomorrow." The secrecy was not his idea, he told reporters. To say anything more, he joked, would be to risk a court-martial himself.[15]

The biggest excitement of the first day of the trial for the press was the fleeting appearance in the Justice Department of the twenty-four-year-old girlfriend of Herbie Haupt. The *New York Post* described the dark-haired Gerda Stuckmann as a "vision in white," wearing a white suit, white shoes, and a white turban. Gerda had given reporters her version of her relationship with Herbie, claiming she had turned down his offer of marriage. Underneath the headline "Widow Jilts Haupt, One of 8 Seized Spies," the *Washington Post* quoted Gerda as saying, "He always appeared to be a gentleman, interested in reading and music. He played the piano and was especially fond of the music of Schubert. I knew he liked Hitler's policies, but that was a couple of years ago and we weren't in the war. Now I am ashamed of him and don't want anything more to do with him."[16]

In the absence of hard facts, reporters ran with anything they could. Nolen Bulloch of the *Washington Times-Herald* provided his readers with a front-page description of the scene inside the D.C. jail as the saboteurs arrived. An FBI investigation later established that the reporter was "serving a short sentence in the District jail for drunkenness" at the time and was therefore "in a position to observe what was going on and obtain a scoop."[17]

Hoover was so worried about leaks that he ordered all his agents to refrain from discussing the trial in restaurants or other public places.[18] One source of his concern was a memo from a deaf Justice Department employee who reported that he had been able to gather information about the trial by reading the lips of his fellow agents as they discussed the case in the office cafeteria.

Just how much information should be relayed to the press was the subject of heated arguments within the government. On June 13, the day Dasch and his men landed at Amagansett, the president had responded to complaints by journalists about the lack of reliable information from the army by setting up the Office of War Information (OWI) under Elmer Davis, a former journalist and well-known radio commentator. The media saw the saboteur case as the first test of the credibility of the government's new information chief.

Davis wanted to be as open as possible with the press, while preserving necessary military secrecy. He felt "Americans are entitled to know everything that the enemy knows; that the better they understand what this war is about, the harder they will work and fight to win it."[19] This led him to favor some press coverage of the sabotage trial, either by a small group of pool reporters or a member of his staff. All reports would be subject to military censorship, thus ensuring that nothing was released that could be helpful to the enemy. It was unreasonable, Davis thought, to expect newspaper editors and reporters to agree to voluntary censorship if they were not given some information about this most sensational of trials.

From the army's point of view, any information about the trial might be damaging, as it would provide clues to American intelligence methods and reveal flaws in U.S. coastal defenses. The Germans should be led to believe that the coastline was impregnable, which would deter them from mounting future sabotage missions. The military argued that there was no satisfactory way of editing the testimony for public release without disclosing sensitive information, either directly or by omission.

Stimson, in particular, was scathing about civilian meddling in military matters, and refused to permit an OWI representative to attend the tribunal hearings. When a reporter asked whether Davis would be supervising the release of military communiqués, he inquired with sarcasm, "Is Mr. Davis an educated military officer?"[20]

The reporter remarked that the OWI director might be considered "one of those civilian generals." "Yes, there are many of them," the secretary shot back.

BY THE second day of the trial, Roosevelt had become exasperated by all the squabbles arising from the case. The FBI was at loggerheads with the navy and the Secret Service; the secretary of war could not stand the attorney general; the press was clamoring for access to the military tribunal. "I am going to go over to my office and will spend the day blowing up various people," the president told Daisy Suckley after breakfast at the White House.[21]

He had summoned Davis and Stimson to adjudicate their dispute about publicity for the trial. His press secretary, Steve Early, sided with Davis. At first, Roosevelt had also been inclined to allow some limited reporting of the trial, but Stimson had invoked national security. The president now told Davis that reporters should not be permitted to attend the trial. Instead the commission would issue communiqués through OWI.

This was viewed as a concession to the media—until the first communiqué appeared. It announced merely that the military commission had convened in the presence of the defendants and their lawyers, and continued: "The sessions will be closed, necessarily so, due to the nature of the testimony, which involves the security of the United States and the lives of its soldiers, sailors and citizens." Subsequent communiqués were similarly terse.

As Stimson emerged from the Oval Office, he found himself besieged by "self-seeking journalists trying to make trouble."[22] He later complained to his diary that the press had "a vested interest in breaking down secrecy in order to sell more papers." The secretary of war felt the media were picking on him because of his insistence on the need for confidentiality. He blamed Biddle for the unpleasantness.

> The fault of the whole matter lies directly on the doorstep of the Attorney General. It was he who in the first place told me of the absolute necessity for secrecy in regard to the evidence. He told me of the particular evidence which was especially dangerous to have come out and said that he had told it to no one else. But immediately after he had taken this attitude and imposed on me the necessity for defending the secrecy of the court, he has wavered under the impact of the

assaults of the press and has been rushing into publicity himself. His subordinate, Hoover, gave before the trial elaborate interviews as to the facts and Biddle himself has done the same thing in press conferences. This has made it very unfair and very hard on me.

For his part, Biddle felt the censorship was "overdone."[23] The Germans must have known "the substance of the evidence," and there was "little if anything that had to be concealed, except the confessions of Dasch and Peter Burger." But opinion polls suggested that the American public sided overwhelmingly with Stimson and the military on the need for secrecy.[24] Of those questioned in a Princeton University study, 69 percent said the tribunal proceedings "should be kept secret," while only 27 percent felt that reporters should be permitted to attend.

Stimson did make a couple of minor concessions. He permitted U.S. Army Signal Corps photographs of the hearing to be distributed to the press. He also allowed a group of twelve reporters to visit room 5235 during a break in the hearing. The reporters were not permitted to talk to anyone, but were free to report what they saw. At least they were getting their first glimpse of the saboteurs.[25] The effect was deflating.

"Instantaneous reaction was that the mysterious Hitler agents were no Nazi supermen but merely a group of most ordinary looking individuals," reported Lewis Wood of the *New York Times*. "Not one of these men charged with a desperate plot suggested in the slightest a burly booted Storm Trooper, a brutal U-boat captain or, indeed, anything resembling the vital, ruthless blond German glorified by Hitler. On the contrary, they were most inconspicuous physically."

Dillard Stokes of the *Washington Post* reported that "the spies flinched" as their names were read out by General Cox for the benefit of the journalists. Dasch "sat tensely forward on his chair and took notes on a pad on his knee." Kerling "gave the reporters a long, cold, level stare." Neubauer clasped his hands "so tightly together that his knuckles were white." The unshaven Haupt "chewed gum vigorously and his mouth curled into a sneer." Quirin's "wide-set eyes glared." Thiel returned "stare for stare as long as he was under scrutiny." Heinck "did not want to be seen at all and crouched behind a pillar until General Cox ordered him to lean forward."

The reporters were also allowed to inspect objects on the evidence table, which included dirty socks and oil-stained dungarees, a pair of

German army boots, a "fatigue cap with a swastika emblem," spades, and other articles, all neatly tagged with green labels. After fifteen minutes, the journalists were escorted from the room, and the trial resumed.

INSIDE ROOM 5235, the trial was turning into a contest of gladiators. Both Biddle and Royall were experienced trial lawyers. They had both studied law at Harvard, and they were both physically imposing. Biddle was six feet two, Royall a towering six feet five. In other respects, however, they were very different, both physically and in the way they approached the case. Biddle wore a neatly cropped mustache in the middle of his round face, with a few strands of carefully combed hair struggling to conceal a bald pate. With his air of noblesse oblige, dazzling white suit, and ever-present pocket handkerchief, Biddle could have been a European dandy strolling the boulevards of Paris. Royall, by contrast, dressed in a loosely fitting military uniform. He had a soft, pleasant voice tinged by a deep-chested North Carolina drawl, and a country boy personality that disguised an intensely competitive nature. He was better prepared and more incisive than Biddle, with an ability to go quickly to the heart of a complicated legal argument.

Although he had the more effective courtroom manner, Royall also had the weaker case. The defense strategy rested on exploiting a series of legal technicalities and procedural irregularities, which might have made an impression on a civilian court or even a regular court-martial, but were largely irrelevant to a military tribunal that made up its own rules. Under the "reasonable man" standard decreed by the president, the judges were not even bound by the rules of evidence outlined in the courts-martial manual. Biddle made the most of his extraordinary latitude to introduce evidence that would have been inadmissible in a civilian trial.

Key to the prosecution's case were the "confessions" elicited from the saboteurs by the FBI, in which each defendant incriminated not only himself but the others. Royall argued in vain that the courts-martial manual forbade the use of such pretrial statements against other members of an alleged conspiracy. Biddle dismissed the defense argument as an irrelevant technicality. Royall then rose to invoke the centuries-old legal traditions of the Anglo-Saxon world, which "stood in sharp contrast" to the legal system of totalitarian states like Nazi Germany. To rely on "the unsworn, unexamined, and uninvestigated" declaration of one defendant as evidence against the remaining seven, Royall said, would undermine the most basic principles of American justice. His passionate rhetoric notwithstanding, the judges sided with Biddle and declared the evidence admissible.

In fact, Biddle was selective in his use of confessions. He opposed the reading of Dasch's 254-page statement into the record on the grounds that it was superfluous and "self-serving." He preferred to have an FBI agent summarize the document. Seated by the wall, Dasch could scarcely restrain himself. He felt the statement would demonstrate that he had fully cooperated with the American authorities in uncovering the sabotage plot. Ristine relayed to the tribunal Dasch's demand that the whole document be read aloud, adding plaintively, "It is his freedom that is at stake, not mine." This time, the judges agreed with the defense. Since the statement was so long, the task of reading it aloud was assigned to relay teams of junior lawyers and FBI agents. It took three days of rapid-fire recitation to complete the job.

Ristine did not help his client's case with his cross-examination of Duane Traynor, the FBI agent who had spent five days interrogating Dasch after he first came to Washington. At first, Traynor told the commission, he had been impressed by Dasch's "sincerity and truthfulness," but came to have doubts about his informant. He cited Dasch's erratic behavior in first insisting that nothing be said about his role in going to the FBI because he wanted to protect his parents from retribution by the Nazis and later deciding that he wanted the world to know about his actions. There were times, Traynor added, when Dasch seemed to be deliberately holding back information.

The reading of confessions was occasionally interrupted by demonstrations of sabotage paraphernalia. The FBI explosives expert, Donald Parsons, invited the judges to marvel at the ingenuity of the bomb-making equipment recovered from the beaches of Amagansett and Ponte Vedra. Sometimes, his enthusiasm ran away with him, as when he offered to assemble an "American fountain pen" set cunningly designed to conceal a delay mechanism for detonating explosives. "I think it had better be unassembled, so as to put it in a safe condition," a tribunal member commented dryly.

A few days later, another FBI agent demonstrated the system of secret writing used by the saboteurs. He produced the white handkerchief confiscated from Dasch, stretched it tautly over a frame, and exposed it to an uncorked bottle of ammonium hydroxide.

"Can the commission see?" Biddle asked, as red letters appeared on the handkerchief.

"The commission can see and smell," replied McCoy.

Biddle wound up his case with a plea for a commonsense approach to the evidence, ignoring the legal quibbles raised by the defense. "These men, not having an opportunity to talk it over, on the whole made confessions entirely bearing out what each other said. Dasch supports Burger, Burger supports Kerling and so on, down the line." He compared the powers of the military commission to administrative tribunals such as the Securities and Exchange Commission that were not bound by the hearsay rule. It was difficult to conceive, he said, that "a body of reasonable men" would reject confessions that bore "the obvious marks of truthfulness."

This gave Royall an opening. The prosecution, he told the judges, was trying to apply the standards of "a dollar-and-cents controversy" to a capital case. "If that is the law, we are losing mighty near all of our vaunted system of criminal justice." The judges were unimpressed by his eloquence. Shortly before noon on July 20, McCoy ruled that the confessions of the defendants were valid evidence "for all purposes."

"The prosecution rests its case," Biddle concluded.

DEPRIVED OF news from the trial, Americans devoured information about sabotage plots, real or imagined. Books about saboteurs and subversives shot to the top of the best-seller lists. Suddenly, everyone in the country was on the lookout for German agents. The FBI was swamped with offers of assistance, tips, derogatory information about next-door neighbors, and suggestions on how to deal with the "Nazi rats."

"Why waste bullets or electricity on them?" was a typical sentiment, expressed by Theodore Piaszczyk of South Carolina soon after the trial began.[26] "I am not rich, just a shipfitter at the Charleston navy yard, but I will donate $5 a head to the government, if you will give me the privilege of putting the rope around their necks, by my own hand. I am not the man to kill a chicken, but I would like to get my hands on those rats."

An anonymous message from New York City apologized for bothering Hoover on the July 4 holiday, and then added: "We don't want to be alarmists. But please investigate 306 West 99th Street. Hates women tenants. Lets men with shortwave sets keep them on all night."

"The entire country owes you a big vote of thanks," a Miss M. R. Shaeffle wrote Hoover from San Francisco. "When I think of the damage these men could have done if you hadn't caught them, it fairly makes me sick. I sincerely trust they get what is coming and get it quickly!" E. C. Newman, a Baltimore businessman, called for the saboteurs to be given a "fair trial" and then be "shot at sunrise."

Hoover kept a file of cartoons and newspaper editorials about the case. When a cartoon struck his fancy, he requested the original to hang in his den at home. One drawing he particularly liked showed a Hoover vacuum cleaner labeled "FBI" sucking up panicked enemy agents across a map of the United States. The FBI director made sure that the more blood-curdling editorials—such as "Shoot them" (New Orleans States) or "Give them death" (El Paso Times)—were forwarded to Biddle.

Anyone who expressed the slightest sympathy for Germany or the saboteurs was marked down as a possible subversive. A Los Angeles woman named Alice Haskell wrote a letter urging the president "to show that we have not lost all sense of justice and decency in our treatment of the fine German people who have not harmed us in any way, but who on the contrary have helped this nation mightily since revolutionary days." Hoover instructed his agents to investigate the woman for security violations and report back "in the immediate future."

Opinion polls showed the American public turning even more strongly against ethnic Germans. Fifty-one percent of those questioned in a government survey in July described German-Americans as the "most dangerous" ethnic group in the country, up from 46 percent in April.[27] By contrast, 26 percent of those questioned were most concerned by Japanese-Americans, and only 1 percent by Italian-Americans.

First to feel the brunt of public outrage were the family members and friends of the saboteurs. Anyone who had dealt with the V-men during their two weeks of freedom was called in for questioning. On July 13, Biddle announced the arrest of "fourteen individuals" who "provided shelter" to the saboteurs or served as their "immediate contacts."[28] Those arrested included Kerling's wife, Marie; his mistress, Hedy Engemann; his Bund friend, Helmut Leiner; most of Haupt's relatives in Chicago; and the Jaques couple, who had agreed to look after Neubauer's money belt. Dozens of Bundists and suspected Nazi sympathizers were rounded up for questioning.

Haupt's parents took their disgrace particularly badly. A tearful Hans Haupt told reporters that it never entered his head that Herbie was a spy.

"We cannot believe that our boy would turn against the country we taught him to love," he pleaded.[29] After his own arrest, he broke down completely, suffering hallucinations, refusing to eat, and slashing his wrists in a suicide attempt. One of the main accusations against the elder Haupt was that he purchased an automobile for his son, to be used for "sabotage activities," including the recovery of the Florida arms cache.

The paranoid public mood affected ethnic Germans who had nothing at all to do with the saboteurs. Soon after the trial began, the Justice Department issued an order for the dismissal of German, Italian, and Japanese waiters, barbers, and busboys in the Washington area for fear they might overhear gossip from their well-connected clientele. The *Washington Post* reported that high officials were "deeply concerned about the amount of loose talk in Washington."[30] The front-page story noted that Germans were likely to be particularly hard hit by the dismissal order, as they were considered the "best waiters and are to be found in all first-class hotels."

AMERICANS TOO GARRULOUS
Loose Patrons' Tongues to Cost
Alien Waiters Here Their Jobs
Quiet, Please

Roosevelt shared the nation's concerns about the dangers of subversion, and understood the thirst for retribution. The maneuverings of Royall and the other defense lawyers did not matter very much to him. If necessary, he told Biddle, he was prepared to follow the example of Abraham Lincoln during the Civil War, and simply refuse to recognize the authority of the civilian courts.[31] The fact that the president was meant to review any sentences issued by the military tribunal did not prevent him from discussing the verdict with members of his inner circle while the trial was still in progress.

"What should be done with them?" he asked his aide, William Hassett, when they got back to Hyde Park. "Should they be shot or hanged?"[32]

"Hanged by all means," replied Hassett, who knew that George Washington had turned down a request by the British spy Major John André to be shot by firing squad because it was "too honorable" a death.

"What about pictures?" the president asked.

"By all means," said Hassett enthusiastically, recalling the photographs of Mrs. Surratt and the other Lincoln conspirators swinging from the gallows in the hot summer sun. A good picture was worth "a million words."

"Hope the findings will be unanimous," FDR concluded. Hassett did not doubt he meant "unanimously guilty."

FOR THE first two weeks of the military tribunal, the eight saboteurs had sat quietly along the corridor wall of room 5235, barely reacting to the arguments between Biddle and Royall. Now, for the first time, it was their turn to speak.

Royall decided to put Herbie Haupt on the witness stand first, depicting him as a naïve American boy who got dragged into the sabotage plot through a series of chance occurrences. Prodded by his attorney, Haupt described how he had run away from home to avoid getting married and wound up in the bureaucratic nightmare of Nazi Germany. He recalled the seemingly insane questions of the police and Gestapo—"how many fillings did I have in my teeth, where did I get them"—the impossibility of finding work, and finally the seemingly providential chance of returning to America on a secret mission.

He never intended to go through with the sabotage plan, Haupt insisted. Instead he planned to turn the other saboteurs over to the FBI on July 6, when Dasch and Kerling were due to arrive in Chicago following their meeting in Cincinnati. As for his purchase of a car, it had nothing to do with traveling back to Florida to pick up the sabotage gear, as the prosecution alleged. He wanted it for pleasure and to take his girlfriend Gerda on a honeymoon, after they got married. He had missed having an automobile in Germany.

Why wait until July 6 before going to the FBI, Biddle wanted to know when the time came for cross-examination. It was the obvious question, and Haupt's answer was complex. In part, he said, he was "nervous" and did not want to be bothered. He also wanted to talk the matter over with the others when they came to Chicago. He did not believe that any of them—at least the members of the Florida group—intended to blow anything up. "After what Neubauer told me in Chicago, I knew he was not going through with it. I knew how nervous Kerling and Thiel were, and knew they would not go through with it. I would be a lovely fellow to go to the FBI and save my neck, and have these men shot."

"Were you going to have your honeymoon after July 6 or before?" Biddle asked incredulously.

"After."

"You thought, of course, that the FBI, after you had given the confession, would say, 'Go off on your honeymoon.'"

Why not? If he told the FBI everything, Haupt said, "there would be no reason to be guilty of anything."

Gerda Stuckmann was one of several witnesses called by the defense to support Haupt's claim that he did nothing to implement the sabotage plot while in Chicago. She described how he had asked her to marry him, and had given her $10 for a blood test. She had been playing for time, she told the judges. "I wanted to talk to him a little more about where he had been."[33] At Haupt's insistence, Royall also called his mother to the witness stand. Speaking in a voice so soft that the judges could scarcely hear, Erna Haupt said she knew nothing about her son's activities in Chicago, except that he had registered for the draft and tried to get his old job back at the Simpson Optical Company.

Haupt was followed to the stand by Neubauer, who depicted himself as a victim of circumstance. "As a soldier, you are not supposed to think," he told Royall. "I just got the order. I didn't know what for." When he learned that he was being sent to the United States as a saboteur, he didn't like it. "In the first place, my wife was born here in the States, and the family of my wife is here in the States. And another thing, if you have been a soldier or are a soldier, you don't think much of an agent or saboteur." When Biddle asked Neubauer why he didn't immediately go to the FBI, he said he feared that word would get back to Germany and his family would suffer reprisals.

Next was Thiel, who also insisted he was "just following orders." His mind had been very muddled when he accepted Kappe's invitation to go on a mission to America. One of his brothers had lost an eye fighting the Germans and another had been killed in the Ukraine. At first, he thought Kappe planned to use him as a propaganda agent. It was only after he got to the school in Brandenburg that he realized he was to be trained as a saboteur. By then it was too late to back out.

Kerling, the leader of the Florida group, was the most forthright and unrepentant. He described how he joined the Nazi Party in 1928, with a membership number of around 70,000, making him part of the Old

Guard. But even Kerling had his doubts and hesitations. He had privately told his defense lawyers that the sabotage plot was doomed to failure as long as "a crackpot" and "egomaniac" like Dasch was in charge.[34] His plan had been to stay in the United States long enough to convince his superiors in Germany that he had made an attempt at sabotage and failed, and then escape to a country like Argentina, where the Nazis were "running the show." He repeated much the same story to the tribunal, without the explicit criticism of Dasch.

When Biddle asked Kerling to say whether or not he was "a loyal Nazi," he squirmed. "I would say I am a loyal German." He did not like the way old party members had been pushed aside by newcomers and careerists, and he also felt let down by the slipshod preparations for Operation Pastorius. "I can say that I have tried to be a loyal party member until I got into this thing, but when they used me, used the power they held over me, I doubt my loyalty."

The tribunal tried to untangle the story of Kerling's complicated love life by listening to testimony from both his wife and his mistress. Marie Kerling had little to add as she had not even seen Eddie since his return from Germany: he was arrested while on his way to a meeting with her. Hedy Engemann confirmed that Kerling had asked her to go to Florida with him, a potentially damaging admission since the prosecution contended that the purpose of the trip was to retrieve the explosives from Ponte Vedra Beach. Kerling was able to meet briefly with both women after they testified. "There was so much to say, and no chance to let you know how I felt," he wrote Hedy later. "But it was good to hold your hand, trembling as it was."[35]

Neither Heinck nor Quirin added very much to their previous statements to the FBI; each was on the stand for only about an hour. Heinck said that the day before his arrest, he had dreamed of "Dasch standing in the FBI office" and revealing everything. Quirin acknowledged he was a loyal Nazi, but claimed he had no intention of blowing anything up. This provoked a series of questions from McCoy, as president of the commission, about the Nazi chain of command.

"George Dasch was your leader, I take it."

"Yes, sir."

"And you obeyed all his orders?"

"Yes, sir."

"Would you have obeyed his orders to spy in this country?"

"No, sir."

"He was your führer, was he not?"

"Yes."

"You would have obeyed all his orders to commit sabotage?"

"I am not sure about that."

Biddle wanted to know what Quirin would have done if Hitler personally had ordered him to blow up American factories.

"I don't know. I never met the Führer. I don't know what kind of man he is. How can I answer that?"

THE LAST defendants to testify were Dasch and Burger, the two turncoats. Royall had saved Burger for last, as he was the most impressive witness, both factual and concise. Dasch, by contrast, was verbose and had trouble answering questions without making long speeches. "We will be here for a week if this kind of thing goes on," Biddle complained. "I have never heard any evidence like this in my life."

The prosecution could hardly deny an obvious fact: Dasch had reported voluntarily to the FBI and blown the whistle on Operation Pastorius. The question was, what had led him to betray the others? Biddle argued that his decision was essentially opportunistic, made on the spur of the moment, after running into the Coast Guard on Amagansett Beach and realizing that the sabotage plan would not work. He pointed to Dasch's intimate involvement in the planning stages of the operation back in Berlin, when he worked closely with Kappe in selecting the saboteur teams. Dasch maintained that he had intended to betray Operation Pastorius right from the start, in order to fight Nazism, and had only pretended to cooperate with Kappe to protect himself and ensure he became part of the mission.

Without knowing Dasch's state of mind while he was still in Germany, it was impossible for even the most fair-minded judge to fully resolve this dispute. Ristine emphasized that his client had never been a member of the Bund and had phoned the FBI office in New York the day after his arrival on Long Island. In his concluding arguments, Ristine also mentioned an important detail that seemed to support Dasch's claim that he decided to betray the sabotage operation long before landing on Amagansett Beach. Back in Berlin in mid-May, Kappe had asked Dasch to give Kerling an address through which he could be contacted in the United States. In response, Dasch provided a fictitious address for his younger brother Ernst in New London, Connecticut, rather than Astoria, New York, where he actually lived. Kerling had written the false address for Ernst Dasch in secret ink on his pocket handkerchief.[36] It is difficult to explain why, if Dasch was really committed to Operation Pastorius, he would make it impossible for the other group leader to reach him in an emergency.

In his cross-examination, Biddle zeroed in on the weakest point in Dasch's defense: the delay of six days before he finally turned himself in. Why, Biddle wanted to know, didn't he go to the FBI "right away"?

"I had three reasons, sir. May I explain all three reasons?"[37]

"Surely, do them quickly—all three."

First, said Dasch, he was "a mental and nervous wreck." Second, he wanted to be "human" toward members of the Kerling group, particularly "this little kid Haupt" who had family in the United States. He could not just run to the police and deprive Haupt of the chance to demonstrate his innocence. "That would have been merely for the sake of my own self-protection. That would have been the rottenest thing in the world. To be a real decent person I had to wait."

Dasch never got to explain his third reason, as Biddle returned to his favorite line of questioning. "Are you a loyal German or a loyal American?"

"I am loyal to the people of Germany."

"How about the people of America? Are you loyal to them, too?"

"Yes."

"You are loyal to everyone, aren't you?"

Dasch's version of events was supported by Burger, who testified that Dasch was a most unlikely leader of a sabotage mission. He would routinely do the opposite of whatever he was asked to do by his superiors. He was both contrary and incompetent. He had even lost his papers on the train from Paris to Lorient. Put simply, Dasch was no soldier and no saboteur. The other V-men were all suspicious of Dasch because he acted so "queerly."

Royall succeeded in showing that Burger had plenty of reason to hate the Nazis. Asked how he was treated by the Gestapo, Burger choked up, and was unable to answer. He finally replied that it was not the way he was treated that hurt him, but the way his wife was treated.

"They knew my wife expected a baby. They had her come down to [Gestapo headquarters] several times and told her that I had stolen money; that I [could get] eight years on a chain gang, that she should get a divorce."

He went on to describe how his wife had had a miscarriage, but still refused to get a divorce. "They told her she should bring my uniform down to Gestapo headquarters so I could wear it and they could rip off my epaulets. She refused that also. After that, they made me write a farewell letter to my wife, telling her I would never come back." At that moment, Burger told the judges, he had decided to find some way out of Nazi Germany.

Royall questioned Burger about a trail of evidence he had left on Amagansett Beach—a half-smoked pack of German cigarettes, a bottle of schnapps, a raincoat, a vest—that had helped lead the Coast Guard to the arms cache. This suggested a premeditated decision to sabotage the sabotage operation. The defense lawyer noted that his client's version of events was "corroborated one hundred percent by the Coast Guard." Burger had mentioned leaving the items on the beach in his original statement to the FBI, at a time when he had no way of knowing they had already been found by the Coast Guard.

As defense counsel for all the saboteurs with the exception of Dasch, Royall recognized that he was in a tricky position. By emphasizing Burger's role in wrecking Operation Pastorius, he was drawing attention to the passivity of his other clients. It was a clear conflict of interest that violated a fundamental concept of American justice: the right of defendants to separate counsel. Reflecting on the case six decades later, as the sole surviving member of the prosecution team, Washington lawyer Lloyd Cutler would conclude that this alone would probably have been "sufficient cause for a mistrial" in any normal legal proceeding.[38]

But a military commission was not a normal legal proceeding.

EVER SINCE the trial opened, tensions had been building within the government over who should take the credit for breaking the case. As the man who had announced the arrests of the saboteurs, J. Edgar Hoover was the public face of the investigation. On the third day of the trial, the FBI director went on the radio to denounce the saboteurs as "Nazi scoundrels," boast that his G-men men had foiled "a diabolical scheme . . . to paralyze American industry," and warn that Hitler would "try to send more destructionists to our shores."[39]

Hoover's attempts to grab all the glory for the FBI were deeply resented by other government agencies, particularly the Coast Guard, which felt that its men deserved at least some recognition. But whenever the Coast Guard tried to draw attention to the role played by Cullen and others, it ran afoul of the Bureau's efficient and aggressive public relations outfit. Hoover's top publicist was the energetic Louis Nichols, who had come to the FBI from the advertising industry and liked to tell his boss about the strong-arm tactics he used to slap down his bureaucratic rivals.

When the Coast Guard public relations people complained that Hoover's radio script made no mention of Cullen, Nichols knew exactly what to do. After clearing his approach with Hoover, he told his Coast Guard counterpart, "on a purely personal basis," that it would be very unfortunate if the whole story came out.[40] If the Coast Guard insisted on making Cullen a hero, it might have a difficult time explaining why so little was done to raise the alarm, why the saboteurs were able to board a train to New York from Amagansett, why the FBI was not informed until a long time afterward. The FBI had avoided mentioning Cullen only because it wanted to save the Coast Guard "any embarrassment." How the Coast Guard handled the matter was its own business, of course, but the FBI believed that "we have enough to do to fight the enemy without having fights among ourselves."

For a while, everything seemed to go Hoover's way. Nichols had a tame senator, James M. Mead of New York, propose a congressional medal for the FBI director, an idea enthusiastically seconded by Hoover's main ally in the media, Walter Winchell. But then the Coast Guard struck back, in classic Washington fashion, with a leaked newspaper story:

OLD VEST HELPED
TO TRAP NAZIS
ON TRIAL HERE

———

*Coast Guard Officer
Cracked Case With
Aid of N.Y. Police*[41]

In the front-page *Washington Post* report, credit for breaking the case went to the Coast Guard, not the FBI. Cullen, "a department store delivery boy before he joined the Coast Guard," had surprised the saboteurs on the beach. Cullen had then led Coast Guard intelligence officers to a buried arms cache, and a vest with a telltale laundry tag. The intelligence officers had tracked down the owner of the vest through "skillful detective work," handing over a dossier on the case to the FBI, which proceeded to round up the saboteurs. The only thanks the Coast Guard had received from the FBI for its input was a demand from Hoover that the two intelligence officers be fired for "holding out the vest."

Much of the account was fiction—the laundry tag on the vest had proved to be a false lead—but what most upset Hoover and Nichols about the story was the implication that the FBI's role had been peripheral. While the presses were still running, Nichols demanded a correction, and the *Post* agreed to amend the headline to read: "Coast Guard Officer Cracked Case with Aid of N.Y. Police *and FBI*." Unsatisfied with this minor victory, Nichols briefed the Bureau's "established friends" in the media the following day. The beneficiaries of the counterleak included the *New York Times*, which ran a story headlined:

FEDERAL SERVICES
CLASH IN SPY TRIAL

———

Hoover of FBI Declares That
the Coast Guard Fails to
Cooperate Properly

———

VEST OF NAZI AN ISSUE

———

Officer and Others Alleged to
Have Retained the Garment
for Several Days[47]

By this time, Hoover was spitting mad. He rejected a truce proposal from the Office of War Information, which suggested a joint statement "approved by both the Coast Guard and the FBI setting forth the chronological developments of the case." Such a statement, he told his aides, would only reward the Coast Guard, which "had nothing to do with this case other than to obstruct and interfere with it," and was now putting out "false and erroneous stories."[43]

The way to end the sniping, Hoover snapped, was "for the Coast Guard to shut up."

THE BUREAUCRATIC warfare was soon forgotten as Americans, young and old, were swept up in what the press described as "the greatest manhunt in

American history."[44] On July 25, the FBI announced a nationwide search for Walter Kappe, Reinhold Barth, and Joseph Schmidt, who were reported to be planning fresh sabotage missions against America. Hundreds of thousands of wanted posters were printed, and nailed up in public places. Soon saboteur sightings were coming in from all over the country.[45]

The Los Angeles office of the FBI received seventy-five tips the first day alone. A nine-state police alarm was ordered after the reported sighting of all three wanted men on Napeague Beach, Long Island, not far from Amagansett, but the suspects turned out to be street entertainers. The commanding officer of Fort Myer, Virginia, reported a rumor that Kappe had been inducted into the U.S. Army "under the name of Herbert Smith." Foreign middle-aged men traveling in threesomes aroused particular suspicion. In Freeport, Long Island, three Norwegian seamen were detained after someone heard them talking animatedly "in German"; it turned out that their ship had been sunk by a German U-boat. In Boston, three Frenchmen were arrested, and only released after they proved that they worked for the French consul.

Suspects were hauled off trains, airline flights, and ships. Secretaries turned in their boyfriends, bus drivers reported on their passengers, elderly matrons scoured the public parks for anyone acting suspiciously. A Chicago woman wrote Hoover to complain about the "curious looking tramps" she had seen on a visit to Florida, "not the usual run of bums often seen during the past few years, but very distinctive looking ones" dressed in full "tramp paraphernalia." One of these so-called "tramps," she felt sure, was Joseph Schmidt.

Each sighting was duly investigated, swelling the FBI's already voluminous files on Kappe, but none was ever corroborated. Which was hardly surprising: the suspects were all in Germany.

CHAPTER THIRTEEN

EQUAL JUSTICE UNDER THE LAW

(JULY 29–AUGUST 1)

LAMBDIN P. MILLIGAN was one of those Americans, like Dred Scott and Ernesto Miranda, who lead unremarkable lives but are nevertheless destined to achieve immortality in legal textbooks. If it were not for the Supreme Court decision that bears his name, he would be forgotten entirely: a small-town lawyer from Indiana known to his friends as a fine conversationalist, an ardent supporter of states' rights, and a Northerner who sympathized with the South during the Civil War. Lincoln supporters dubbed people like Milligan "copperheads," after a particularly venomous snake that strikes without warning. But what made this particular copperhead a historic figure—and what made his case relevant to the case of the Nazi saboteurs nearly eight decades later—were the constitutional arguments that raged over his trial by a military commission.

Back in 1862, when the United States was fighting for its very survival, Lincoln issued a presidential proclamation establishing military commissions to try "all Rebels and Insurgents" as well as "their aiders and abettors." The decree effectively suspended the centuries-old legal tradition of habeas corpus that obliged the government to turn over suspected criminals to civilian courts for trial. Lincoln argued that it was sometimes necessary to resort to "otherwise unconstitutional" measures to save the nation and constitution, like cutting off a limb to save the body. The president's opponents accused him of behaving like a tyrant. Under Lincoln's decree, the authorities could sentence troublemakers to long terms of imprisonment or even death with a minimum of fuss. It was the perfect weapon to use against Milligan, who was suspected of conspiring with other copperheads to distribute arms to draft resisters. Within weeks of his arrest in October 1864 on charges of inciting insurrection and "giving aid and comfort to the enemies of the United States," he was duly sentenced by a military commission in Indiana to death by hanging.

A lawyer himself, Milligan knew that his best chance of a reprieve was to appeal his "unlawful imprisonment" to the federal courts. By the time the case came before the Supreme Court, the Civil War was over, and radical Republicans were using the assassinated president's 1862 decree to impose military justice on the newly conquered South. Milligan's lead defense counsel was James A. Garfield, a future president of the United States. He argued that the government had violated the Constitution by imposing martial law in regions of the country far from the actual fighting. The Supreme Court agreed with Garfield, ruling that martial law could only be imposed in cases of obvious necessity, such as a foreign invasion shutting down the civilian courts. As long as the civilian courts were operating normally, as they were in Indiana in 1864, defendants were entitled to a civil trial. By a 5–4 majority, the Supreme Court issued one of the most vigorous defenses of civil liberties in American legal history:

> The Constitution of the United States is a law for rulers and people, equally in war and in peace, and covers with the shield of its protection all classes of men, at all times, and under all circumstances. No doctrine, involving more pernicious consequences, was ever invented by the wit of man than that any of its provisions can be suspended during any of the great exigencies of government. Such a doctrine leads directly to anarchy or despotism . . .[1]

While often criticized as being too sweeping, *Ex parte Milligan* had never been overruled. As counsel for seven of the eight saboteurs, Royall understood immediately that this seventy-six-year-old case offered the best hope of saving his clients from execution. Like Milligan and Garfield before him, he would appeal to the Supreme Court. The question was, how?

In normal times, appeals to the Supreme Court proceed according to a leisurely timetable. A case must wend its way through a multitude of lower courts—district court, appeals court, perhaps a state supreme court— before it becomes eligible for consideration by the highest court in the land. On this occasion, Royall understood that there was no time to lose:

Roosevelt's order setting up the military tribunal made no provision for an appeal process, meaning that a verdict could be implemented without delay. By the time the Supreme Court got around to hearing the case, the saboteurs could already be dead.

Royall knew that the quickest way of getting the Supreme Court to hear an appeal was to apply to an individual justice for a temporary writ asserting jurisdiction. But the Court was already in summer recess, and most of the justices were on vacation. Only one justice was available in Washington: Hugo Black, a Roosevelt appointee known as an ardent defender of civil liberties. Encouraged by Black's reputation, Royall went to see him, and asked him to issue a writ to review the saboteur case in light of *Milligan.*

"You mean the case of these German spies?"[2]

"We don't call them spies, but I suppose that's the case you are talking about."

"I don't want to have anything to do with that matter."

"Mr. Justice, you shock me. That's all I can say to you."

Royall tried to reach several other justices, including Felix Frankfurter, his old Harvard law professor, but they were all unavailable. On Monday, July 20, he read in the *Washington Post* that Justice Owen Roberts, a former federal prosecutor appointed to the court by Herbert Hoover, was in town to attend the funeral of a former colleague. In the absence of Chief Justice Harlan Fiske Stone, who was on vacation in New Hampshire, Roberts was the senior member of the Supreme Court in the Washington area.

Royall immediately went to the justice's chambers and waited for Roberts to return from the funeral. Roberts agreed that the saboteur case raised important constitutional issues that merited review. Before taking any action, however, he wanted to consult his eight brethren, including Black. He invited Royall to come to his Pennsylvania farmhouse later in the week together with Biddle to discuss the case.

The following day, Tuesday, Royall and Dowell formally notified the military commission of their decision to appeal to the Supreme Court. They warned McCoy and his colleagues that there was a risk that some of the arguments developed behind closed doors in room 5235 could become public as a result of a Supreme Court hearing. Dowell, in particular, was worried that an open Supreme Court session would generate enormous publicity that could harm the war effort. "As a soldier," he told the commission, "I cannot bring myself to the point of doing that."[3]

Dasch's lawyer, Colonel Ristine, said he had come to the case late, without fully investigating the constitutional issues involved. As a serving army officer, he did not feel he was "authorized" to appeal to the Supreme Court.

As they had at the beginning of the trial, Royall and Dowell were trying to strike a balance between their responsibilities as defense lawyers and their duties as military officers. They were giving their superiors a chance to order them back into line, on national security grounds. In the event, the military commission followed the example set by the president a few weeks earlier, when informed that the defense was planning to challenge his decree denying the saboteurs access to the civilian courts. After a short break, McCoy announced that "the Commission does not care to pass on that question."

Once again, the two defense lawyers were on their own.

AFTER CONSULTING with the White House, Attorney General Biddle agreed to accept a full-scale challenge to the president's proclamation. It seemed preferable to argue the case before the Supreme Court than to risk being accused of flouting the Constitution. On Thursday morning, Biddle and Royall flew to Philadelphia on a military plane. An FBI car met them at the airport, and drove them to Justice Roberts's farm at Chester Springs, to the west of the city.

Roberts was a gracious host. He served the prosecutor and defense counsel crackers, cheese, and fresh farm milk as he listened to their arguments in favor of a hearing.[4] He then invited them to take a tour of the farm while he got in touch with his colleagues. Stone had already agreed in principle to take the case. Roberts was able to persuade Black, who was staying with him as a houseguest, to drop his earlier objections. The other justices signaled their agreement by phone. By the time Royall and Biddle returned from their stroll, the question had been settled. The Supreme Court would interrupt its summer recess for the first time in twenty-two years, and convene in Washington the following Wednesday, July 29, to consider the saboteur case.[5]

Announcement of the decision was delayed until Monday evening, and greeted with general astonishment. The *Washington Times-Herald* hailed the extraordinary Supreme Court session as "a smashing climax" to the saboteur trial that would pit the authority of the judiciary against the power of the presidency.[6] Not everybody, however, was happy. The trial had already dragged on for three weeks, far longer than most observers anticipated, and many people felt that it was getting bogged down in legal nitpicking. "There is nationwide grumbling over the length of time it is taking to convict the eight Nazi saboteurs who landed on our coasts from German submarines," noted the *Richmond Times-Dispatch.*[7] "It is greatly to be hoped that the court will find no ground for granting these writs, and that all the would-be dynamiters and murderers will be promptly executed, including the double-crosser who is said to be trying to save his skin by turning against his pals."

Before the court could convene, it needed a decision it could formally adjudicate. Royall took care of that on Tuesday evening by filing writs for habeas corpus with a district court in Washington. Habeas corpus—Latin for "you have the body"—is one of the most venerable and venerated legal procedures in the Anglo-Saxon world. It prevents the king or other executive authority from holding people unlawfully by demanding that they be turned over to a legally constituted court. In the words of the Magna Carta of 1215, negotiated between King John of England and his barons, "no free man shall be taken or imprisoned . . . or exiled or in any way destroyed except by the lawful judgment of their peers or by the law of the land." The Founding Fathers considered the principle of habeas corpus to be so important that they reaffirmed it in article 1 of the Constitution, rather than relegating it along with other civil liberties to the Bill of Rights. The Constitution states that "the privilege of the writ of habeas corpus shall not be suspended, unless when in case of rebellion or invasion the public safety may require it."

Filed on behalf of all the saboteurs except Dasch, the petitions for habeas corpus were couched in traditional, centuries-old language. "I am unjustly and unlawfully detained and imprisoned by color of the authority of the United States," each petition stated. "Wherefore, I pray that a writ of Habeas Corpus be issued by this Court, directed to Brigadier General Albert L. Cox, Provost Marshal General of the United States Army, Military District of Washington, commanding him to produce my body before your Court."[8]

It took District Judge James W. Morris only a few minutes to reject the petitions, citing the presidential proclamation of July 2 that denied "subjects, citizens or residents of a nation at war with the United States" the right to be heard in regular U.S. courts. The stage was now set for a landmark Supreme Court hearing. The case would become known as *Ex parte Quirin,* after Richard Quirin, one of the seven petitioners.

WHATEVER ITS constitutional significance, the extraordinary Supreme Court session was Washington's event of the season. Stimson, the crotchety secretary of war, was taken aback to be told by Felix Frankfurter that the Court was "being deluged with applications for entrance" from serving army officers, among other prominent Washingtonians.[9] Determined to prevent "a public show," he ordered the army chief of staff, George Marshall, to station a man at the door to prevent the entry of all uniformed officers, other than those directly connected with the trial.

The following morning, long lines of would-be spectators snaked around the Supreme Court, an imposing building opposite the Capitol completed just seven years earlier on the site of a federal prison. The legal gladiators ascended the gleaming white marble steps of the west portico, beneath a frieze depicting "Authority" and "Liberty" and the inscription "EQUAL JUSTICE UNDER THE LAW." For the most part, they arrived two by two, pausing for photographers in the sweltering summer sun. The two defense counsel, Royall and Dowell, both in loosely fitting colonels' uniforms, one very tall, the other short. The two government lawyers, Biddle in his trademark white suit, his assistant Oscar Cox in owlish round glasses. The nation's two top G-men, J. Edgar Hoover and his ever-present companion Clyde Tolson, in snap-brim hats, sharp suits, and crisp pocket handkerchiefs, Tolson precisely one step behind his boss. Only the saboteurs themselves were missing: the Supreme Court hearing would take place without them.

Inside the courthouse, Stone walked around the table in the wood-paneled conference room, shaking the hands of his brethren, a symbolic reminder of the court's unity in diversity. Eight justices were present. The ninth, William O. Douglas, was still on his way back from Oregon. Word had already reached the justices via Biddle that FDR planned to execute the saboteurs, whatever the Supreme Court decided.

"That would be a dreadful thing," said the chief justice.[10]

Despite the outward appearance of harmony, Stone's court was already known for its acrimonious divisions. The chief justice referred to his colleagues as "my wild horses."[11] The most strong-willed of them all was Frankfurter, a former professor of law at Harvard. Short in stature, pugnacious in manner, at once brilliant and arrogant, Frankfurter was contemptuous of anyone who did not share his opinions. He faulted Stone for an excessive preoccupation with legal formalities. He referred to the trio of liberal justices—Black, Douglas, and Frank Murphy—as "the Axis."[12] A European-born Jew, Frankfurter believed that the United States was fighting "a war to save civilization itself," and treated those who disagreed with him about the need for strong executive power as not only wrong-headed but potentially treasonous.[13] A dazzling conversationalist and correspondent, Frankfurter was on intimate terms with many members of the government, beginning with Roosevelt. Earlier in his career, he had served on Stimson's staff as U.S. attorney for the Southern District of New York, and they had remained close friends.

At conference, Frankfurter quickly moved to disqualify Murphy from any role in the hearing. A few weeks before, Murphy had accepted an army commission as a lieutenant colonel, and had attended a military training camp. A photograph had appeared on the front page of the *New York Times* of the justice in army uniform, cradling a submachine gun. Frankfurter argued that this created a clear conflict of interest, since the army was a party to the saboteur case. Murphy agreed to step aside. What Frankfurter failed to tell his colleagues was that he had himself talked about the case with his friend the secretary of war, and had even urged Stimson to set up a military tribunal "entirely composed of soldiers."[14] Had this been known at the time, it likely would have been grounds for Frankfurter's own disqualification from the Supreme Court hearing, in the opinion of many legal observers.[15]

At noon precisely, the marshal of the court shouted the traditional announcement for a new session: "Oyez, oyez, oyez"—Hear ye, hear ye, hear ye. The heavy purple drapes of the court's main chamber parted, and the black-robed justices settled into their nail-studded leather chairs, dwarfed by the huge white marble columns behind them. When the building was first inaugurated, one justice complained that he and his colleagues would look like "nine black cockroaches in the Temple of Karnak." It was an apt description, except that only seven "black cockroaches" were present on this occasion. An unhappy Murphy sat behind the curtain as an observer, and Douglas would not arrive until the following day.

Royall scarcely had time to approach the wooden lectern in front of the chief justice and introduce himself as counsel for the saboteurs when he was interrupted by his old Harvard law professor. Justice Frankfurter noted that writs for habeas corpus normally went from the district court to an ordinary appeals court, not the highest court in the land. Why should the Supreme Court even have jurisdiction in this case? Because of its urgency, replied Royall. Under the procedure laid down in the presidential proclamation, a verdict could be delivered and a sentence carried out without any kind of appeal. "A man has a right to an appeal," he said. Frankfurter seemed unconvinced, but Biddle supported Royall, saying the government did not object to the Supreme Court considering the case.

The preliminaries out of the way, Royall launched into his main argument, which was that Roosevelt's proclamation establishing a military commission was unconstitutional. He conceded that the saboteurs had been transported to America in a German U-boat, but argued that the government had failed to show sufficient reason to try them by military tribunal. The Articles of War reserved two crimes for military jurisdiction: espionage and "assisting the enemy" in an area of combat operations. Neither charge applied to his clients.

"They constituted, I suppose, an invading force?"[16]

This from Justice Robert Jackson, who would later serve as the chief U.S. prosecutor of Nazi war crimes at Nuremberg. His words echoed around the cavernous chamber, bouncing off the marble floors. Spectators at the back of the hall had to lean forward to hear what the justices and opposing counsel were saying through the faulty acoustics.

"No, sir," replied Royall. He noted that several defendants claimed that they had only pretended to go along with the sabotage plan in order to escape from Germany and return to America. Furthermore, Long Island and Florida, where the saboteurs originally landed, could hardly be described as areas of combat operations.

Justice James Byrnes took Royall's argument and reduced it to absurdity: "Your contention is that if the Führer and seven generals of the Army of the Reich should land from a submarine on the banks of the Potomac, having discarded their uniforms, they are entitled to every right you have discussed in the application for a writ of habeas corpus?"

"My argument would have to carry that fact, and does," Royall acknowledged. Under *Milligan*, unless an enemy soldier was detained within a theater of combat operations, he was entitled to the same legal rights as anyone else simply because he was "a person in America."

But surely, Frankfurter insisted, the enemy determined "the theater of operations" through his acts of aggression. "If a parachutist should come into this building, or near this building, would this not be a theater of operations?"

Royall conceded that this was so. His clients, however, arrived "unarmed." That is to say, they came with explosives, but "they did not engage in any actual combat operations."

"I am glad to know what 'unarmed' is," rejoined Frankfurter, as the chamber erupted in laughter.[17]

UNDER NORMAL circumstances, it is impossible to tell what the justices of the Supreme Court are thinking as they sit on the bench, weighing the arguments of opposing counsel. A few months later, however, Frankfurter would offer a running commentary of his views "on the issues of the saboteur case ever since my mind came to rest upon them." He did so in the form of a fictional dialogue between himself and the saboteurs, which he circulated to his fellow justices. Entitled "F.F.'s Soliloquy," it is one of the most unusual documents in Supreme Court history.[18]

> **Saboteurs:** Your Honor, we are here to get a writ of habeas corpus from you.
> **F.F.:** What entitles you to it?
> **Saboteurs:** We are being tried by a Military Commission set up by the President although we were arrested in places where, and at a time when, the civil courts were open and functioning with full authority and before which, therefore, under the Constitution of the United States we were entitled to be tried with all the safeguards for criminal prosecutions in the federal courts . . .
> **F.F.:** You damned scoundrels have a helluvacheek to ask for a writ that would take you out of the hands of the Military Commission and give you the right to be tried, if at all, in a federal district court. You are just low-down, ordinary, enemy spies who, as enemy soldiers, have invaded our country and therefore could immediately have been shot by the military when caught in the act of invasion. Instead you were humanely ordered to be tried by a military tribunal convoked by the Commander-in-Chief himself, and the verdict of that tribunal is returnable to the Commander-in-Chief himself to be acted upon by himself. To utilize a military commission to establish your guilt or innocence was plainly within the authority of the Commander-in-Chief.

Frankfurter was equally unimpressed by Royall's secondary arguments. The defense maintained that even if the president had a right to set up a military commission to try the saboteurs, he had failed to abide by the *Manual for Courts-Martial.* Article 46 of the manual provided for a review of tribunal proceedings by the judge advocate general. Article 50½ stated that such a review must be completed before the trial record and sentence were sent to the president for execution. The president's proclamation, Royall argued, short-circuited these established procedures. Frankfurter, by contrast, believed that the courts-martial manual did not apply to enemy agents. All the saboteurs were achieving by their appeal to the Supreme Court was endless legal trouble:

> You've done enough mischief already without leaving the seeds of a bitter conflict involving the President, the courts and Congress after your bodies will be rotting in lime. It is a wise requirement of courts not to get into needless rows with the other branches of government by talking about things that need not be talked about if a case can be disposed of with intellectual self-respect on grounds that do not raise such rows. I therefore do not propose to be seduced into inquiring what powers the President has or has not got, what limits the Congress may or may not put upon the Commander-in-Chief in time of war, when, as a matter of fact, the ground on which you claim to stand— namely, the proper construction of these Articles of War—exists only in your foolish fancy. That disposes of you scoundrels.

All in all, Frankfurter concluded, such abstract constitutional debates were a waste of time and national energy, a pastime better postponed "until peacetime." For the moment, however, he kept these thoughts to himself.

"MAY IT please the Court," Biddle began, when it was his turn to address the justices. "The United States and the German Reich are now at war. That seems to be the essential fact on which this case turns and to which all of our arguments will be addressed."

Not only was this war, the attorney general contended, it was "total war." It was impossible to compare the "East Coast of today" with the "Indiana of Milligan in 1864." Milligan was arrested far from the front lines. Modern war was "fought on the total front, on the battlefields of joined armies, on the battlefields of production, and on the battlefields of transportation and morale, by bombing, the sinking of ships, sabotage, spying, and propaganda." It was impossible to distinguish one battlefield from another. "We know that the two submarines were able to cross our lines and land these men on our patrolled shores. We know that our whole East Coast is a theater of operations in substantially the same sense as North Atlantic or the British Isles."

Biddle had made a valid point. The Articles of War, which governed military commissions, were written in the eighteenth century at the time of the Revolutionary War. They were designed to deal with the type of situation that arose when Major André was discovered "lurking" behind American lines close to West Point after contacting Benedict Arnold. In modern times, however, unlawful belligerents could turn up anywhere. They would not restrict themselves to "lurking or acting as a spy in or about . . . the fortifications, posts, quarters, or encampments of the armies of the United States," in the language of the Articles of War.

On the other hand, as Royall pointed out, the government's definition of "total war" was so elastic that it could be stretched to cover virtually any crime committed in wartime that might conceivably "aid the enemy." If the battlefield was everywhere, then military tribunals could also be established everywhere. A worker who went on strike in a defense plant could be hauled before a military commission on the grounds that he had helped the enemy on "the battlefield of production." There had to be some limit on the "total war" theory, Royall argued, "or we have very few constitutional guarantees left when we go to war."

At first, the justices listened respectfully to the attorney general as he rebutted Royall's arguments, sometimes saying "war of law" when he meant "law of war."[19] But soon they were challenging him to define where he drew the line between crimes that could and could not be tried by military commission.

Justice Black wanted to know what would happen if a U.S. citizen was "picked up on the street" several months after landing in the country as part of a group of enemy saboteurs. Would he be tried by military tribunal? "That is Haupt's case perfectly," Biddle replied. "Haupt landed, left his stuff buried in the sand, got away, and was arrested in the internal part of the country." In such a case, he had no problem arguing that the military should have jurisdiction.

"Suppose," said Black, "that a man had been accused of trying to interfere with work in a defense plant, and it was said that in some way he had received instructions from a foreign country. Under the [president's] order, would he be tried by a court-martial?"

"It is right on the edge," the attorney general replied.

"Where is the line?" asked Justice Jackson.

Biddle was reluctant to be precise. But he was sure of one thing, he told the justices. The line had to be drawn to include groups of saboteurs who invaded "the coast of the United States," evading patrols that were specifically on the lookout for enemy submarines and invaders. Furthermore, these particular saboteurs had taken off their uniforms, and were therefore not entitled to the privileges traditionally conferred on prisoners of war.

"The mere absence of uniforms makes a difference?" asked Justice Stanley Reed.

"All the difference in the world."

The following day, Thursday, Biddle turned his attention to the *Milligan* case, which he described as "bad law" because it interfered with the responsibility of the commander in chief to defend the country. It was "preposterous" to argue that the president could not take "proper steps to repel and capture" invaders. But even if the justices were reluctant to completely overturn *Milligan*, Biddle thought there were still grounds for carving out an exception for the saboteurs. Milligan was the citizen of a state that had kept out of the Civil War fighting. The saboteurs were enemy invaders.

In his rebuttal, Royall pointed out that the saboteurs had not blown up anything, and had never sought to retrieve the explosives they buried when they first came ashore. He continued to insist that the saboteurs had not passed through a "zone of combat operations."

"I don't quite get your distinction," interrupted Justice Black. "What about the planes that fly over foreign countries and drop bombs and destroy property far removed from the scene of battle?"

"If it was a military plane, that is generally accepted as a means of fighting or of combat."

"A submarine is, too."

"A submarine is, but these submarines in this case did not do anything but transport."

Winding up for the plaintiffs, after nine hours of debate spread over two days, Royall agreed with Biddle that the United States was fighting a war for its very survival. He then paraphrased the majestic words of Justice Davis in *Ex parte Milligan*. "The Constitution is not made for peace alone, it is made for war as well as peace. It is not merely for fair weather. The real test of its power and authority, the real test of its strength to protect the minority, arises only when it has to be construed in times of stress."

"The Court stands adjourned until twelve noon tomorrow," announced the chief justice, rapping his gavel on the table in front of him.

"MEMBERS OF the Commission, this has been a most unusual case," declared Judge Advocate General Myron Cramer on the morning of July 31, when the military tribunal reconvened to hear closing arguments. As the army's senior law enforcement officer, Cramer was assisting Biddle with the prosecution. The case was unusual, Cramer said, because it was the first time a military commission had met in seventy-seven years. It was even more unusual because the accused all claimed to be innocent of the charges against them, while admitting to doing all the things the prosecution said they did.

"They claim that instead of being invaders, they are refugees." The judge advocate general injected a note of sarcasm into the word "refugees." Such a claim was preposterous, he said. Not only were they trained saboteurs, they had passed through a theater of naval operations and "came and landed in the darkness of night on our shores." Had the beaches of Long Island and Florida been better protected, the U.S. Army would have had every right to shoot the prisoners down "as an invading force." For these reasons, Cramer urged the commission to sentence all the defendants to death.

Winding up for the defense, Royall had the tricky task of assuring the judges that he had complete confidence in their "wisdom and fairness" only hours after pleading with the Supreme Court to declare the military tribunal unconstitutional. Implicitly recognizing that the commission was likely to find his clients guilty, he sought to spare them from the death penalty. His main argument was that the defendants "did not blow anything up." The law had always drawn a clear distinction between intention and accomplishment, Royall noted. A man who bought a pistol "with intent to kill" would be fined no more than $50 "in most jurisdictions."

It was important, Royall insisted, for America to remain true to its own system of justice, even at times of greatest stress and crisis. "We want to win this war, and we are going to win it, but we do not want to win it by throwing away everything we are fighting for."

The defense arguments were cut short by the need to return to the

Supreme Court for the habeas corpus decision. At 11:40 a.m., McCoy declared a recess to allow both sides to keep their noon appointment in the shiny marble palace on Capitol Hill.

As THEY mulled over *Ex parte Quirin* in the conference room, the justices were unanimous in concluding that they should do nothing that would interfere with the war effort. This was not the time to undermine the authority of the president. On the other hand, they were reluctant to over-turn *Milligan,* as the attorney general seemed to want.

Although they agreed on where they should end up, the justices were divided about how to get there. Some of them, like Frankfurter, had little patience for abstract constitutional debates at a time when civilization hung by a thread. Others, like Roberts, were dubious about the legality of the president's proclamation denying the saboteurs access to civilian courts.[20] If they were going to preserve a public show of unanimity, they had to find a way of papering over these deep-seated differences.

As chief justice, Stone was a stickler for legal procedures and judicial independence. A few weeks earlier, he had turned down a request by Roosevelt to chair a government inquiry into the rubber crisis precisely because of his fervent belief in the separation of powers. While agreeing with much of what Biddle had to say about the nature of modern war, Stone was also impressed by some of the points raised by Royall. In partic-ular, he felt that the government should abide by the appeals procedures for military courts outlined in the Articles of War. In order to draw atten-tion to his concerns, he proposed including the following paragraph in the draft opinion:

> Even if petitioners are correct in their contention that Articles of War 46 and 50½ require the President, before his action on the judgment or sentence of the Commission, to submit the record to his staff Judge Advocate or the Judge Advocate General of the Army and even if that question be reviewable by the courts, nothing in the President's order of July 2, 1942, forecloses his compliance with such requirement and this Court will not assume in advance that the President would fail to conform his action to the statutory requirements.[21]

Translated into plain English, this was a way of serving notice on the president that he should comply with the Articles of War. But when Stone circulated the language at conference on Friday morning, some of his colleagues raised objections, on the grounds that it might cast doubt on the president's powers. As the justices debated the question, the hands on the clock on the mantelpiece in the conference room crept around to noon.

There was no time to resolve the dispute before the court announced its decision. Reluctantly, Stone agreed to omit the controversial paragraph. A couple of minutes later, he and the other justices filed back into the great hall of the Supreme Court. The chief justice picked up two typewritten sheets and proceeded to read a "per curiam" decision, meaning that it was a consensus document on behalf of the entire court. Interrupted briefly by the roar of a low-flying airplane, he announced that the justices had concluded that the military commission was "lawfully constituted" and that the "petitioners are held in lawful custody."[22]

"The motions for leave to file petitions for writs of habeas corpus are denied. The orders of the District Court are affirmed."

Surrounded by journalists on the steps of the court, Biddle pronounced himself "elated." A disappointed Royall would say only, "The Court has acted."[23] In fact, the Supreme Court had acted in a very curious fashion. The justices had agreed on a verdict without agreeing on the reasons for the verdict, a reversal of normal procedure that would cause Stone and his colleagues great agonizing in the months ahead.

"I want to talk briefly about the individual cases," Royall told the military judges, when the commission resumed work later that afternoon. He ran down the list of his clients, trying to say something exculpatory about each one. Kerling had "a triangular matrimonial difficulty" that helped explain why he was anxious to get back to the United States. His conflicting motives were sufficient to "raise a doubt" about whether he would have gone ahead with the sabotage plan. Heinck was just "a fellow who followed orders." Although Quirin had displayed greater initiative than Heinck, he too had done nothing to carry out the plan. Neubauer had been severely wounded on the eastern front, and "was hardly himself when he got into this thing." Thiel floated through life with little grasp of what was going on. Royall used a North Carolina mountain expression to describe his dim-witted client: a man who spent his time "chinking wood, to fill in between the chinks of log cabins."

Before Royall could speak about his two other clients, Burger and Haupt, Ristine rose to urge the judges to acquit Dasch on all charges. He dismissed the prosecution's argument that Dasch only went to the FBI because he was afraid of getting caught after his encounter with the Coast Guard on Amagansett Beach. Far from being afraid of Cullen, Ristine said, Dasch had allowed him to live rather than killing him in accordance with his orders. Everything that Dasch did was consistent with a "pre-arranged, thought-out plan on his part to come back to the United States and expose the whole thing and not carry it out."

Ristine dismissed the prosecution's complaint that Dasch had failed to report the sabotage plot to the proper authorities for six whole days, arguing that it took his client that long to calm his nerves. He reminded the judges that Dasch had telephoned the FBI in New York the day after he landed: he could hardly be blamed for the Bureau's failure to follow up on this call. Ristine concluded by recalling the FBI's offer of a presidential pardon for Dasch in return for a guilty plea. If the FBI believed that Dasch deserved a pardon, the military commission should too.

It was not until Saturday morning that Royall was able to wind up the case for the defense. In talking about Haupt, he emphasized his youth and thoughtlessness. Haupt, he told the commission, was a naïve American boy who got into trouble with a girl, and skipped out of town. "That is a bad thing to do, but it happens every day." Through a chain of bizarre circumstances, Haupt had ended up in Nazi Germany, where he became desperately homesick. "He tried to get back to America, and this was the only way in which he could do so." Once back in America, he had moved around quite openly. The only reason he did not immediately report to the FBI was that he was waiting for everyone to get together on July 6.

Turning finally to Burger, Royall reminded the commission that his client had cooperated voluntarily with the FBI, which never once challenged any of his statements. His mistreatment by the Gestapo suggested a compelling motive to leave Germany and secure his revenge by wrecking Operation Pastorius. "Can it be that Burger is in a situation where he can be put to death by Germany for being a traitor, as he certainly was, and put to death by us as a traitor?" he asked the commission. "That is an impossible situation."

The last word went to the prosecution. Judge Advocate General Cramer reacted scornfully to the claim that at least some of the saboteurs viewed Operation Pastorius as a means of escaping Nazi Germany. Perhaps the defendants had been charged with the wrong offense, Cramer suggested sarcastically. If the defense version of events was to be believed, the charges should have been amended to read something like "In that, Burger and all the rest of these defendants, with intent to defraud the German government, did, in Quenz, Germany, in or about the month of May, 1942, unlawfully pretend to said German government that they, well knowing the said pretenses were false, and by means thereof, were saboteurs, and by means thereof did fraudulently obtain from the said German government the sum of $180,000 in money, four or eight boxes full of explosives, and a free trip across the Atlantic in a submarine."

After a pause for laughter, Cramer proceeded to argue that death sentences for all the defendants were the best way of deterring future groups of saboteurs. The defense case rested on the assumption that Walter Kappe, the mastermind of the sabotage operation, was so stupid that he selected only incompetent "morons" to take part in Operation Pastorius. But Kappe was "not the dumbbell that these men would have you believe." On the contrary, the former Bund chief was "smart" and "knew his men."

Cramer hinted that "one or two of the defendants," presumably Dasch and Burger, might benefit from presidential clemency. But this was not a matter for the tribunal to decide, as it had no way of knowing how much assistance each man had given to the FBI. The only question for the military commission was whether the defendants were guilty.

At 2:25 p.m., McCoy declared the trial over. The verdict would be sealed and sent to the president.

GEORGE DASCH was a very bitter man. He considered the charges against him "crazy" and the concluding remarks of Cramer "grossly unjust."[24] The tribunal, he would later write, was "not my idea of an honest American trial." But what upset him most was his treatment by the FBI. He thought he would be hailed as a hero for betraying Operation Pastorius; instead he was shunned and ignored.

As Dasch was escorted out of room 5235 for the Saturday lunchtime recess, he turned to an FBI agent and asked whether Director Hoover would be back. The agent refused to provide any information. As the agent later reported to Hoover, Dasch "stated before the guards took him away that he had risked his life to give a full story to the Director and had been here for over a month and the Director had not even spoken to him and he wanted to tell the Director thank you. He was most sarcastic."[25]

Melodramatically, Dasch told his defense counsel that he wanted to be taken out and shot if found guilty.

Most of the other saboteurs reserved their anger for Dasch rather than the FBI. It was against regulations for the prisoners to communicate with the outside world during the trial; they were not even meant to have access to writing materials while in prison. They were, however, permitted to make notes during the trial, and some used the opportunity to write hastily scribbled letters to friends and family, accusing Dasch of betrayal.

"Dasch and Burger . . . told everything," Kerling complained in a note written on the final day of the trial.[26] "All other six men stood up well but could not deny anything in face of statements of traitors." Kerling persuaded one of the guards to mail the letter to his best friend in Germany after the war was over, but it was intercepted by the FBI. Although Kerling said he had been "treated very good" by his captors, he had no illusion about what would happen to him. "Am waiting for the sentence of court, which propably [sic] is death . . . Have done my duty and given my life for our country."

Heinrich Heinck wrote his wife Anna and eight-month-old son Harm back in Germany that as a result of the treachery of Dasch and Burger, "it was a small matter for the FBI—American Gestapo—to arrest us." Unlike Kerling, Heinck still felt "some hope," even though he was prepared for the worst. "Dear Anna, you are the only one who must suffer, and Harm, who will probably miss his Papa very much. Should I be executed or given life imprisonment, darling, I would not expect you to remain faithful to me. It would probably be better if Harm had another Papa. I leave that to you."[27]

"Please don't judge me too hard," Herbie Haupt told his parents in a penciled note.[28] "While I was in Germany I worried night and day wondering how you were getting along . . . I tried to get work in Germany but I could not, and when they told me that they had chosen me to go back to the United States you don't know how happy I was. I counted the days and hours until I could see you again and probably help you . . . Dear Mother, I never had any bad intentions. I did not know what a grave offense it is to come here the way I did in wartime. They are treating me very well here, as good as can be expected.

"Dear Mother and Father, whatever happens to me, always remember that I love you more than anything in the world. May God protect you, my loved ones, until we see each other again, wherever that may be. Love, your son, Herbie."

Royall and Dowell had done everything they could for their clients under the Articles of War, fighting all the way to the Supreme Court. The only recourse left was to appeal directly to the president.

They drafted two more appeals. The first was on technical grounds, requesting an independent review of the military commission proceedings, as stipulated by the Articles of War. They reminded Roosevelt that the Supreme Court had yet to issue its final opinion. It was quite possible that the Court would agree with the defense that a review was mandatory. If the president refused a review, the prisoners would have a legal basis for challenging the validity of the commission proceedings.

Their second appeal was on the grounds of the practical conduct of the war. Royall and Dowell noted that Nazi Germany had not imposed "the extreme penalty" on Englishmen captured in similar circumstances behind German lines. Writing on behalf of the defendants, they told the president that ordering capital punishment in the present case would be "unfair," as well as against the interests of American soldiers and sailors, "many of whom will doubtless engage in similar missions, in civilian clothes or disguise, in German territory during the war."

Both lawyers had attracted public criticism for their vigorous defense of their unpopular clients. Royall, in particular, came under harsh attack. An editorial in the *Charlotte News,* in his home state of North Carolina, described him as a "braying ass," and suggested he be put on trial himself. A California woman sent him a dime so that one of his clients could buy a cigar to celebrate his "mockery" of the United States.[29]

At the same time, the defense team also won plaudits from some unlikely quarters. While the trial was still going on, FDR's secretary, Marvin McIntyre, remarked to Hoover that the defense lawyers were showing "a lot of courage."[30] Soon after the Supreme Court hearing, Royall received a letter from his old Harvard law professor, Justice Frankfurter, congratulating him on the "admirable manner in which you discharged the difficult and uncongenial task entrusted to you by the Commander-in-Chief." "You were in the service of both War and Law," Frankfurter wrote, "and you served both with distinguished fidelity."[31] Justice Jackson praised Royall for demonstrating that "the right to counsel in our democracy is neither a fiction nor a formality."

But the most gratifying compliment to Royall and Dowell came from the men they defended. After the Supreme Court hearing, Kerling drafted a statement thanking the defense lawyers for their efforts. "We have been given a fair trial," he wrote.[32] "Before all we want to state that the defense council . . . has represented our case as American officers unbiased, better than we could expect and propably risking the indignation of public opinion." He affixed a note stipulating that the statement "may not be used by Dasch and Burger!!!"

The final statement bore the signatures of Edward Kerling, Herbert Haupt, Werner Thiel, Hermann Neubauer, Richard Quirin, and Heinrich Heinck.

CHAPTER FOURTEEN

DEATH ROW

(AUGUST 2–11)

PRESIDENT ROOSEVELT spent the weekend at Hyde Park. Before leaving Washington, he had served as best man as his friend and confidant Harry Hopkins married Louise Macy in the first wedding ceremony to be held at the White House in twenty-five years. The next day, he was "not surprised" to hear that the Supreme Court had ruled against habeas corpus for the saboteurs. He told his aide William Hassett he hoped the military commission would recommend death by hanging.

In the absence of any other appeal mechanism, the president was meant to act as a final reviewing authority for the case. But as he perused the Sunday papers in his bedroom, Roosevelt had pretty much made up his mind. He felt the case had already consumed far too much time and energy. "It's always hard for generals to act as judges," he mused. "I hope they don't string it out too long. They ought to bring in a verdict just like a jury." Knowing the way generals worked, however, he braced himself for a "wordy report."[1]

"A veritable bale of papers" duly arrived at Hyde Park late on Monday afternoon, transported from Washington by military plane. The package included the 2,967-page transcript of the trial and a series of guilty verdicts. The military judges had sentenced all eight defendants to death by electrocution. However, they also suggested clemency for Dasch and Burger in recognition of the assistance they had provided to the FBI. In Dasch's case, the commission recommended imprisonment for thirty years with hard labor; in Burger's, imprisonment for life.

Although no records have survived of the commission's deliberations, it seems unlikely there was much debate over the verdicts. In their questioning of the prisoners, the judges were uniformly hostile to the defense. Neither McCoy nor his subordinates showed any patience with the legal points raised by defense attorneys. From their point of view, technical legal arguments were irrelevant, as they were under instructions from the president to apply a "reasonable man" standard to the evidence. Royall got the impression from the beginning that "the Commission was against us," which was why he put so much stock in his appeal to the Supreme Court.[2]

Roosevelt had heard from Biddle two weeks earlier that Dasch and Burger "were helpful in apprehending the others and in making out the proof."[3] He was unaware of the full extent of their cooperation, although Biddle had suggested that it might be useful to make Dasch "somewhat of a hero, thus encouraging other German agents to turn in their fellows, and making all agents suspect each other." The attorney general noted that Burger did not want any publicity at all, and "prefers death to endangering his family." By the end of the trial, Biddle was so exasperated with Dasch that he dropped the idea of turning him into a hero.

The president mulled over what to do with the saboteurs on the overnight train back to Washington. When he reached the White House on Tuesday morning, he summoned his legal advisers for a review of the case, which lasted much of the afternoon. By this time, he had already decided to accept all the military commission's recommendations, including use of the electric chair as the means of execution, despite his earlier preference for hanging. He had no intention of submitting the trial record to the judge advocate general's office, as the defense lawyers were urging. But appearances had to be maintained. When the meeting with his lawyers wound up at 4:10 p.m., Roosevelt called reporters into the Oval Office and told them he was busy reviewing the "voluminous" evidence in the case. It would likely take "two or three days" to "finish my labors."[4]

"Are you more or less, sir, putting everything else aside during that period?" a reporter wanted to know.

"Oh my, no," replied Roosevelt cheerfully, looking the picture of relaxation in a tieless white shirt and seersucker trousers.

By this time, the Justice Department had already alerted General Cox, the provost marshal, that the president would order "execution by electrocution" for six of his prisoners.[5] Cox would be in charge of the most dramatic mass execution in American history since the hanging of the Lincoln conspirators. He had to find executioners, chaplains, and medical officers; arrange for a supply of additional electric current; and make sure that "Old Sparky," as the D.C. jail's venerable electric chair was known, was in good working order. He also had to plan for disposal of the bodies.

What was more, everything had to be done in total secrecy.

As THEY waited in solitary confinement in the women's section of the D.C. jail, the prisoners were fast losing hope. They displayed little outward emotion and spent long periods of time alone in their cells, smoking and staring at the walls. Occasionally, against prison regulations, the guards asked them to sign souvenirs. "To a fine American soldier," Richard Quirin scrawled on a paper cup presented to him by a military policeman.

Early on in the trial, some of the saboteurs complained they could not get to sleep because of the harsh lighting in their cells.[6] Cox ordered the lighting to be dimmed, but never entirely turned off, as he was determined to keep the prisoners under twenty-four-hour observation to prevent suicide attempts.

The saboteurs tried to put their affairs in order as best they could while waiting for the verdict. The most energetic was Eddie Kerling. Always a prolific correspondent, he wrote lengthy farewell letters to his wife, his mistress, his best friend, and to Miriam Preston, the American girl living in Massachusetts with whom he had been friendly. "Our fate is up to the President," he told his wife Marie, who was herself in FBI custody in New York City.[7] "This means the end of my life. We have to part. I know you can't grasp that. Neither can I." He had always been ready to die a soldier's death for the Fatherland. His only regret was that he was sent on "a hopeless mission where we could not be of any service to our country."

As he prepared for his death, Kerling tried to make sense of the confused love triangle between himself, Marie, and Hedy Engemann. He blamed himself for "not being a better husband while I had the chance" and asked Marie's "forgiveness for all the headaches and sorrow I have caused you." He admitted his feelings for Hedy, but insisted that his wife remained dearer to him than anyone in the world. "When I have to go on my last walk, I'll think of you, my Marie. I know you'd give your life to see me happy. I was a fool not to have seen it. When I realized what I had left behind, it was too late." His final advice to Marie was to stick close to Hedy.

His next letter was to Hedy, "my very dear friend." He told her that he had just finished a long letter to Marie in which "I tore my heart out to let her know how much I love her." His main reason for taking part in Operation Pastorius was to "help" his wife and "win her back." He knew from the beginning that the sabotage mission would fail. "I cannot explain why! Yet I hoped to be able to hide until the war blew over." He thanked Hedy for testifying on his behalf before the military tribunal. "Hedy, you have helped me, but our case was too hopeless. So it is all over now . . . Remember me as you have known me in happier days, forget the tragic end."

He apologized to Helmut Leiner, the tuberculosis patient from Astoria, for getting him in trouble with the FBI "after those two years you have spent in a hospital bed fighting for your life." Leiner was one of several dozen German-Americans accused of cooperating with the saboteurs. "I tried to keep you out of it, but they already knew about you." After thanking Leiner for arranging meetings for him in New York with Marie and Hedy, he gave him one final piece of advice. "Helmut, get that girl [Hedy] for yourself. You both will be happy."

Writing to his friend Miriam, he asked that she not judge him too harshly. "I did bring some dynamite, but not any hate for America or Americans." He complained of the power of propaganda—in both Germany and the United States—and pleaded for her respect and understanding. "I have done my duty to my country as any American would for his [and now] we have to take the punishment for it. It is foolish to say that it is easy to take. But I hope that we manage to make a decent show of it."

Quirin, who had left a wife and twenty-month-old daughter behind in Germany, struck a note of resigned stoicism in a farewell letter to a German-American friend. "Just at the time when my life started to look bright for me with my little girl and all, I was approached by these men, and of course I couldn't say no," he wrote. "I think that fate meant this for me."[8] The former Volkswagen worker asked his friend to pass a message to his wife after the war was over. "The people who sent me here on this mission have promised to take care of her and the child and I hope they will live up to their promise. In the event that the worst should happen, which I hope against hope won't, tell her good buy for me."

Herbie Haupt wrote to his girlfriend, Gerda Stuckmann, mentioning the baby he never saw and relatives who "froze to death" on the Russian front. Just as Kerling had done with Marie, he told Gerda he had come back to America in order to make things up to her and his parents. "But I brought nothing with me but *Horror* for my Parents and trouble for you. I have managed to put my Mother, Father, and Uncle into jail, decent People who never have done a thing wrong in their life." He had learned a bitter lesson from his time in Germany. "Dearest Gerda, it breaks my heart to write you this, but I will not be able to see you any more. You see, Gerda, this is *war*. You people in this country don't realize that yet, but we who have been in Europe have felt it. You see Gerda those people face Death every day, they know it and finally they don't fear it at all."

Outside the jail, excitement was mounting. Newspapers and radio stations competed frantically for any scrap of news about the saboteurs. Neither the White House nor the War Department had provided any indication about the verdict from the military commission. It was generally agreed they would be found guilty, but opinions were divided over how they would be executed, and who might receive a pardon. The reporter with the best information about the case was Jack Vincent of the International News Service. Early on Thursday morning, Vincent reported that the military commission had sentenced all eight saboteurs to death, but had recommended clemency for two or three.

Reporters kept a vigil outside the jail all night, looking for telltale signs such as the appearance of lights in the corridor leading to the death chamber. On Friday morning, Vincent wrote that six saboteurs would die in the electric chair, but that the president had commuted the sentences of Dasch and Burger. The executions were to have taken place overnight on Thursday, but there was a twenty-four-hour postponement at the last moment.

Vincent's information was substantially correct, although he did not know exactly when the executions would occur. As Cox later noted, it was "impossible" to keep news of an imminent electrocution from spreading around a prison.[9] An early tip-off was a request to the prison kitchen for a large bag of salt. Longtime inmates knew that executioners use a salt solution to paint the legs and shaven heads of condemned men to ensure a proper electrical contact when the electrodes are attached. "Among old prison hands," Cox wrote, "the secret spread, but not to our prisoners."

IN BERLIN, Nazi leaders were scrambling to repair the damage caused by the saboteurs. The news from America could hardly have been worse. Colonel Lahousen noted in his war diary for August 4 that on the basis of American radio reports "it must be assumed that all participants in Operation Pastorius have been sentenced to death by a special court instituted by President Roosevelt. No news yet about the passing of the judgment."[10] He added that all Abwehr agents had been instructed to draw the necessary lessons from the "failure" of the sabotage plot. The Rankestrasse safe house would have to be given up.

In the meantime, belated efforts were under way to save the saboteurs from their seemingly inevitable fate.[11] Legal experts for both the Abwehr and the Foreign Ministry did the best they could to make the case that the V-men should be treated as prisoners of war. A Foreign Ministry lawyer suggested informing the U.S. government that the V-men were regular soldiers who had somehow become detached from their units and landed on American soil by mistake.

According to reports filtering back to Berlin via the U-boats that transported the saboteurs to America, the eight men had all worn German military caps when they went ashore. In the opinion of the German legal experts, these caps should have been sufficient to identify them as soldiers if they got into trouble. They believed they could make an argument that all eight men were lawful combatants. Burger and Neubauer were German soldiers, while the other six V-men were acting under the orders of the German High Command, signed by Admiral Canaris.

Should these arguments fail to convince Washington, Berlin had another card to play. The High Command had been keeping a list of American citizens convicted in Germany on a variety of offenses. If the Americans refused to treat the V-men as prisoners of war, the Abwehr could use these American prisoners as bargaining chips for the saboteurs.

The Foreign Ministry lawyers drafted a diplomatic protest, accusing the United States of violating the 1929 Geneva Convention. The note would be dispatched to the Department of State via a Swiss diplomat in Washington responsible for looking after German interests in the United States. American legal experts had already anticipated such protests. Under the U.S. interpretation of the Geneva Convention, the saboteurs were "unlawful belligerents," as they were caught behind the lines in civilian clothes.[12] Furthermore, they had been given a "full and fair trial," in contrast to the "arbitrary executions" that took place in Nazi Germany.

The German protests would prove to be academic. By the time they were delivered, it would be too late.

LATE ON Friday evening, Roosevelt's naval aide, Captain John McCrea, phoned General Cox at his home to give him his orders. The executions would take place at noon the following day, Saturday, August 8. The president's order specified that each of the six condemned saboteurs would "suffer death by electrocution by having a current of electricity of such intensity pass through his body to cause death, the application to be continued until he is dead."[13]

Cox arrived at the jail at dawn and assembled his team, which included six military chaplains, three Catholic, three Protestant. Beginning at 7:30, he visited the prisoners in their cells to inform them of their sentences. He started with Herbie Haupt. The youngest saboteur seemed to freeze as Cox read out the president's order, but said nothing. One of the chaplains stayed with him in his cell. Cox repeated the same procedure with the other condemned men. The only one to display any emotion was Werner Thiel, who "looked as though an electric current went through him," after which he dropped his head and closed his eyes.[14]

Next, Cox visited Dasch and Burger, to tell them that their death sentences had been commuted to long prison terms. Dasch immediately began babbling incoherently about his family, until Cox silenced him and walked out of his cell. He then became "very morose." His moroseness eventually turned to bitterness. He could not understand why the military commission had found him guilty at all.

Since the end of the trial, Burger had withdrawn almost completely to himself. He was lying on his bed reading the *Saturday Evening Post* when Cox entered his cell. He looked up from his magazine long enough to say "Yes, sir" as the provost marshal informed him that he had been sentenced to life in prison, and then resumed reading his magazine.

The men were given paper and pencil and a last chance to communicate with their loved ones. Instead of writing another letter, Haupt told the chaplain that he wanted to bequeath his diamond ring to Gerda Stuckmann, a wish that was later fulfilled by the FBI. Haupt also sent greetings to his mother and father. "I was with your son, Herbert Haupt, as spiritual adviser until the last moment," the chaplain, Lieutenant William B. Adams, later wrote Hans Haupt. "Through me, he sends his love, requests that you not take it hard, and that his last thoughts were of his mother."[15]

Quirin wrote to his wife Ann and daughter Rosie. "These are the last lines I can write to you. I should like to tell you that I have always loved you and that I came here to make a better life for you, my dear ones. But, unfortunately, God willed it otherwise . . . Tell Kappe or one of his people that George Dasch and Peter Burger betrayed us. Begin a new life and think of me often."[16]

"I only have a few hours left in this life," Hermann Neubauer, the soldier wounded on the Russian front, told his parents. "I and my comrades are dying for you and for Germany. I know that our Führer will bring Germany to victory . . . When I heard my sentence I could not grasp it at first. But my nerves are strong enough. I am quite at ease now. Just as thousands of German men lay down their lives every day at the front, so also shall I die courageously as a German soldier."[17]

To his American wife, Alma, who had followed him back to Germany, Neubauer wrote, "Never thought they would take our life away. But as I write these lines I have control of my nerves again." He had lived for Germany, and was going to die for Germany. "If it only would not hurt so much, it would not be so hard. But I shall try to be brave, and take it as a soldier . . . A priest is with me, and he will be with me to the last minute. So my Alma, chin up, because I want you to, be good and goodbye, until we may meet in a better world, may God bless you! I love you, Your Hermann."

Eddie Kerling had the most to say in death, as he had in life. "I was not a good Catholic, but I believe in a God," he told his parents. He permitted the Catholic priest who was with him to formally "reconcile" him to the Church by intoning the last rites. He wrote two other letters, this time in German, to his Nazi Party comrades and the wife he had repeatedly betrayed.

> Marie, my wife—I am with you to the last minute! This will help me to take it as a German! Even the heaven out there is dark. It's raining. Our graves are far from home, but not forgotten. Marie, until we meet in a better world! May God be with you. My love to you, my heart to my country.
>
> Heil Hitler!
> Your Ed, always.[18]

After writing their letters, the men underwent final preparations for execution. These included the complete shaving of their heads, a bath, and a last meal, with wine. As Haupt was having his head shaved, he broke down and cried. Neubauer was "so nervous that he had difficulty in holding a cigarette." Quirin was "calm and reserved during his preparation for the execution, although his hands were shaking slightly." The other three men displayed no outward emotion at all.

At 10 a.m., Cox ordered that the condemned men be taken to the death cells, in another section of the prison. The walk was quite long, down a flight of stairs and along a hundred-yard corridor. A little procession formed for each prisoner, beginning with Haupt, the first in alphabetical order, and ending with Thiel. "A guard was at either side of each prisoner, a chaplain behind him, and behind the chaplain two guards carrying a litter—just in case," Cox later wrote. "But there was no hesitancy on the part of any of the prisoners, nor any utterances, as they walked erect to their doom."[19]

OUTSIDE THE jail, the atmosphere was becoming ever more frenzied, with reporters trying to find out what was happening inside. Overnight, three American soldiers and a sailor had arrived at the jailhouse door and volunteered their services as a firing squad, explaining, "We want to see those Jerries die."[20] Guards turned them away. The journalists reported a succession of officials arriving at the jail, including Cox, the chaplains, and the city coroner.

The reporters had learned from friendly guards that the surest sign of an execution taking place would be the momentary dimming of lights in the rest of the jail, because of the sudden diversion of current to the electric chair. But they were deprived of even this source of information when, toward the end of the morning, all lights were turned off at the front of the jail facing the street.

To while away the waiting hours, the reporters fed ham sandwiches to a stray dog they named Jake, and exchanged folklore about the electric chair that would be used for the executions.[21] "Old Sparky" had been installed in 1925, replacing the gallows as the standard method for carrying out executions in the District of Columbia, and had been used twenty-four times since then, most recently in 1941. At first, the chair had been stored in an alcove of the prison dining room, in full view of the inmates every time they had a meal. The sight had so sickened a previous attorney general that he ordered it removed to a new, specially constructed death wing of the jail.

Somehow, from jailhouse gossip, the reporters learned that there would be four executioners.[22] The executioner and his chief assistant would receive $50 for each person put to death. Two more assistant executioners would receive half that amount, a total of $150 each. The total bill paid by the Justice Department for "confidential expenses" in connection with the trial—court transcripts, Supreme Court briefs, meals, electrocution services, and burial expenses—would come to $9,525.09.

It rained heavily all morning.

TWO PRISON officials escorted Haupt, the first saboteur to face the electric chair, to the execution chamber at 12:01 p.m. as the sound of an air raid siren wailed across the city. After his earlier crying fit, he had fully regained his composure and "walked to the chair like a real man," a witness later recalled.[23] He was strapped into the chair, and electrodes were applied to his head and his leg through a slit that had been cut in his trousers. Seated in a room next to the execution chamber, a dozen government witnesses could see Haupt through a darkened glass window, but he could not see them.

At 12:03, executioners applied two thousand volts of electricity to Haupt. When the current first hit him, he tightened up, raised his body, and turned slightly to the left. There were some further spasms but, after a minute or so, his body completely relaxed. At 12:11, the coroner walked over to the chair, and pronounced Haupt dead. Orderlies placed the body on a stretcher, covered it up with a sheet, and wheeled it out of the room. The next man, Heinrich Heinck, was then brought in.

It took just over an hour to complete all six executions. Only Kerling had any comment to make. As he was being led to the execution chamber from the death cell, he told his guards he was "proud to be a German" and would do the same thing again if given the opportunity.

The bodies were taken down to the basement. When the masks were removed from the men, one of the army witnesses noticed, their faces were "completely white" and "in a horribly contorted condition with their mouths open." Guards loaded the bodies into ambulances and twenty steel-helmeted soldiers took positions outside the gates to hold back the crowd of the curious. Soon a grim cortège was winding its way through the damp streets, from the D.C. jail on the Anacostia River to Walter Reed Army Hospital in northwest Washington.

"They're gone," a bystander shouted out.[24]

"It's over!"

"The spies are dead!"

"Nothing to say, boys, nothing at all," the coroner told reporters as he hurried to his car.

"Mum's the word," said General Cox.

THE OFFICIAL announcement of the executions—and the first public word of the verdicts of the military commission—came from White House press secretary Steve Early at 1:27 p.m. Reading from a typewritten sheet, annotated with Roosevelt's handwriting, Early told reporters that "the sentences were carried out at noon today. Six of the prisoners have been executed. The other two have been confined to prison." At the president's insistence, he added, "the records in the eight cases will be sealed until the end of the war."[25]

Half an hour after the announcement, Roosevelt left the White House for his new retreat in the Catoctin Mountains in Maryland, a two-hour drive north of Washington. He called it Shangri-La because of the secrecy that surrounded the place and its isolated, invigorating quality. (Later presidents would know the retreat as Camp David.) Although Roosevelt loved to go to Hyde Park, it was becoming increasingly difficult for him to make the overnight train trip to upstate New York. Shangri-La was close enough to Washington that he could go there most weekends with a few friends, in an atmosphere of informality and relaxation.

On this particular weekend, the president was accompanied by his usual circle of intimates: Daisy Suckley, his secretary Grace Tully, and his friends Samuel Rosenman and Archibald MacLeish, together with their wives and a few Secret Service men. It was still raining heavily when they got to Shangri-La, and inspected their rustic quarters. Roosevelt "gleefully" informed his guests that they would all have to share a single bathroom with a door that never closed quite securely. As president, he claimed the master bedroom with attached bathroom. They would all share the casual living-dining room and screened-in porch with a magnificent view overlooking a valley.

That evening, Roosevelt busied himself with a much-loved ritual, mixing cocktails. At dinner, he reminisced about his days as governor of New York, when he had to decide whether to pardon murderers with the help of Rosenman, his longtime legal adviser and speechwriter. He also entertained his guests with a series of gruesome stories inspired by the executions of the six saboteurs.[26]

One of the stories the president related with gusto was about a barber during the final days of the siege of Paris, in 1871. Everybody was starving, but somehow the barber managed to supply excellent "veal" to the local butcher. Throwing his huge head back with laughter, Roosevelt described how suspicions spread that the "veal" had come straight from the barber's chair as a number of his customers had gone missing. He piled detail on grisly detail, until Ada MacLeish began to shiver. The wife of the poet and librarian of Congress remarked that she might also make good "veal," as she was slightly plump.

The guests understood that telling such stories was a way for the president to unburden himself from the cares and responsibilities of his office. American troops had just landed at Guadalcanal in the Solomon Islands, on the first stage of what would be a three-year island-hopping campaign in the Pacific. Casualties were high. Reports were also coming in of a disastrous naval engagement near Savo Island, where the Allies had lost four cruisers.

The next morning, after receiving a briefing from his naval aide, Captain McCrea, about the progress of the war, Roosevelt resumed his macabre tales. He retold one of his favorites, about a wealthy Chicago widow who died in Moscow while on a world tour. Her coffin was shipped back to Chicago for burial but, when it arrived, her relatives were horrified to discover the body of a dead Russian general in full military regalia. They sent a telegram to the U.S. embassy in Moscow to find out what had gone wrong, and received the following reply: "Suggest you close the casket and proceed with the funeral. Your grandmother was buried in the Kremlin with full military honors."

Mrs. Rosenman asked the president what would happen to the bodies of the saboteurs. Roosevelt avoided giving her a direct answer. That was one of the matters he had just been talking about with Captain McCrea, he said.

THE PRESIDENT was determined that no trace remain of the saboteurs. He did not want their graves to become a place of ghoulish pilgrimage for Nazi sympathizers. At his instructions, all the clothing that had belonged to the V-men, including the new suits they had bought in New York, Jacksonville, and Chicago, was incinerated.[27] Contrary to normal regulations, no reports of their deaths were filed with the public health authorities in Washington.

After lying for two days in the morgue of the army medical center, the bodies were placed in plain pine boxes at 6 p.m. on Tuesday, August 11. A light truck took the coffins under armed guard to a graveyard for unclaimed bodies on the southernmost edge of the District of Columbia, on a lonely hill adjoining the sewage disposal facility of Blue Plains. Six graves had been prepared with crude wooden headboards marked only with numbers, from 276 to 281. A six-foot-high wire mesh fence separated the saboteurs' graves from the paupers' graves. A stench of sewage wafted up the hill, which lay high over the Potomac River.

At 7:30 p.m., two army chaplains, one Protestant, one Catholic, said some prayers as the bodies of the six saboteurs were laid to rest. No photographs were taken, and no information given to the press. Only two copies were made of the report on the disposal of bodies. One went to the president, the other to the secretary of war. Both were stamped SECRET.[28]

Operation Pastorius—the high-risk gamble that Hitler hoped would lead to the crippling of the American war machine—had come to an ignominious and unmourned end.

SURVIVORS

G EORGE DASCH and Peter Burger learned about the fate of their six companions when they were taken on their regulation fifteen-minute walk around the cell block. The cells previously occupied by the men who had trained with them in Brandenburg were empty. Both Dasch and Burger were tortured by the thought that they had sent their fellow saboteurs to their deaths.

Dasch kept asking the army guards if he did "the right thing" by reporting the sabotage plot to the FBI. On Saturday night, he had trouble getting to sleep, as he thought about everything he had done since arriving in America eight weeks earlier. "I have died six deaths," he told one of his guards.[1] On Sunday morning, however, he ate a "hearty breakfast" and began talking more coherently to the guards about his own situation.

He was still "extremely pale and haggard looking," almost ghostlike, when the two FBI agents who had most to do with his case, Duane Traynor and Mickey Ladd, visited the D.C. jail on Wednesday morning.[2] He could not get used to the idea that he had been sentenced to thirty years in prison, and broke down when he realized that the agents had not come to let him out of jail. "You may think you came over here to help us, but you have to understand the attitude of the American people and the U.S. government," they told him. "As far as Americans are concerned, you were a saboteur who landed from an enemy submarine."

Burger also felt remorse about informing on his comrades. The two FBI men tried to allay his conscience by claiming they knew in advance that Dasch was coming over to America. They told Burger that it was only a "question of time" before they rounded everybody up, and therefore he should not feel responsible for the deaths of his comrades. Hearing this, Burger felt better.

Both the surviving saboteurs said they wanted to do everything in their power "to fight Hitler." The agents promised to pass their ideas "to the right places," but gave them little hope of early release from prison. A few days later, the prisoners were transferred to the newly vacated "death house" of the D.C. jail, where they occupied adjoining cells.[3] They were allowed to talk to each other and their guards—in English—but otherwise were kept isolated from the rest of the prison. After a few weeks, they were sent to the federal prison in Danbury, Connecticut.

In October, Burger appeared as the star prosecution witness in the treason trial in Chicago of the Haupts, the Froehlings, and the Wergins. (Dasch was considered too unreliable to testify.)[4] All six defendants were found guilty, largely on the basis of their incriminating statements to the FBI. Judge William Campbell sentenced the three men to death, and the three women to twenty-five years in prison and $10,000 fines. The harsh sentences earned Campbell, a hard-line former U.S. attorney, the plaudits of the press and the nation, but were reversed on appeal, partly because of the controversy over whether FBI statements could be admitted as evidence. Haupt was eventually sentenced to life imprisonment, but was released in 1957; Walter Froehling and Otto Wergin got five-year prison terms; Erna Haupt was interned; the other two women were released.

Trials of people who cooperated with the saboteurs also took place in New York. Anthony Cramer and Hermann Faje were sentenced to nine and five years respectively for "trading with the enemy." Kerling's friend Helmut Leiner received eighteen years for trading with the enemy and concealing treason, and was released on parole in 1954. Hedwig Engemann spent three years in prison on a similar charge.

Marie Kerling was freed without a trial. Fortunately for her, the FBI had arrested her husband half an hour before she was due to meet with him. She had no case to answer.

ONE OF the justices involved in the *Ex parte Quirin* ruling, William O. Douglas, liked to quote the dictum of one of his predecessors: in the Supreme Court, cases are decided 90 percent on emotion, only 10 percent on the law.[5] There are few better illustrations of what he meant than the case of the Nazi saboteurs. Eight months after Pearl Harbor, none of the justices was willing to dispute the extraordinary war powers claimed by the president. In denying habeas corpus to the saboteurs, and partially overturning *Ex parte Milligan,* they first decided what they should do, and then searched for the legal texts to support their decision.

As chief justice, Harlan Stone assigned himself the task of writing a unanimous opinion that would keep all his "wild horses" riding together. Immediately after the saboteur ruling, he returned to his summer retreat in New Hampshire. Drafting the opinion was an agony for him, both physically and mentally. He was suffering from a severe bout of lumbago, contracted from "an extremely cold Pullman car" on the train from Washington and two days of strenuous mountain hiking.[6] By the time he started work on the opinion, he was in such pain he had to dictate his correspondence to his wife.

Sorting through the intricacies of the Constitution, the *Manual for Courts-Martial,* and various international conventions codifying the practices of war was "a mortification of the flesh" for the chief justice.[7] He was unimpressed by the hastily written briefs that Biddle and Royall had submitted to the Supreme Court, and wanted to establish a more solid legal ground for a ruling in favor of the government than the attorney general had been able to provide. "I certainly hope the military is better equipped to fight the war than it is to fight its legal battles," he wrote his law clerk, Bennett Boskey, in some irritation. Since Stone did not have a proper law library at his country retreat, he relied on Boskey, who was still in Washington, to document his conclusions with the relevant legal footnotes.

Most troubling of all to Stone was the thought that the saboteurs might have been executed illegally, without the mandatory review stipulated by the Articles of War. He very much regretted agreeing to drop the paragraph in the per curiam ruling that indirectly urged the president to comply with the review procedures. The paragraph in question would not have been eliminated, he told Boskey, "if we had had a little more time to consider it; as it was, we went into Court a little late."[8] But it was too late to do anything about this now, and none of the justices wanted to give the two surviving saboteurs grounds for appealing their sentences. In the end, Stone decided to pass over the matter in his final opinion "to avoid indecent exposure of some very worthy gentleman."[9]

On the central issue of why the *Milligan* ruling should not apply to the saboteurs, the chief justice described them as "unlawful belligerents," in contrast to Milligan, who was neither a belligerent nor a member of the enemy armed forces.[10] The fact that at least one of the saboteurs, Haupt, was a U.S. citizen was irrelevant, he decided. Haupt's offense, Stone wrote, was that he entered the country as an unlawful belligerent for a hostile purpose, "which constitutes a violation of the law of war." Unlike Haupt, Milligan did not cross enemy lines.

While supporting the president's right to establish a military commission to try the saboteurs, Stone also upheld the saboteurs' right to appeal to the civilian courts. He did so, however, in an extremely cryptic way, claiming there was "nothing" in the presidential proclamation that precluded the petitioners from taking their case to the Supreme Court. In order to maintain the court's unanimity, Stone deleted a much stronger sentence from an earlier draft explicitly asserting the saboteurs' constitutional right to a hearing. "There were so many eggs in the case which I felt it necessary to avoid breaking," he wrote a friend, "that I am afraid the opinion was not good literature. I hope you noticed that the opinion flatly rejected (as unobtrusively as possible) the President's comment that no court should hear the plea of the saboteurs. That, I thought, was going pretty far."[11]

Formally issued on October 29, 1942—twelve weeks after Quirin and his five comrades walked to the electric chair—Stone's opinion in *Ex parte Quirin* has reverberated through the decades. In the aftermath of the ruling, Biddle wrote to Roosevelt claiming that the inconvenient *Milligan* precedent was "out of the way" for all practical purposes and "should not bother us any further."[12] Once the war was over, however, several justices had second thoughts about the case. The saboteur trial was "not a happy precedent," Justice Frankfurter noted in 1953, after casting a losing vote in favor of a stay of execution for Julius and Ethel Rosenberg.[13] In 1962, Justice Douglas told an interviewer that the saboteur case showed it was "extremely undesirable" to announce a decision without issuing an opinion to explain it. Once the search for grounds to justify a decision gets under way, Douglas noted, "sometimes those grounds crumble."

The sharpest criticism of *Ex parte Quirin* came from a legal scholar who served as law clerk to Justice Black at the time of the saboteur hearing. John P. Frank complained that Black and the other justices had allowed themselves to be "stampeded" by the executive branch. If judges are to "run a court of law and not a butcher shop," Frank wrote in a 1958 book, "the reasons for killing a man should be expressed before he is dead; otherwise the proceedings are purely military and not for [the] courts at all."

This contrasted with the opinion of a leading constitutional scholar, Robert Cushman, a few months after the six saboteurs were executed. "The Supreme Court stopped the military authorities and required them, as it were, to show their credentials. When this had been done to the Court's satisfaction, they were allowed to proceed."[14] Cushman hailed the court's action as "a wholesome and desirable safeguard to civil liberty in time of war."

Views about *Quirin* and *Milligan* tend to veer back and forth, depending on whether America is at war or at peace. In times of peace, pressure mounts for curbs on executive power. In times of war, the pendulum swings in the opposite direction. After the attacks on the World Trade Center and the Pentagon on September 11, 2001, the Bush administration cited the *Quirin* decision as a legal basis for establishing military tribunals to try al-Qaeda terrorists.

Reflecting on the relationship between the two branches of government in wartime, Chief Justice William Rehnquist noted in a 1999 speech that both Lincoln and FDR had put a higher value on prosecuting the war than obeying the Constitution. By and large, the courts had gone along with the president. "To lawyers and judges, this may seem a thoroughly undesirable state of affairs, but in the greater scheme of things it may be best for all concerned," Rehnquist concluded. "While we would not want to subscribe to the full sweep of the Latin maxim *Inter Arma Silent Leges* (In a time of war, the laws are silent), perhaps we can accept the proposition that, though the laws are not silent in wartime, they speak with a muted voice."[15]

WITHIN THE prison system, Burger was known as Special Prisoner A and Dasch as Special Prisoner B. As Nazi saboteurs who expressed their hatred of Nazism, they were anomalies, and it was difficult to deal with them fairly. The Bureau of Prisons wanted to send them to Alcatraz Island to protect them from Nazi sympathizers or an "overpatriotic American prisoner who might feel they got off too easily."[16] This alarmed the FBI, which feared that the harsh penal regime at Alcatraz would turn Dasch into a "mental case" and might cause Burger to attempt suicide.

Instead of Alcatraz, the two special prisoners were sent to the federal penitentiary in Atlanta in February 1943. It was an unhappy experience, particularly for Dasch. The prison psychiatrist diagnosed Dasch as "an obsessive, compulsive, neurotic personality type," who frequently complained of "depressive trends, nervousness, insomnia, and vague pains."[17] During an interview on November 3, Dasch "cried and rung his hands. He repeatedly stated that he did not mind being in prison but that he was hurt by the way it was done; that he has terrific prejudice and anger and that he feels he cannot go on long this way."

Dasch was disliked by prisoners and prison authorities alike. "He is a loquacious individual who likes to brag about his activities as an espionage agent and his connections with the Nazis," reported the Atlanta prison warden, Joseph Sanford.[18] "He goes out of his way to antagonize [other prisoners] by belittling their intelligence." When his fellow inmates staged a prison rebellion in January 1945, they threatened to shove Dasch off the roof unless their demands were met. He was lucky to escape with his life after hours of patient negotiation.

Even Burger, who initially asked to be imprisoned with Dasch because he wanted company, soon began to tire of his endless chatter. By the end of the war, he had come to detest Dasch, and even threatened to kill him if he revealed information that could jeopardize the safety of his family back in Germany.[19] Like Dasch, Burger felt aggrieved that the U.S. government had failed to make more use of his talents in the propaganda war against Nazi Germany. But he expressed his complaints more mildly, and retained the respect of everyone who dealt with him.

After the war ended, the Atlanta prison warden wrote a glowing testimonial for Burger, saying he had "cooperated with me and the institutional officials in every respect, and has courage equal to any man I have ever known."[20] Sanford considered Burger to be "straightforward," "honest," "diligent," and "a walking encyclopedia" on the Nazi Party, deserving of better treatment from the United States than he received. By contrast, Sanford had "no confidence" in Dasch, whom he described as "a communist troublemaker" who would likely head for the Russian zone of Germany as soon as he was released.

One of the few people to feel at all sorry for Dasch was his old FBI handler, Duane Traynor, who was perhaps more aware than anybody else of the role he had played in rounding up the other saboteurs. When the war ended, Traynor wrote a letter to Hoover arguing in favor of a presidential pardon for both Dasch and Burger because of the help they had given to the FBI. "As you know," he told Hoover, "I feel that I personally, and the Bureau as a whole, owe a moral obligation to Dasch."[21]

Traynor received a very cold reply from Hoover, who had long since decided that Dasch was both "communistically-inclined" and "a mental case." "Your personal opinion . . . relative to the granting of consideration to Dasch," the FBI director told his subordinate, "is, to say the least, ill-advised."

For the time being, both Dasch and Burger would stay in prison.

ONE OF the lessons of the saboteur affair is that it is very difficult to fight a war and respect legal niceties at the same time. From the government's point of view, much of the benefit of using a secret military commission to try the saboteurs was offset by the speculation surrounding the case and the publicity generated by the Supreme Court hearing. Roosevelt and his advisers believed that the release of any information on how the saboteurs were captured could reveal the porous state of America's coastal defenses. Despite the secrecy, the Germans were fairly well informed about what happened to their agents on the basis of American press reports and the debate in the Supreme Court. Nazi leaders concluded while the trial was still going on that Dasch and Burger had turned traitor.[22]

In retrospect, there was an obvious inconsistency in the way the government handled the saboteurs, as Eugene Rachlis pointed out in his 1961 book on the case, *They Came to Kill*.[23] If Biddle was correct in arguing that America was engaged in "total war" and the saboteurs were "illegal combatants," then why go to the bother of giving them even the pretense of a fair trial? To take Biddle's argument to its logical conclusion, the saboteurs should have been arrested, tried, and sentenced in secret, with the press only being informed after the event, if at all. This, in fact, was the way similar cases were handled in Britain, the country where habeas corpus originated. Under British wartime regulations, the press was prohibited from publishing any uncensored information about enemy espionage activity.[24] Had such a procedure been followed in the saboteur case, the Germans would truly have been left guessing about the reasons for the failure of Operation Pastorius.

If, on the other hand, Royall was correct in insisting that the saboteurs had legal rights guaranteed by the U.S. Constitution, then surely those rights were flouted by the manner of their trial. The outcome was virtually predetermined, both in the military commission and in the Supreme Court. Rules of evidence that would apply to normal defendants, even before a military court-martial, were ignored. Justice Frankfurter was so prejudiced against the saboteurs that he called them "damned scoundrels" in a memorandum to his fellow justices. President Roosevelt, who appointed himself the court of final appeal for the saboteurs, decided at the outset that they were "as guilty as can be."

After American soldiers landed in Normandy in June 1944, and fought their way through France and Germany, the U.S. government rethought its attitude toward high-profile trials for saboteurs. Now that American agents were routinely being sent behind enemy lines in civilian clothes, the U.S. Army did not want its own "unlawful belligerents" to suffer the fate of the Nazi saboteurs. A practical test of American attitudes came in November 1944, when two more German agents, William Colepaugh and Erich Gimpel, were landed by U-boat on the Maine coast near Mount Desert Island.

Like their predecessors, Colepaugh and Gimpel arrived with lavish funds—$60,000 in cash plus a cache of small diamonds—which they proceeded to spend away in New York nightclubs. As with the original saboteurs, one agent (Colepaugh) betrayed the other (Gimpel), and turned himself in to the FBI. On this occasion, however, the government decided to deal with them as quietly as possible. Anything resembling the 1942 trial "would be entirely too spectacular," a Pentagon memorandum noted. "All the fanfare over the last trial is out of place now that thousands of our men are being killed from week to week. It should be on a routine, purely military basis."[25] With a minimum of publicity, a military commission sentenced the two agents to death, but immediately commuted their terms to life imprisonment.

PRESIDENT HARRY S. Truman finally agreed to pardons for Dasch and Burger in April 1948, and they were both deported to Germany. They arrived in Stuttgart handcuffed to one another, amid a blaze of press publicity, despite American assurances that everything would be done to ensure their "quiet absorption" into the German population.[26] The country was ruined and it was practically impossible to find jobs. Many Germans regarded Dasch and Burger as traitors for sending their fellow agents to their deaths.

Soon Burger was feeling nostalgic for prison. In an October 1948 letter to Hoover from the southern German town of Würzburg, he described scrounging for food from garbage cans, and doing without winter clothes, underwear, and shoes. He was sharing a room fifteen feet by ten feet with his sister and brother-in-law. His entire prison savings of $250 had been converted into German marks at a very unfavorable exchange rate, and were now worth less than a carton of cigarettes. His wife, Bettina, had disappeared into the maw of the Russian concentration camp system. He was interrogated by German denazification courts, and was "pushed around by anyone who feels like it."[27]

Dasch, meanwhile, had crossed illegally into the Russian zone in October 1948, exactly as the Atlanta prison warden had predicted.[28] His motives for leaving the American zone were not so much ideological as personal. He wanted to collect affidavits from people he had known during the war, testifying to his anti-Nazi credentials, as part of his campaign to secure a full rehabilitation in the United States. By telling his story to the Russians, he might also be able to secure a measure of revenge for the way American authorities had treated him. The Cold War was beginning to heat up, and Dasch believed Moscow might be interested in exploiting his story for propaganda purposes. But the Soviets soon tired of their difficult guest, and ordered the East German secret police to keep a close watch on him. "We are firmly convinced that this man is an American agent," a supervisor noted in Dasch's secret police file. "He should not be permitted to move freely."[29] After debriefing him fully, and holding out false promises of a job, the Soviets expelled him back to the American zone in January 1949.

"Everybody mistrusts me," Dasch complained to acquaintances before leaving Berlin.

THE FBI tried to track down the masterminds of Operation Pastorius after the war ended, but U.S. government interest in the case was almost exhausted by the time Dasch and Burger returned to Germany. The Bureau formally closed its investigation of Walter Kappe and his associates in December 1946. This created a strange anomaly. The men who sent the Nazi saboteurs to America were able to go free, while the men who betrayed the operation to the American authorities were kept in prison for another sixteen months.

In December 1948, eight months after he returned to Germany, Burger was surprised to wander into a U.S. government office in Stuttgart, and come face to face with Kappe's right-hand man, Reinhold Barth, one of his instructors at the Quenz Lake sabotage school. He did some investigating, and found out that Barth had used his excellent knowledge of English and background with the Long Island Rail Road to get a job as a U.S. Army liaison officer with the German railway system. The impoverished, jobless Burger—who had received lessons from Barth in blowing up American railroads—was chagrined to learn that his former instructor occupied a "splendid office" in Stuttgart and was on the U.S. government payroll.

This was too much for even the phlegmatic Burger to take. "You will see the humor in the situation," he wrote Hoover.[30] While Burger found it "impossible to make a living," Barth had a job that allowed him to monitor the movement of U.S. troops and military supplies all over Germany. If he wanted to carry out acts of sabotage against the United States, the former Abwehr official was now in an ideal position to do so.

Burger told everybody he could about Barth's dubious past—the FBI, military intelligence, the U.S. occupation authorities—but no one was interested. It was difficult to find Germans who spoke good English with as much expertise in their field as Barth. Operation Pastorius belonged to the past. A new Germany was rising from the ashes of history.

In the fall of 1950, Dasch was struggling to come to terms with a lifetime of soaring dreams and bitter defeats. He was forty-seven years old, and he had failed at practically every endeavor he had ever undertaken. His disappointments ran the full arc of the ideological spectrum. He was raised as a Catholic, only to be thrown out of seminary; he pursued the American dream but left America bankrupt and disillusioned; he came to see Hitler as a savior but then turned against him; he was selected to lead a sabotage expedition but betrayed his own men; he dreamed of using the money he had been given for Operation Pastorius to lead a propaganda war against Nazism, only to be rebuffed by the Americans; he offered his services to the Soviets as a lecturer and writer, but was thwarted in that dream too.

He now divided his time between writing petitions to Washington for his readmission to the United States, a totally futile effort, and trying to earn enough money to survive from day to day. Most days, he could be found standing in a busy shopping street in Mannheim, a German city south of Frankfurt, hawking wool to housewives from a collapsible table covered by an umbrella.

One day, Dasch was walking through the streets of Mannheim when he came across someone who looked very familiar. The middle-aged man was gaunt and disheveled, but the outlines of his fleshy jowls and thick bull neck were still quite visible. He was balder than Dasch remembered, and he waddled rather than walked. It was Walter Kappe.

Kappe seemed startled to see his former agent, and shivered a little as he looked at him. Ever talkative, Dasch invited him to visit his "store," but Kappe showed no interest in conversation, and soon slipped back into the crowds. "He was surprised and shaky like hell," Dasch recalled.[31]

Since the end of the war, Kappe had lived on the lam, convinced that the Americans were hunting him down.[32] He enjoyed the conspiratorial life, holding meetings in the forest with former associates and members of his family. He later changed his name to König, and got a job with the British army as a personnel officer. When he met Dasch on the street, he was still running away from the Americans, even though they had lost interest in him.

One of the most puzzling aspects of Operation Pastorius is why the Nazi spymasters placed so much trust in Kappe, and why Kappe in turn put so much trust in Dasch. For all the energy that he had displayed as a leader of the German-American Bund, the affable, fun-loving Kappe was a terrible judge of men. By selecting Dasch to lead the first team of saboteurs to land in America, he practically guaranteed the failure of the sabotage operation.

Part of the answer to the conundrum probably lies in Nazi bureaucratic politics. Kappe wore a gold button in his lapel, meaning that he joined the Nazi Party long before it achieved political power. He rose to prominence as a Nazi propagandist in America, which meant that his enemies were in America, rather than in Germany. His personal failings were largely unknown to his fellow bureaucrats at the Nazi Party's Ausland Institut in Berlin, which enthusiastically supported his plan for a sabotage operation in the United States and lobbied for it with Hitler.

Dasch was adept at playing on Kappe's vanity and taste for high living. In Berlin, he plied Kappe with gifts of wine and rum and flattered him shamelessly, in addition to impressing his boss with his intimate knowledge of American ways.[33] In return, Kappe brushed aside criticism of Dasch from the other V-men. By the time the saboteurs reached the French port of Lorient, where Dasch lost his identity papers, Kappe had probably realized his mistake. By then, however, it was too late for him to get rid of Dasch without exposing himself to ridicule and jeopardizing the entire operation. All he could do was hope for the best.

During the seventeen-day submarine voyage, Dasch spent much of his time lying in his bunk worrying that the captain of *U-202* would receive a message from navy headquarters ordering him to return to Lorient. He was convinced that Kappe suspected him of planning to turn traitor. But his luck held, and the message never came.

THE MOST obvious flaw in Operation Pastorius was the lack of ideological commitment and cohesion among its principal protagonists. Although most of the saboteurs either were Nazi Party members or had Nazi connections, they lacked the ideological zeal to sacrifice themselves for the cause. The only one among them who believed in the mission wholeheartedly was Kerling, the leader of the Florida group, and even he had personal reasons for coming to America. To varying degrees, the saboteurs were all seduced by American plenty, which contrasted so starkly with the poverty of wartime Germany. "In Germany, you couldn't buy a pair of shoes, a piece of meat," recalled Haupt's friend Wolfgang Wergin, who was offered a place on the sabotage team by Kappe, but declined. "Everything was rationed. Nobody in his right mind was going to go from a country like that to a country with everything, like America, and start blowing things up. You'd have to be nuts."[34]

Six decades later, of course, a group of Islamic terrorists would do precisely that, and plot the destruction of the World Trade Center at the very time they were leading the life of American suburbanites, ordering pizzas, visiting shopping malls, and dropping into video stores. The Nazi saboteurs were as well trained and just as well funded as the September 11 hijackers. They had the logistical support of the German armed forces. So why did one plot succeed and the other fail? One reason is that Osama bin Laden's brand of militant Islamic fundamentalism is more myth than reality. Until the bin Laden myth is discredited in practice, it will remain a rallying point for the resentful and the deprived. By contrast, by 1942 the Third Reich was not just a myth; it was a very grim reality, and a much less attractive one than the reality of wartime New York and Chicago.

Even so, Operation Pastorius was hardly doomed to fail. A wartime study by the Office of Naval Intelligence concluded that Kerling, supported by others like him, might well have succeeded in carrying out its mission.[35] America's coasts were poorly defended against saboteurs. The freedom with which Haupt moved around Chicago, and the fact that none of his friends or relatives gave him away, suggested there was a sizable German-American population willing to offer shelter to Nazi agents.

There is a fine line between success and failure when it comes to sabotage operations. The difference between a triumph and a fiasco can often boil down to one false move or unfortunate coincidence. In different circumstances—with better luck, better planning, and, above all, better leadership—Hitler might have pulled off his gamble, and brought a war that had already engulfed much of the rest of the world onto American soil.

ADMIRAL WILHELM CANARIS, *the Abwehr chief who signed the order for Operation Pastorius, was executed by the Nazis in the courtyard of the Flossenberg concentration camp on April 9, 1945, along with four other prominent opponents of Hitler. He was strung up naked on a hastily erected gallows, and his body was then cut down and left to rot.*

General Erwin von Lahousen, the head of the sabotage division of the Abwehr, who supervised Operation Pastorius, appeared as a witness for the prosecution in the Nuremberg trials of Nazi war criminals. After two years in Allied military prisons, he returned to his native Austria, where he died in 1955.

Walter Kappe became a trade union official in Hanover. As he got older, he drank ever more heavily, and took a succession of increasingly minor union jobs. He ended up running a souvenir shop outside a U.S. Army base in Frankfurt, and died in 1958.[36]

Peter Burger lost his job as manager of a U.S. Army motor pool in Würzburg in 1951 following an Associated Press article that drew attention to his past. He kept in touch with the FBI for many years, submitting regular reports on the activities of his former companions and sending Christmas cards to J. Edgar Hoover. The last mention of him in FBI records is in 1961, when he was reported to be employed by the Bayer pharmaceutical company in Cologne and in good health after recovering from a heart attack.[37]

George Dasch failed in his repeated attempts to get back into the United States, largely because of Hoover's vehement opposition. "This is outrageous," the FBI director scrawled on a March 1958 State Department memorandum recommending a visa for Dasch. "Make as strong a case against Dasch as possible."[38] Dasch published his account of Operation Pastorius in 1959 under the title Eight Spies Against America. *It received little attention. He died in Germany in 1992.*

Acknowledgments

One of the joys of writing narrative history is the opportunity to follow in the footsteps of your characters. In researching this book, I was able to reconstruct the extraordinary wartime journey taken by the eight Nazi saboteurs by visiting places they visited while reading extensive archival material about their adventures. My travels took me from the grounds of a former Nazi sabotage school in Brandenburg, Germany, to a windswept beach in Amagansett, Long Island; from Hitler's bunker in the lake district of northeastern Poland to the streets of downtown Chicago, where the saboteurs played cat and-mouse games with their FBI pursuers.

Everywhere I went, I benefited immeasurably from extraordinary acts of assistance and hospitality. Some of the people who helped me were friends, others complete strangers. Some knew nothing about the strange story of the Nazi saboteurs; others had been researching the case for much longer than I. But all were generous with their time, and to all of them I want to say thank you.

Pride of place in these acknowledgments must go to those who had direct, firsthand knowledge of the saboteur case, and are either characters in this book or participated in the events described here. Given the fact that these events took place more than six decades ago, I count myself fortunate to have been able to conduct as many interviews as I did. In particular, I want to thank John Cullen, the coastguardsman who ran into the saboteurs on Amagansett Beach the night they came ashore, and Duane Traynor, the lead FBI investigator in the case. Both men sat with me patiently through hours of interviews, providing valuable insights and anecdotes, which I have incorporated into the narrative. My gratitude also goes to Lloyd Cutler, the sole surviving member of the prosecution team at the military tribunal; Wolfgang Wergin, who shared many of the adventures of saboteur Herbert Haupt; Bennett Boskey, law clerk to Supreme Court Chief Justice Harlan Stone; and Heinrich Fischer, a crew member of *U-584*, one of the submarines that transported the saboteurs to America.

One circle further out, I owe a debt to relatives and acquaintances of the characters in this book, including Gerhard Kappe, son of Walter Kappe, and Christel Engemann, daughter of Hedy Engemann. My understanding of George Dasch was enriched by my conversations with researcher Jonathan Mann, who traveled to Germany to meet with the last surviving saboteur before his death. Other people who have fallen under the spell of the Nazi saboteur story include Richard Cahan, who wrote a splendid article on the subject for *Chicago* magazine and gave me a tour of saboteur sites in the Windy City, including the street corner where Herbert Haupt proposed to Gerda Stuckmann. Peter Hansen, a writer for *Classic Trains*, helped me locate the photograph of *U-584* that I have used in this book.

In Amagansett, I was able to soak up the atmosphere of the now-defunct lifeboat station thanks to a kind invitation from Isabel Carmichael, whose parents bought the old house many years ago and moved it to its present site on Bluff Road. Tony Prohaska of The History Project allowed me to look at interviews he had made with retired coastguardsmen. My friend Celestine Bohlen gave me a place to stay in New York a couple of blocks from Grant's Tomb, one of the secret meeting places of the saboteurs. In Washington, NBC reporter Jim Popkin helped me locate the final resting place of six of the saboteurs, on a wooded hill that overlooks the Potomac River and a city sewage plant.

It would have been impossible to write this book without access to extensive records on the saboteur case, the most important of which are housed at the National Archives in College Park, Maryland. At the Archives, I would particularly like to thank Greg Bradsher, who whetted my interest in the case by giving me a tour of the stacks where the Dasch records are held; Amy Schmidt, for guiding me through the intricacies of captured German records; John Taylor, an inexhaustible fount of information on World War II; David Van Tassel, for opening up thousands of previously secret FBI records on Walter Kappe; and Timothy Mulligan, for helping me understand the operations of a German U-boat. In Berlin, I owe a special debt of gratitude to a very capable researcher, Shannon Smiley, who tracked down numerous records on my behalf, including letters from U-boat survivors and Dasch's old East German Stasi file, and introduced me to the incredibly helpful Hans-Georg Kohnke, director of museums for the city of Brandenburg.

Once again, I have benefited from the indulgence and encouragement of my longtime employers, the *Washington Post*. I want to thank the editors, Len Downie and Steve Coll, for allowing me to take a nine-month book leave and teach a course on media and politics at Princeton University. In addition to introducing me to some wonderful teachers and students, Princeton was also an ideal place to carry out much of the research for this book.

My agent, Rafe Sagalyn, was a pillar of support from beginning to end, along with my editor, Ash Green, who jumped on the idea of writing a book about the Nazi saboteurs when I first proposed it in the summer of 1991. At Knopf, I would also like to thank Luba Ostashevsky and Kevin Bourke for shepherding this book to publication so professionally.

Most of all, as with my previous books, I am grateful to my family for sharing my enthusiasms, pointing out my failings, and forgiving my frequent absences. For these reasons, and so many others, I dedicate this book to my oldest daughter, Alex, a never-ending source of pride, joy, and inspiration.

Notes

NOTE ON SOURCES

I first became interested in the case of George Dasch and the Nazi saboteurs after stumbling across a treasure trove of research material at the National Archives in College Park, Maryland. The FBI records of the Dasch case include forty boxes of original material, each containing thousands of pages of memoranda, photographs, letters, interrogation reports, newspaper clippings, and other memorabilia. Since this was one of the FBI's most important cases, anything of relevance to the investigation was preserved, including the handkerchiefs with secret writing that Dasch and Kerling used to list each other's contacts and letters written by the saboteurs to their families on the day of their execution. The records are a researcher's dream.

Unless otherwise stated, the notes below refer to the FBI records at NARA, which can be found in Record Group 65, FBI Headquarters Files. The main file number for the Dasch case is 98-10288. When available, I have provided the subfile number, e.g., 98-10288-3472. (In this example, 98 is the FBI headquarters reference number for all sabotage cases, 10288 is the Dasch case, and 3472 is a report on the postwar interrogation of Wilhelm Ahlrichs, a German Naval Intelligence officer.)

While the FBI records contain the most exhaustive information on the Nazi saboteur case, many other agencies kept records on the case, including the Department of Justice, the Coast Guard, the Office of the Secretary of War, the U.S. Army and Navy, and the Secret Service. The Franklin D. Roosevelt Library at Hyde Park has its own saboteur collection. Transcripts of the military commission can be found in several places, including the FDR Library, the Records of the Army Staff (RG 319), and the Records of the Judge Advocate General (RG 153). I have used the following abbreviations in the source notes:

AP   Associated Press
BdU   *Befehlshaber der Unterseeboote*, Commander in Chief of U-boats
ESF   Eastern Sea Frontier

FBI   Federal Bureau of Investigation
FDR   Franklin Delano Roosevelt
NARA   National Archives and Records Administration
NYT   *New York Times*
ONI   Office of Naval Intelligence
OWI   Office of War Information
PRO   Public Record Office, London
RG   Record Group
WP   *Washington Post*

PROLOGUE

1. Lahousen/Abwehr diary for April 16, 1942, NARA, RG 238, Reference Files 1933-1946 (Entry 2), Box 18.
2. Roger Manvell and Heinrich Frankel, *The July Plot,* 102. For description of the Wolf's Lair, see also Constantine FitzGibbon, *20 July,* 10–17.
3. Max Seydewitz, *Civil Life in Wartime Germany,* 100–101.
4. FDR radio address, December 29, 1940; see also State of the Union address, January 1, 1942.
5. H. R. Trevor-Roper, *Hitler's Table Talk, 1941–44,* 180.
6. Ibid., 188.
7. Ibid., 179, 545.
8. Ibid., 279.
9. Don Whitehead, *The FBI Story,* 199.
10. Karl Heinz Abshagen, *Canaris,* 183–190, Charles Wighton and Günter Peis, *Hitler's Spies and Saboteurs,* 42–48, and Erwin Lahousen interview with AP reporter George Tucker, December 6, 1945, NARA, reprinted in part in *NYT,* December 10, 1945. The Wighton and Peis book must be treated with caution as it includes clearly fabricated dialogue, even though it is based on interviews with Lahousen and extracts from the Abwehr war diary.
11. Abshagen, 186–187; Lahousen AP interview.
12. Interrogation of Wilhelm Ahlrichs, German naval intelligence officer, NARA, RG 65, FBI headquarters file 98-10288-3472. The complete file is contained in Boxes 18–58.
13. Abwehr war diary, April 7, 1942.
14. Clay Blair, *Hitler's U-Boat War: The Hunters, 1939–1942,* 562.
15. Lahousen AP interview. See also Abwehr war diary, April 16–17, 1942.
16. Lahousen AP interview.

CHAPTER ONE: SCHOOL FOR SABOTAGE

1. Burger FBI statement, FBI file 98-10288-1172, June 23, 1942, 11; FBI memorandum, October 12, 1942.
2. Dasch FBI statement, FBI file 98-10288-1163, June 19–24, 1942, 145.

3. Author visit, September 2002. Quenz Lake Farm has been absorbed into the grounds of a steel mill, but the original farm buildings still exist.

4. Dasch FBI statement, 57a.

5. Burger, 12.

6. Heinck FBI statement, June 23, 1942; Dasch FBI statement, 144; Burger drawing, FBI files 98-10288, Box 41.

7. Military Tribunal Transcript, 2530, NARA, RG 153, Records of Office of Judge Advocate General, Court-Martial Case Files, Entry 1009, Boxes 17–21. For Burger account, see Tribunal, 2664.

8. Dasch FBI statement, 130.

9. George Dasch, *Eight Spies Against America,* 78.

10. Burger, 23; Dasch FBI statement, 193.

11. Interview with Hans-Georg Kohnke, Museum im Frey-Haus, Brandenburg; see also Michael Dobbs, *WP,* November 30, 1998, A1.

12. FBI memo, August 21, 1942, 98-10288-1586.

13. Kappe FBI file, 98-11449-240.

14. Burger, 23; Dasch FBI statement, 147.

15. Tribunal, 2309.

16. Burger, 13.

17. Ibid., 14.

18. FBI memo, August 21, 1942.

19. Dasch FBI statement, 98. Dempsey's real name was William Braubender.

20. Burger, 17–22.

21. Tribunal, 2049, 2468; Dasch, Burger, Quirin, and Heinck statements to FBI.

22. Burger, 23.

23. Burger, 24; Heinck, June 23, 1942, 11.

24. Burger, 31. See also testimony by FBI expert, Tribunal, 212–220.

25. Burger, 40–41.

26. Ibid., 26.

27. Quirin statement to FBI, June 25, 1942, 11.

28. Ibid., 12.

29. Dasch FBI statement, 146.

30. Ibid., 106–109; Burger, 35–36.

31. Dasch FBI statement, 107; Heinck, June 23, 1942, 10.

32. Kerling letter to Miriam Preston, December 22, 1940, FBI file 98-10288-1102.

33. Kerling letter to Miriam Preston, November 25, 1941, loc. cit.

34. Tribunal, 2374.

35. Burger, 33.

36. Tribunal, 2321.

37. Dasch FBI statement, 24; Tribunal, 2550–2552.

38. Dasch FBI statement, 102.

39. Dasch, *Eight Spies Against America,* 83.

40. Tribunal, 2321.

41. Dasch FBI statement, 68–69; Burger, 40.

42. Burger, 34.
43. Dasch FBI statement, 110.
44. Tribunal, 2469.
45. Quirin, June 25, 1942, 13–14; see also Burger, 29.
46. Heinck, June 23, 1942, 27.
47. Burger, 44.
48. Dasch FBI statement, 147.
49. Burger, 37.
50. Dasch FBI statement, 155.
51. Harry N. Holmes, *Strategic Materials and National Strength*, 31.
52. Dasch FBI statement, 94; Roosevelt address to Congress, January 6, 1942.
53. Hoover letter to attorney general, July 10, 1942. See also FBI files 98-10288-578 and 146-7-4219.
54. Burger, 41, 44.
55. Ibid., 41.

CHAPTER TWO: FAREWELLS

1. Haupt letter to parents from prison, July 1942. Bureau of Prisons, Notorious Offenders Files, RG 129, NARA; FBI report on Walter Froehling, July 3, 1942; FBI report, August 4, 1942, 98-10288-1605.
2. Burger, 43.
3. Dasch interview with FBI official W. C. Hinze, June 21, 1942.
4. Dasch FBI statement, 113.
5. Ibid., 2.
6. Ibid., 8–9.
7. Notorious Offenders, Dasch file, September 29, 1942, NARA, RG 129.
8. Marie Dasch statement, April 20, 1943, FBI file 98-10288-2809.
9. Dasch FBI statement, 11.
10. Ibid., 12.
11. Hoover memo to attorney general, October 28, 1944, FBI 146-7-4219.
12. Dasch FBI statement, 15.
13. Ibid., 16.
14. Ibid., 19.
15. Ibid., 23.
16. Ibid., 24.
17. FBI interview with Alma Neubauer, November 14, 1946, 98-10288-3597; see also Neubauer FBI statement, June 23, 1942.
18. Tribunal, 2208.
19. Burger drawing, FBI file 98-10288.
20. Dasch FBI statement, 57.
21. Ibid., 116.
22. Burger, 46.
23. Reinhold Barth FBI file, 98-11448-1373.

24. Haupt, FBI statement, June 29, 1942, 8; see also Dasch FBI statement, 157–159.
25. Dasch FBI statement, 161.
26. Ibid., 161.
27. Burger, 39–40.
28. Dasch FBI statement, 164.
29. Ibid., 36.
30. Tribunal, 2050–2052, 2149–2152.
31. Burger, 43
32. Dasch FBI statement, 204.
33. Ibid., 194; for Schmidt outfit, see Burger, 21.
34. Dasch FBI statement, 133.
35. Burger, 35.
36. Burger, 46; Quirin, June 25, 1942, 15; Tribunal, 204–236; FBI report NY 65-11065, July 1, 1942, 84.
37. Dasch FBI statement, 65, 207.
38. Ibid., 199–200.
39. Ibid., 166–167; Kerling statement to FBI, 98-10288-1174, June 30, 1942, 3; Memo from FBI agent E. P. Coffey, June 22, 1942, 98-10288-230.
40. Dasch FBI statement, 34.
41. Alexandra Richie, *Faust's Metropolis: A History of Berlin*, 522.
42. Dasch conversation with FBI agent W. C. Hinze, June 20, 1942.
43. Dasch FBI statement, 236.
44. Burger, 48.
45. FBI memo, October 24, 1942; Dasch FBI statement, 37.
46. Dasch FBI statement, 90.
47. Ibid., 142; Burger, 46.

CHAPTER THREE: "THE MEN ARE RUNNING WILD"

1. Tribunal, 2207.
2. Kappe FBI file, NY 98-870, 6.
3. Kappe FBI file, NY 98-870, 13.
4. Kappe FBI file, 98-11449-240.
5. Kappe FBI file, NY 98-870, 29.
6. Kappe FBI file, NY 98-870, 36, quoting *WP* magazine article, September 2, 1934.
7. Kappe FBI file, NY 98-870, 60, quoting *United Progressive News*.
8. Dasch FBI statement, 140; Dasch, *Eight Spies Against America*, 72.
9. Dasch FBI statement, 37.
10. Quirin, June 25, 1942, 15.
11. Burger, 47.
12. Tribunal, 2688-2689, 2373-2374.
13. Ahlrichs FBI interview.
14. Ahlrichs FBI interview; for Haupt outfit, see Burger, 20.
15. Burger, 14.

16. Tribunal, 2326.

17. Dasch FBI statement, 50–51.

18. Ahlrichs FBI interview.

19. Dasch FBI statement, 92.

20. Ibid., 75.

21. Ibid., 102.

22. Burger, 44.

23. Dasch FBI statement, 61.

24. Quirin, FBI statement, June 25, 1942, 16.

25. *Berliner Lokal-Anzeiger,* May 13 and May 15, 1942.

26. *Berliner Illustrierte Zeitung,* April 23, 1942.

27. Ahlrichs FBI interview.

CHAPTER FOUR: ACROSS THE ATLANTIC

1. Timothy Mulligan, *Neither Sharks nor Wolves,* 3.

2. British Admiralty report, PRO, ADM 186/808.

3. Dasch FBI statement, 180.

4. German BdU War diary, May 26, 1942.

5. Account of crew member Otto Wagner, *U-boot Archiv,* Cuxhaven.

6. Clay Blair, *Hitler's U-Boat War: The Hunters,* 57–59.

7. Dasch FBI statement, 39.

8. Dasch FBI statement, 39; Burger, 51.

9. Stephen Budiansky, *Battle of Wits,* 234–236.

10. Bletchley Park decrypt, PRO, HW 18/323.

11. Haupt FBI statement, June 28, 1942, 10.

12. Dasch FBI statement, 181.

13. Ibid., 173.

14. Mulligan, *Neither Sharks nor Wolves,* 18.

15. Dasch FBI statement, 184; Burger, 50.

16. Mulligan, *Neither Sharks nor Wolves,* 63.

17. Burger, 50.

18. Dasch FBI statement, 173.

19. Blair, *Hitler's U-Boat War: The Hunters,* 58.

20. Dasch FBI statement, 183.

21. FBI interrogation of Hermann Faje, June 29, 1942.

22. *U-202* log, NARA, Microform Room, May 28–30, 1942.

23. Dasch FBI statement, 102.

24. Ibid., 2.

25. Ibid., 4.

26. Burger, 1–3.

27. FBI memo, August 24, 1942, 98-10288-1974.

28. Dasch FBI statement, 40.

29. Ibid., 185.
30. *U-202* log, June 2, 1942.
31. Dasch FBI statement, 41.
32. Tribunal, 1993.
33. *NYT,* June 13, 1942.
34. Dasch FBI statement, 86–88.
35. Ibid., 142.
36. FBI memo, August 24, 1942, loc. cit.
37. Report from Radioman Kuenne, *U-boot Archiv;* see also Burger, 35; *U-202* log, June 15, 1942.
38. Dasch FBI statement, 42.
39. Ibid., 41, 171.
40. Burger, 15, 50.
41. Ibid., 51.
42. Otto Wagner account, loc. cit.
43. Budiansky, *Battle of Wits,* 237.
44. Dasch, *Eight Spies Against America,* 95.
45. Burger, 52.
46. Dasch FBI statement, 42; Burger, 53; *U-202* log, June 13, 1942.
47. Ahlrichs FBI interrogation, 98-10288-341.
48. Otto Wagner, loc. cit.
49. Dasch FBI statement, 117.
50. Ibid., 43.
51. Dasch, *Eight Spies Against America,* 97.
52. Burger, 54.
53. Dasch FBI statement, 42.

CHAPTER FIVE: THE BEACH

1. Stetson Conn et al., *The U.S. Army in World War II: Guarding the United States and Its Outposts,* 97.
2. Henry Landau, *The Enemy Within,* 77–80.
3. Materials for Joint Chiefs of Staff meeting, March 30, 1942.
4. Memorandum from FDR naval aide John McCrea, April 6, 1942, to Admiral Ernest King.
5. Author interview with John Cullen, January 2002; see also *New Yorker,* "Talk of the Town," July 25, 1942.
6. Confidential U.S. Coast Guard memorandum 602, New York District, April 11, 1942.
7. Cullen interview.
8. Cullen interview; Tribunal, 101–107; Cullen statement to FBI, 98-10288-2139; Dasch FBI statement, 43–44; Tribunal, 2533–2534; Cullen statement to FBI agent Connelley, June 19, 1942, FBI file 146-7-4219.
9. Dasch FBI statement, 126–128.

10. Carl Jennett interview, 1997, the History Project, Inc., 14; Jennett FBI interview, 98-10288-2139.

11. In his testimony to the military tribunal, Cullen estimated the elapsed time at around twenty minutes, but the Office of Naval Intelligence reported that he did not get back to the beach until 0105. (NARA RG 38 ONI Security classified administrative correspondence, June 18, 1942.)

12. Cullen interview; Cullen statement to FBI, loc. cit.

13. FBI memorandum, 98-10288-347.

14. Otto Wagner account, *U-boot Archiv,* Cuxhaven; Günther Gellermann, *Der Andere Auftrag,* 67.

15. *U-202* log, June 13, 1942.

16. Ibid., June 15, 1942.

17. Dasch, *Eight Spies Against America,* 102; Burger, 55.

18. Dasch FBI statement, 45, 125–128.

19. Ibid., 45.

20. Burger, 56; Dasch FBI statement, 118.

21. Author interview with Fred W. Nirschel Jr., August 2002.

22. Eastern Sea Frontier war diary, chapter 4, June 1942, NARA, RG 38, Box 332; see also Third Naval District intelligence office memorandum, June 29, 1942; Coast Guard intelligence memorandum, June 18, 1942, NARA RG 38 ONI Security classified administrative correspondence.

23. ESF war diary, chapter 4.

24. Ibid., chapter 5, July 1942.

25. Ibid., chapter 4.

26. Jennett interview, the History Project.

27. Warren Barnes statement to FBI, 98-10288-2139.

28. Otto Wagner account, *U-boot Archiv.*

29. Carl Jennett statement to FBI, 98-10288-2139.

30. Tribunal, 125.

31. ESF war diary, July 1942.

32. Tribunal, 110.

33. Jennett interview, the History Project.

34. FBI interviews with Barnes and Jennett, 98-10288-2139.

35. FBI memorandum, June 17, 1942, 146-7-4219; Cullen interview with FBI, 98-10288-2139.

36. Coast Guard Intelligence report on "activity vicinity of Amagansett Lifeboat Station," June 18, 1942.

37. Burger, 56.

38. Dasch FBI statement, 46. Although Dasch estimates that the distance to the railroad station was "two or three miles," maps and an on-site inspection show that it was around a mile.

39. FBI file 98-10288-1827.

40. Louise Maunsell Field, ed., *Amagansett Lore and Legend,* 70; Dasch FBI statement, 133; Field, 71.

CHAPTER SIX: NEW YORK, NEW YORK

1. Dasch, *Eight Spies Against America*, 104.
2. Tribunal, 977.
3. Dasch FBI statement, 46, 133; *NYT*, June 13, 1942.
4. Burger, 58.
5. Dasch FBI statement, 133.
6. Governor Clinton Hotel letterhead; FBI memorandum, June 20, 1942, 98-10288-43. The hotel has since been renamed the Southgate Tower.
7. Coast Guard press release, July 15, 1942.
8. White House memorandum, June 26, 1939.
9. FBI memorandum, July 21, 1942, 98-10288-1055; *NYT*, June 14, 1942.
10. FBI memorandum, June 25, 1942, 98-10288-389; Coast Guard intelligence office memorandum, June 18, 1942.
11. Dasch admission summary, September 29, 1942, Bureau of Prisons.
12. Dasch FBI statement, 137.
13. Full-page ad, *NYT*, June 14, 1942.
14. *NYT*, June 14, 1942.
15. FBI memorandum for attorney general, June 17, 1942; FBI laboratory report, July 2, 1942.
16. Hoover memorandum, June 15, 1942, 98-10288-25; Tribunal, 203–236.
17. Hoover memorandum, June 15, 1942, loc. cit.
18. FBI memorandum, June 15, 1942, 98-10288-40.
19. Author interview with Cullen, January 2002.
20. FBI memorandum, June 25, 1942, 98-10288-389.
21. Coast Guard intelligence memorandum, June 18, 1942.
22. ESF war diary, chapter 4, June 1942.
23. Dasch FBI statement, 138; Dasch, *Eight Spies Against America*, 106.
24. Burger, 58; Dasch FBI statement, 16.
25. Burger, 8.
26. Burger, 58; Tribunal, 2537.
27. Dasch, *Eight Spies Against America*, 106.

CHAPTER SEVEN: HIGH STAKES

1. Tribunal, 2537; Dasch, *Eight Spies Against America*, 111.
2. Tribunal, 2676.
3. Burger, 58.
4. Ibid., 59.
5. Ibid., 3–9, 60.
6. Dasch FBI statement, 49; Burger, 60.
7. Dasch FBI statement, 49.
8. Ibid., 130.
9. Burger, 61.

10. Ibid., 61.

11. Tribunal, 2481; Burger, 61; Dasch FBI statement, 49.

12. McWhorter memo, June 14, 1942, FBI NY file, 65-11065-79.

13. Dasch FBI statement, 52; see also Burger, 67, and Tribunal, 2578.

14. William Sullivan, *The Bureau*, 183.

15. Hoover memo, June 19, 1942, 98-10288-27.

16. *U-202* log, June 13, 1942.

17. Lahousen war diary, June 15, 1942.

18. Tribunal, 2538, 2560–2562, 2614.

19. FBI interview with Joseph Mayer, July 21, 1942, 98-10288-1272.

20. FBI memo, August 15, 1942, 98-10288-1810.

21. Ibid.

22. Ibid.

23. Tribunal, 2560–2562; Dasch, *Eight Spies Against America*, 109–110.

24. Letter from Hermann Lamby, former *U-584* crew member, *U-boot Archiv*, Cuxhaven.

25. FBI statements of Hermann Neubauer, July 2, 1942, and Herbert Haupt, June 28, 1942, NARA, 98-10288.

26. FBI statement of Edward Kerling, June 28, 1942, 98-10288-1174.

27. Miami FBI report, October 24, 1942, 98-10288-2213.

28. FBI statements of Kerling and Haupt, op. cit.

29. Haupt FBI statement; FBI property list.

30. Tribunal, 2414.

31. Burger, 63.

32. Ibid., 63.

33. Tribunal, 2679.

34. Burger, 64.

35. Heinck letter to family, FBI file 98-10288, July 1942; Heinck FBI biography; Quirin FBI statement, July 3, 1942; FBI New York report, July 1, 1942, 146-7-4219. See also FBI memo, 98-10288-1827.

36. Dasch FBI statement, 55.

37. FBI memo, July 21, 1942, 98-10288-1055.

38. Curt Gentry, *J. Edgar Hoover,* 179; see also Hoover *NYT* obituary, May 3, 1972.

39. Hoover memo to FDR, June 2, 1942, FDR Library.

40. Hoover memo to White House aide Edwin M. Watson, June 16, 1947, FDR Library.

41. Francis Biddle, *In Brief Authority,* 327.

42. Author interview with Duane Traynor, January 2002.

43. Hoover memo, June 15, 1942, 98-10288-25.

44. Hoover memo, June 17, 1942, 98-10288-8; Hoover letter to ONI director, June 22, 1942.

45. Hoover letter to ONI director, June 20, 1942; see also Hoover memo, June 17, 1942, 98-10288-9.

46. ESF war diary, chapter 4.

CHAPTER EIGHT: A STORY TO TELL

1. Dasch FBI statement, 55.
2. Washington FBI report, July 1, 1942, 98-10288-408.
3. Dasch letter to Burger, June 19, 1942, FBI files.
4. Dasch FBI statement, 57.
5. Washington FBI report, July 1, 1942.
6. FBI interview with Heinrich Heinck, June 21, 1942.
7. Burger, 65.
8. Duane Traynor memo, June 25, 1942, FBI file 98-10288-128.
9. Dasch FBI statement, 58.
10. Author interview with Traynor, January 2002.
11. Dasch note, June 19, 1942, FBI file 98-10288-14.
12. Washington field office report, July 1, 1942, op. cit.
13. Author interview with Traynor.
14. Author interview with Traynor; memo, June 25, 1942, op. cit.
15. Biddle memorandum for FDR, June 19, 1942, FDR Library; Biddle, *In Brief Authority*, 327.
16. Winston S. Churchill, *The Second World War: The Hinge of Fate*, 377.
17. James MacGregor Burns, *Roosevelt*, 235.
18. Churchill memorandum to Roosevelt, June 20, 1942, in Warren F. Kimball, ed., *Churchill and Roosevelt*.
19. Weekly gains and losses of Allied shipping, 1942, FDR Library.
20. Tribunal, 2210, 2235.
21. Ibid., 2208–2209.
22. Ibid., 2211.
23. Ibid., 2236.
24. Ibid., 1857.
25. Dasch activity log, 98-10288-128.
26. Washington field office report, July 11, 1942, op. cit.
27. Hoover memos, June 19, 1942, 98-10288-26, 98-10288-27.
28. Author interview with Cullen, January 2002.
29. Connelley memo, June 19, 1942, FBI file 146-7-4619, NY file 65-11065.
30. Burger, 19.
31. Tribunal, 2062.
32. FBI interview with Erna Haupt, July 2, 1942, 98-10288-227.
33. FBI interview with Hans Haupt, July 3, 1942, 98-10288-398.
34. Author interview with Wolfgang Wergin, May 2002.
35. FBI interview with Hans Haupt.
36. FBI interview with Walter Froehling; Tribunal, 2063.
37. FBI interview with Hans Haupt.
38. Burger, 65.
39. Heinck interviews with FBI, June 21 and 23, 1942.
40. Author interview with Traynor.

41. Hoover memo, June 19, 1942, 98-10288-28.
42. Author interview with Traynor; FBI memo, June 20, 1942, 98-10288-44; Tribunal, 1856.
43. Washington field office report, July 11, 1942, op. cit.

CHAPTER NINE: *THE INVADERS*

1. Burger, 65.
2. FBI memorandum, June 20, 1942, 98-10288-43.
3. Burger section, FBI file, 147-7-4219.
4. Burger section, FBI file 146-7-4219.
5. FBI memo, June 21, 1942, 98-10288-276.
6. Quirin interrogation, June 20, 1942.
7. FBI log of Dasch movements, 98-10288-128.
8. Dasch FBI statement, 57b.
9. FBI NY file, 146-7-4219, 66.
10. Dasch FBI statement, 68.
11. Ibid., 65.
12. Ladd memorandum, June 20, 1942, 98-10288-48.
13. *Chicago Daily Tribune,* June 20, 1942.
14. Survey of Intelligence Materials, no. 30, OWI, July 1, 1942, FDR Library.
15. Hans Haupt FBI interview, 98-10288-398.
16. Author interview with Wolfgang Wergin, May 2002; statement to U.S. Army, May 20, 1945, FBI file 98-10288-3456.
17. Herbert Haupt FBI interview, July 3, 1942.
18. *The Invaders* was a 1942 movie also released under the title *The Forty-ninth Parallel;* see also Lucille Froehling FBI interrogation, 98-10288-436.
19. Tribunal, 2213, 2069, 2070.
20. FBI surveillance report, July 23, 1942, 98-10288-262.
21. The Commodore has since been rebuilt as the Grand Hyatt New York.
22. Edward Kerling letter to Miriam Preston, November 25, 1941, RG 65, NARA.
23. Kerling letter to Preston, November 25, 1941.
24. Edward Kerling letter to Marie Kerling, August 3, 1942, 98-10288-2089.
25. Kerling letters to Helmut Leiner, Hedy Engemann, and Marie Kerling, August 3 and August 8, 1942.
26. Tribunal, 2284-2286; Kerling FBI interviews, June 28 and June 30.
27. Traynor memo, FBI file 98-10288-73.
28. Dasch FBI statement, 160.
29. Ibid., 110–111.
30. FBI memo by E. P. Coffey, June 22, 1942, 98-10288-236.
31. Dasch FBI statement, 166.
32. Hoover memo, 98-10288-173.
33. Herbert Haupt FBI statement, June 29, 1942; FBI memo, June 22, 1942, 98-10288-194.

34. FBI memo, June 21, 1942, 98-10266-276.
35. FBI surveillance report, July 23, 1942, loc. cit.
36. FBI interrogation of Hedwig Engemann, June 30, 1942; see also Leiner interrogation, June 30, 1942.
37. Tribunal, 2378, 2387.

CHAPTER TEN: WIVES AND GIRLFRIENDS

1. Tribunal, 2261.
2. Marie Kerling interview with FBI, June 28, 1942, 98-10288-391.
3. Tribunal, 2724.
4. Ibid., 2173.
5. Erna Haupt FBI interview, July 2, 1942, 98-10288-227.
6. Confidential letter to FBI from car salesman, 98-10288-585.
7. FBI interview with Gerda Stuckmann, FBI file 98-10288-406.
8. Chicago FBI report, July 5, 1942, 98-10288-406.
9. Dasch letter to Burger, June 22, 1942, FBI files.
10. Author interview with Traynor, January 2002.
11. FBI log on Dasch, June 24, 1942, New York file 65-11065.
12. Dasch FBI statement, 212.
13. Ibid., 189.
14. Cramer letter to Thiel, November 25, 1941, FBI files.
15. Tribunal, 2758–2761; Kerling's version, 2303–2306; Thiel's version, 2264–2265. See also Kerling FBI detention log, June 24, 1942.
16. Kerling FBI interrogation, June 24, 1942.
17. Neubauer FBI statement, July 3, 1942. See also FBI file, 98-10288-1000, and FBI interrogations of Harry and Emma Jaques, 98-10288-390, 98-10288-403.
18. FBI surveillance report, July 23, 1942, 98-10288-262; see also individual agent reports, FBI file 98-19277-1330.
19. *Billboard*, November 5, 1921.
20. Tribunal, 2214; Herbert Haupt FBI interview, June 29, 1942.
21. Hoover memo, June 24, 1942, 98-10288-37.
22. Tribunal, 2305; FBI photographs, NARA.
23. Dasch FBI statement, 252.
24. Traynor memo, June 25, 1942, 98-10288-128.
25. Ladd memo, July 6, 1942, FBI files.
26. FBI log book on Dasch, July 25, 1942; Dasch, *Eight Spies Against America*, 134.
27. FBI interview with Erna Haupt, July 2, 1942, 98-10288-227.
28. Chicago FBI report, July 5, 1942, 98-10288-406.
29. Haupt FBI interview, July 3, 1942.
30. FBI file, 98-10288-1574.
31. FBI surveillance report, July 23, 1942, loc. cit.
32. Tribunal, 1997.
33. New York FBI report, July 1, 1942, 103, loc. cit.

34. Chicago FBI report, July 5, 1942, 84, loc. cit.
35. Neubauer FBI statement, July 3, 1942.
36. Chicago FBI report, July 5, 1942, 90, loc. cit.

CHAPTER ELEVEN: "AS GUILTY AS CAN BE"

1. Donegan memo, June 27, 1942, 98-10288-164; Dasch, *Eight Spies Against America*, 135.
2. Donegan memo, loc. cit.; Tribunal, 541–545, 675–677.
3. Dasch, *Eight Spies Against America*, 137; Donegan memo, loc. cit.
4. Hoover memo, June 24, 1942, 98-10288-37.
5. FBI memo from D. M. Ladd, June 15, 1942, 98-10288-162.
6. FBI memo from E. A. Tamm, June 27, 1942, 98-10288-98. See also 98-10288-134.
7. Biddle, *In Brief Authority*, 327.
8. Maj. Gen. George V. Strong memo, June 28, 1942, RG 165, NARA, Military Intelligence Service.
9. UPI report, June 27, 1942.
10. Biddle, *In Brief Authority*, 328.
11. *NYT*, June 28, 1942.
12. FBI transcript of Winchell broadcast, June 28, 1942.
13. Notes from Margaret Hambley, Daisy Suckley diary, June 27, 1942.
14. Biddle, *In Brief Authority*, 327–328.
15. William D. Hassett, *Off the Record with F.D.R.*, 74.
16. FDR memo, June 30, 1942, Justice folder, FDR Library; FBI file 146-7-4219; Biddle, *In Brief Authority*, 330–331.
17. Author interview with Lloyd Cutler, May 2002.
18. Strong memo, June 28, 1942, loc. cit.
19. MacFall letter to Rear Admiral T. S. Wilkinson, June 29, 1942, RG 381, NARA, ONI Security classified correspondence.
20. Hoover note on August 10, 1942, memo from Assistant Attorney General Wendell Berge, 98-10288-145; see also 98-10288-203, 98-10288-1142.
21. Hassett, *Off the Record with F.D.R.*, 74–75.
22. Memo from FBI agent J. E. Brown, June 27, 1942, Dasch detention log.
23. Dasch, *Eight Spies Against America*, 135.
24. Hoover memo, June 30, 1942, 98-10288-283; see also Ladd memo, June 30, 1942, 98-10288-691; Tribunal, 1873.
25. Addendum to unsigned Dasch statement, July 2, 1942, FBI files.
26. Dasch, handwritten statement, July 3, 1942, 98-10288-624.
27. FBI memo, June 30, 1942, 98-10288-264.
28. Samuel Rosenman, *Working with Roosevelt*, 321.
29. Biddle, *In Brief Authority*, 328.
30. Judge Advocate General memorandum, RG 165, NARA, June 28, 1942, decimal file 383.4.
31. Biddle, *In Brief Authority*, 331.

32. Stimson diaries, Yale University, July 1, 1942.
33. Lahousen interview with AP, December 9, 1945; Lahousen war diary, June 28 and 30, 1940; Wighton and Peis, *Hitler's Spies and Saboteurs*, 77–79.
34. Ahlrichs interrogation, FBI file 98-10288-3472.
35. U.S. Navy Fourth Naval District war diary; Blair, *Hitler's U-Boat War: The Hunters*, 606–607.
36. Author visit to Hyde Park; Doris Kearns Goodwin, *No Ordinary Time*, 43.
37. Hassett, *Off the Record with F.D.R.*, 82–83.
38. Biddle memoranda, June 30 and July 1, 1942, FDR Library; Biddle, *In Brief Authority*, 329.
39. Hoover memo, July 1, 1942, 98-10288-221.
40. Franklin D. Roosevelt, *Public Papers and Addresses*, 1942, 296–298.
41. Albert L. Cox, *The Saboteur Story*, 24.
42. Burger detention log, July 3, 1942, FBI files.
43. Suckley diary, FDR Library; Hassett, *Off the Record with F.D.R.*, 85.

CHAPTER TWELVE: MILITARY TRIBUNAL

1. Tribunal, 2099.
2. Kenneth Royall interview, Columbia University Oral History Collection.
3. Stimson Safe File, Box 5, NARA, RG 107.
4. Biddle memo, July 6, 1942, FDR Library.
5. *Washington Times-Herald*, July 8, 1942.
6. Heinck letter to Anna Heinck, July 1942; Kerling letter to Miriam Preston, August 4, 1942.
7. Hoover memo, July 1, 1942, 98-10288-285.
8. All quotes from tribunal proceedings are taken from the official transcript, copies of which can be found in the FDR Library, Hyde Park, or NARA.
9. Author interview with Lloyd Cutler, May 2002; see also *Time*, November 19, 2001.
10. *New York Sun*, July 14, 1942.
11. Royall interview, loc. cit.
12. Dasch, *Eight Spies Against America*, 53.
13. Author interview with Cullen, January 2002; see also FBI memo, July 9, 1942, 98-10288-618.
14. OWI statement, July 15, 1942, FDR Library.
15. *New York Post*, July 9, 1942; *WP*, July 10, 1942.
16. *WP*, June 29, 1942.
17. FBI memo, July 6, 1942, 98-10288-811.
18. Hoover memo, July 14, 1942, 98-10288-756.
19. Elmer Davis and Byron Price, *War Information and Censorship*, 9; see also Biddle, *In Brief Authority*, 334.
20. *WP*, July 10, 1942.
21. Suckley diary, July 9, 1942, FDR Library.
22. Stimson diaries, Yale University, July 7–11, 1942.

23. Biddle, *In Brief Authority*, 335.
24. Memo from Assistant Attorney General James Rowe, October 8, 1942, FDR Library.
25. *NYT* and *WP,* July 12, 1942.
26. FBI Dasch files, Box 57.
27. OWI Intelligence Report 37, August 21, 1942, FDR Library.
28. Department of Justice press release, July 13, 1942, FDR Library.
29. *WP,* June 29, 1942; FBI memo, December 7, 1942, 98-10288-2574.
30. *WP,* July 17, 1942.
31. Biddle diary entry, July 17, 1942, Biddle Box 1, FDR Library.
32. Hassett, *Off the Record with F.D.R.,* 90.
33. Tribunal, 2137.
34. Letter to Hoover from Maj. William Hummell, December 14, 1942, FBI file 98-10288-2648.
35. Kerling letter to Hedy Engemann, August 3, 1942, FBI file 98-10288-2089. See also Tribunal, 2716–2743.
36. Dasch FBI statement, 81, 114.
37. Tribunal, 2560.
38. Author interview with Cutler, May 2002.
39. *Washington Times-Herald,* July 10, 1942.
40. Nichols memos, July 6 and July 9, 1942, 98-10288-472, 98-10288-681.
41. *WP,* July 21, 1942.
42. *NYT,* July 22, 1942.
43. Hoover memo, July 22, 1942, 98-10288-897.
44. *Philadelphia Record,* July 27, 1942.
45. FBI Walter Kappe file, 98-11449, NARA; *NYT,* July 28, 1942.

CHAPTER THIRTEEN: EQUAL JUSTICE UNDER THE LAW

1. Majority opinion of Justice David Davis, *Ex parte Milligan,* 4 Wallace 2, 71 U.S. 2 (1866).
2. Kenneth Royall, Columbia oral history interview, loc. cit.
3. Tribunal, 2110.
4. W. A. Swanberg, "The Spies Who Came from the Sea," *American Heritage,* April 1970; Eugene Rachlis, *They Came to Kill,* 246.
5. Alpheus T. Mason, *Harlan Fiske Stone,* 654.
6. *Washington Times-Herald,* July 28, 1942.
7. *Richmond Times Dispatch,* July 29, 1942.
8. Habeas corpus petition on behalf of Ernst Peter Burger, FDR Library.
9. Stimson diaries, Yale University, July 28, 1942.
10. David J. Danielski, "The Saboteurs' Case," *Journal of Supreme Court History,* vol. 1, 1996, 69.
11. Melvin I. Urofsky, *Division and Discord,* 13.
12. Ibid., 40.

13. Michael Belknap, *Frankfurter and the Nazi Saboteurs* (Supreme Court Historical Society Yearbook, 1982), 67.
14. Stimson diaries, June 29, 1942, loc. cit.
15. See, for example, Danielski, "The Saboteurs' Case," 69.
16. Unless otherwise stated, all quotes from the Supreme Court hearing are taken from Philip B. Kurland and Gerhard Casper, eds., *Landmark Briefs and Arguments of the Supreme Court of the United States*, vol. 39, 300–666.
17. *WP* and *NYT*, July 30, 1942.
18. Felix Frankfurter Papers, Harvard Law School, also quoted in full in Belknap, *Frankfurter and the Nazi Saboteurs*, 66–71.
19. Author interview with Lloyd Cutler, May 2002.
20. Felix Frankfurter Papers, Harvard Law School; author interview with Bennett Boskey, former Stone law clerk, June 2002.
21. Danielski, "The Saboteurs' Case," 71; Mason, *Harlan Fiske Stone*, 659–660; Stone correspondence with Frankfurter.
22. *WP*, August 1, 1942.
23. *NYT*, August 1, 1942.
24. Dasch, *Eight Spies Against America*, 166.
25. FBI memo, August 1, 1942, 98-10288-1210.
26. Kerling letter, August 1, 1942, FBI file, 98-10288.
27. Heinck letter, July 1942, FBI file, 98-10288-2486.
28. Haupt letter, July 1942, FBI files. 98-10288.
29. Rachlis, *They Came to Kill*, 250.
30. Hoover memo, July 24, 1942, FBI file, 98-10288 989.
31. Rachlis, *They Came to Kill*, 297.
32. Kerling letter, July 31, 1942, Oscar Cox files, FDR Library.

CHAPTER FOURTEEN: DEATH ROW

1. Hassett, *Off the Record with F.D.R.*, 97–98.
2. Kenneth Royall, oral history interview, loc. cit.
3. Biddle memo to FDR, July 16, 1942.
4. Roosevelt press briefing, August 4, 1942.
5. Report of Brigadier General Cox to the president, August 19, 1942.
6. FBI memo, July 9, 1942, 98-10288-941.
7. Letters from Kerling, August 3 and 4, 1942, FBI file 98-10288-2089.
8. Quirin letter, FBI file, 98–10288-2486.
9. Cox, *The Saboteur Story*, 25.
10. Lahousen war diary, August 4, 1942.
11. FBI memo, August 19, 1946, 98-10288-3587; Gellermann, *Der andere Auftrag*, 71–72.
12. See, for example, Biddle letter to secretary of state, September 17, 1942, FDR library.
13. Roosevelt order, August 7, 1942, FDR Library.
14. FBI memo, August 10, 1942, 98-10288-1604.

15. Letters from William B. Adams, FBI file 98-10288-2004.
16. Quirin letter, FBI file 98-10288-2088.
17. Neubauer letter, FBI file 98-10288-2088.
18. Kerling letters, FBI file 98-10288-2088.
19. Cox, *The Saboteur Story*, 25.
20. *WP*, August 9, 1942.
21. *Washington Star*, August 9, 1942; Rachlis, *They Came to Kill*, 287.
22. *Washington Star*, April 8, 1942; George T. Washington papers, Library of Congress.
23. FBI memo, August 10, 1942, loc. cit.
24. *WP*, August 9, 1942.
25. White House press release, FDR Library.
26. Rosenman, *Working with Roosevelt*, 359–355; see also Suckley diary, August 8, 1942.
27. Cox, *The Saboteur Story*, 17; see also *Washington Star*, October 13, 1942.
28. Report to president on disposal of bodies of saboteurs, August 14, 1942, FDR Library.

EPILOGUE: SURVIVORS

1. FBI memo, August 10, 1942, 98-10288-1604.
2. Ladd memo, August 12, 1942, 98-10288-1444.
3. Dasch prison file, RG 129, NARA.
4. Richard Cahan, "A Terrorist's Tale," *Chicago Magazine*, February 2002; Rachlis, *They Came to Kill*, 292–293.
5. William O. Douglas, *The Court Years, 1939–1975*, 33.
6. Letter to Charles Hughes, September 25, 1942, quoted in Mason, *Harlan Fiske Stone*, 658.
7. Ibid., 658–659.
8. Stone letter to Boskey, September 5, 1942, Stone papers, Library of Congress.
9. Stone letter to Frankfurter, quoted in Mason, *Harlan Fiske Stone*, 661.
10. Mason, *Harlan Fiske Stone*, 658–659.
11. Ibid., 664.
12. Biddle memo to FDR, quoted in Danielski, "The Saboteurs' Case," 79.
13. Danielski, "The Saboteurs' Case," 80.
14. Robert E. Cushman, "The Case of the Nazi Saboteurs," *American Political Science Review*, 1942.
15. William Rehnquist, speech to Dickinson College of Law, Pennsylvania State University, November 12, 1999.
16. Letter from Bureau of Prisons director James V. Bennett, September 3, 1942, Dasch prison file.
17. Psychiatric evaluation, November 10, 1943, Dasch prison file.
18. Report by Atlanta prison warden, January 15, 1945, Dasch prison file.
19. FBI memo, October 17, 1942, 98-10288-2125.
20. Report by Atlanta prison warden, July 25, 1947, Dasch prison file.
21. Traynor letter, July 3, 1945, Hoover reply, July 13, 1945, FBI file 98-10288-3479.

22. Lahousen war diary, July 20 and August 9, 1942.
23. Rachlis, *They Came to Kill,* 296.
24. British Joint Staff Mission letter, July 16, 1942, Frank McCoy papers, Library of Congress.
25. Memo for secretary of war, January 5, 1945, Stimson safe file, NARA RG 107.
26. Burger letter to Kenneth Royall, May 12, 1948, NARA RG 165, War Department decimal files 000.536.
27. Burger letter, October 23, 1948, FBI file 98-10288-3675.
28. Burger letter, January 1, 1949, FBI file 98-10288-3685.
29. Dasch East German Stasi file, Berlin, MfS-AS Nr. 598/66.
30. Burger letter, January 6, 1950; see also FBI memo, February 2, 1949, 98-10288-3617.
31. FBI memos, March 15, 1951, and April 13, 1951, Dasch file, 98-10288.
32. Author interview with Gerhard Kappe, May 2002.
33. Dasch memo to FBI, August 20, 1942, 98-10288-2376.
34. Author interview with Wolfgang Wergin, May 2002.
35. Office of Naval Intelligence report, FBI files, 98-10288.
36. Author interview with Gerhard Kappe.
37. FBI memorandum, March 1, 1961, 98-10288.
38. Hoover memorandum, March 10, 1958, FBI file 98-10288-3851.

Bibliography

Abshagen, Karl Heinz. *Canaris*. London: Hutchinson, 1956.

Biddle, Francis. *In Brief Authority*. New York: Doubleday, 1962.

Blair, Clay. *Hitler's U-Boat War: The Hunters, 1939–1942*. New York: Random House, 1996.

Brissaud, Andre. *Canaris*. London: Weidenfeld and Nicolson, 1970.

Buchheim, Lothar-Günther. *Das Boot*. London: Cassell, 2002.

Budiansky, Stephen. *Battle of Wits: The Complete Story of Codebreaking in World War II*. New York: Free Press, 2000.

Burns, James MacGregor. *Roosevelt: The Soldier of Freedom*. New York: Harcourt Brace Jovanovich, 1970.

Churchill, Winston S. *The Second World War: The Hinge of Fate*. Boston: Houghton Mifflin, 1950.

Conn, Stetson, Rose C. Engelman, and Byron Fairchild. *The U.S. Army in World War II: Guarding the United States and Its Outposts*. Washington, D.C.: Office of the Chief of Military History, 1964.

Cox, Albert L. *The Saboteur Story*. Records of the Columbia Historical Society, Washington, D.C., 1961.

Dasch, George. *Eight Spies Against America*. New York: Robert M. McBride Company, 1959.

Davis, Elmer, and Byron Price. *War Information and Censorship*. American Council on Public Affairs, Washington, D.C., n.d.

Douglas, William O. *The Court Years, 1939–1975*. New York: Vintage Books, 1981.

Farago, Ladislas. *The Game of the Foxes: The Untold Story of German Espionage in the United States and Great Britain During World War II*. New York: David McKay, 1971.

Field, Louise Maunsell, ed. *Amagansett Lore and Legend*. Amagansett, N.Y.: Amagansett Village Improvement Society, 1948.

FitzGibbon, Constantine. *20 July*. New York: W. W. Norton, 1956.

Gellermann, Günther. *Der andere Auftrag.* Bonn: Bernard & Graefe Verlag, 1997.

Gentry, Curt. *J. Edgar Hoover: The Man and the Secrets.* New York: Plume, 1992.

Goodwin, Doris Kearns. *No Ordinary Time: The Home Front in World War II.* New York: Simon and Schuster, 1994.

Hassett, William D. *Off the Record with F.D.R., 1942–1945.* Brunswick, N.J.: Rutgers University Press, 1958.

Holmes, Harry N. *Strategic Materials and National Strength.* New York: Macmillan, 1942.

Kahn, David. *Hitler's Spies: German Military Intelligence in World War II.* New York: Macmillan, 1978.

Kimball, Warren F., ed. *Churchill and Roosevelt: The Complete Correspondence.* Princeton, N.J.: Princeton University Press, 1984.

Kurland, Philip B., and Gerhard Casper, eds. *Landmark Briefs and Arguments of the Supreme Court of the United States.* Vol. 39. Washington, D.C.: University Publications of America, 1975–.

Landau, Henry. *The Enemy Within: The Inside Story of German Sabotage in America.* New York: Putnam, 1937.

Manvell, Roger, and Henrich Frankel. *The July Plot.* London: Bodley Head, 1964.

Mason, Alpheus T. *Harlan Fiske Stone: Pillar of the Law.* New York: Viking, 1956.

Mulligan, Timothy. *Neither Sharks nor Wolves.* Annapolis, Md.: Naval University Press, 1999.

Persico, Joseph E. *Nuremberg: Infamy on Trial.* New York: Penguin, 1995.

———. *Roosevelt's Secret War: FDR and World War II Espionage.* New York: Random House, 2001.

Rachlis, Eugene. *They Came to Kill: The Story of Eight Saboteurs in America.* New York: Random House, 1961.

Richie, Alexandra. *Faust's Metropolis: A History of Berlin.* London: HarperCollins, 1998.

Roosevelt, Franklin D. *Public Papers and Addresses.* Volume 11, *Humanity on the Defensive.* New York: Harper, 1938–1950.

Rosenman, Samuel. *Working with Roosevelt.* New York: Harper, 1952.

Seydewitz, Max. *Civil Life in Wartime Germany.* New York: Viking, 1945.

Shirer, William. *The Rise and Fall of the Third Reich.* New York: Ballantine, 1989.

Showell, Jak P. Mallmann. *U-Boats at War.* Shepperton, England: Ian Allen Publishing, 2002.

Sullivan, William. *The Bureau: My Thirty Years in Hoover's FBI.* New York: Pinnacle Books, 1982.

Trevor-Roper, H. R., ed. *Hitler's Table Talk, 1941–44.* London: Weidenfeld and Nicolson, 1953.

Urofsky, Melvin I. *Division and Discord: The Supreme Court Under Stone and Vinson.* Columbia: University of South Carolina Press, 1997.

Whitehead, Don. *The FBI Story: A Report to the People.* New York: Random House, 1956.

Wighton, Charles, and Günter Peis. *Hitler's Spies and Saboteurs.* New York: Henry Holt, 1958.

Index

PERMISSIONS ACKNOWLEDGMENTS

PHOTOGRAPHIC CREDITS

ALSO BY MICHAEL DOBBS

"One of the great stories of our time . . . a wonderful
anecdotal history of a great drama."
—San Francisco Chronicle Book Review

DOWN WITH BIG BROTHER
The Fall of the Soviet Empire

As a *Washington Post* correspondent in Moscow, Warsaw, and
Yugoslavia in the final decade of the Soviet empire, Michael
Dobbs had a ringside seat to the extraordinary events that led to
the unraveling of the Bolshevik Revolution. From Tito's funeral
to the birth of Solidarity, from the tragedy of Tiananmen Square
to Boris Yeltsin standing on a tank in the center of Moscow,
Dobbs saw it all.

The fall of communism was one of the great human dramas of
our century, as great a drama as the original Bolshevik revolution. Dobbs met almost all of the principal actors, including
Mikhail Gorbachev, Lech Walesa, Václav Havel, and Andrei
Sakharov. With a sweeping command of the subject and the passion and verve of an eyewitness, he paints an unforgettable
portrait of the decade in which the familiar and seemingly petri-
fied Cold War world—the world of Checkpoint Charlie and Dr.
Strangelove—vanished forever.

History/Current Affairs/0-679-75151-3

VINTAGE BOOKS
Available at your local bookstore, or call toll-free to order:
1-800-793-2665 (credit cards only)